PHILOSOPHERS
WHO BELIEVE

THE SPIRITUAL JOURNEYS OF 11 LEADING THINKERS

edited by

KELLY JAMES CLARK

D0169577

INTERVARSITY PRESS
DOWNERS GROVE, ILLINOIS 60515

InterVarsity Press
P.O. Box 1400
Downers Grove, IL 60515
World Wide Web: www@ivpress.com
E-mail: mail@ivpress.com

InterVarsity Press® *is the book-publishing division of InterVarsity Christian Fellowship USA*®, *a student movement active on campus at hundreds of universities, colleges and schools of nursing in the United States of America, and a member movement of the International Fellowship of Evangelical Students. For information about local and regional activities, write Public Relations Dept., InterVarsity Christian Fellowship USA, 6400 Schroeder Rd., P.O. Box 7895, Madison, WI 53707-7895.*

All Scripture quotations, unless otherwise indicated, are from the Holy Bible, New International Version® NIV®. *Copyright ©1973, 1978, 1984 by International Bible Society. Used by permission of Zondervan Publishing House. All rights reserved.*

Portions of Alvin Plantinga's essay are from James E. Tomberlin and Peter Van Inwagen, eds., Alvin Plantinga *(Dordrecht: D. Reidel, 1985). Used by permission.*

"A Philosopher's Religious Faith" is reprinted with the permission of Macmillan Publishing Company from A Second Look in the Rearview Mirror *by Mortimer J. Adler. Copyright © 1992 by Mortimer J. Adler.*

Cover illustration: Roberta Polfus; Background: Cowgirl Stock Photography

ISBN 0-8308-1543-0 (pbk.)

Printed in the United States of America ∞

Library of Congress Cataloging-in-Publication Data

Philosophers who believe: the spiritual journeys of eleven leading thinkers/
  edited by Kelly James Clark.
    p.   cm
    Includes bibliographical references and index.
    ISBN 0-8308-1851-0 (hdbk.)
    ISBN 0-8308-1543-0 (pbk.)
    1. Christian philosophers—Biography.   2. Christianity—
Philosophy—History—20th century.   I. Clark, Kelly James, 1956-
BR102.A1P55   1993

190—dc20   *93-36196*
                                                        CIP

22	21	20	19	18	17	16	15	14	13	12	11	10	9	8	7	6	5	4	3	2	1
15	14	13	12	11	10	09	08	07	06	05	04	03	02	01	00	99	98	97			

To
Phyllis Clark,
that mom than which none greater can be conceived
and
Anna Catherine Leech,
grandma extraordinaire

Introduction
The Literature of Confession

KELLY JAMES CLARK

Kelly James Clark is associate professor of philosophy at Calvin College. Prior to his appointment at Calvin College, he taught at Gordon College. The closest he has come to philosophical fame was when he shared a tent with Alvin Plantinga on a climbing trip. His works include Return to Reason *and* Our Knowledge of God: Essays on Natural and Philosophical Theology.

*I*n 1980, *Time* magazine reported a remarkable renaissance of religious belief among philosophers:

> God? Wasn't he chased out of heaven by Marx, banished to the unconscious by Freud and announced by Nietzsche to be deceased? Did not Darwin drive him out of the empirical world? Well, not entirely. In a quiet revolution in thought and arguments that hardly anyone could have foreseen only two decades ago, God is making a comeback. Most intriguingly, this is happening not among theologians or ordinary believers . . . but in the crisp, intellectual circles of academic philosophers, where the consensus had long banished the Almighty from fruitful discourse. Now it is more respectable among philosophers than it has been for a generation to talk about the possibility of God's existence.[1]

These philosophers have developed their theories against the rising tide of strict empiricism, using "a kind of tough-minded intellectualism." Who are these tough-minded intellectuals, and what has led to their return to Christian belief and philosophy?

It would be difficult to overestimate the increase in anti-Christian sentiment among professional philosophers since the time of the Enlightenment. Yet in spite of the march of unbelief, a substantial number of prominent intellectuals has reclaimed intellectual ground for belief in God. This "quiet revolution" has been led by Alvin Plantinga, described in the *Time* article as "the leading Protestant philosopher of God." Battles have been fought and won at Oxford, Cambridge, Yale, Toronto and Calvin College by a mighty host of powerful and creative thinkers.

All of the contributors to this volume enjoy international reputations for their contributions to the discipline of philosophy and for their distinctly Christian approach to philosophy. A visit to any university library or bookstore will reveal the monumental and respected advancements that these thinkers have made. These distinguished scholars hold or have held positions of importance at the greatest institutions of higher learning in the world and have been accorded the prestige and honors that their significant contributions merit.

But the contributors to this volume are distinguished in more ways than one. They are distinguished not only as thinkers at the top of their discipline, but as robust Christians in a field that until recently was scarcely marked by religion of any sort. Those not of a Christian persuasion who read these autobiographical essays may be struck that such estimable intellectuals publicly confess faith in Jesus Christ. The Christian reader, on the other hand, will notice immediately that these writers represent a wide range of Christian thought (Protestant and Catholic) and many different points in the spiritual pilgrimage. As one might expect among philosophers, the writers don't always agree with one another. For that reason and others, the purpose of this book can hardly be to endorse everything said by every writer in the collection. The purpose of telling these stories is instead to demonstrate and exemplify the importance of basic Christian faith—what C. S. Lewis called "mere Christianity"—in the lives and work of several leading philosophers.

The contributors are Mortimer Adler of the Institute for Philosophical Research, Stephen Davis of Claremont McKenna College, Basil Mitchell of Oxford University, Terence Penelhum of the University of Calgary, Alvin Plantinga of the University of Notre Dame, Nicholas Rescher of the University of Pittsburgh, John Rist of the University of Toronto, Richard Swinburne of Oxford University, Frederick Suppe of the University of Maryland, Nicholas Wolterstorff of Yale University and Linda Zagzebski of Loyola Marymount University.[2]

The rising tide of empiricism was thought to sound the death knell of religious belief. Some declared that a God beyond the sensible cannot be known, and others more radically claimed that any talk of God is just nonsense. Among intellectuals an increased dependence on science has seen the waning of religious belief. Nietzsche, Freud and Marx contended that religious belief is nothing but the product of subtle yet powerful processes of self-deception. These combined forces of modernism had put Christian philosophers on the defensive—virtually all of their efforts in the 1940s, 1950s and 1960s went to the defense of the meaningfulness of religious language and the defense of belief in God—and sent most of them into silent retreat. But in this age of scientific imperialism the contributors to this volume have powerfully argued that God-talk is meaningful and that God can indeed be known. Yet beyond this, philosophy has seen a renaissance both of belief in God and of the development of a positive Christian philosophy. Why is it that Christianity has once again become a live intellectual option among philosophers?

One important influence on this revival was the founding of the Society of Christian Philosophers in April 1978 at the Western Divisional meeting of the American Philosophical Association in Cincinnati, Ohio. At the urging of William Alston of Syracuse University, a prominent philosopher of language who had recently returned to the Christian fold, a letter went out from Alvin Plantinga, Robert and Marilyn Adams of UCLA, Arthur Holmes of Wheaton College, George Mavrodes of the University of Michigan, and William Alston to spark interest in a society to provide fellowship and encouragement of philosophical reflection on issues of concern to the Christian community. The society has since grown to over one thousand members and is the largest single-interest group among American philosophers. It meets regularly at the three divisional meetings of the American Philosophical Association and supports annual regional meetings. In 1984 the society initiated its own scholarly journal of philosophical reflection on matters of Christian belief, *Faith and Philosophy*, which is prized for the analytical rigor, originality and diversity of its articles.

A second major factor in the revival of Christian philosophy was the presentation, publication and subsequent discussion of Plantinga's "Advice to Christian Philosophers," his inauguration speech at the assumption of the John A. O'Brien Professorship of Philosophy.[3] Plantinga challenged philosophers not to be Christians who were incidentally philosophers, but to be Christian philosophers: to follow out their Christian commitment in all areas of philosophy. By this he meant that Christians were to develop Christian philosophy independently of the great secular bastions of philosophy; Christians must attempt to understand, develop, systematize and extend the beliefs of their own, Christian, community.

This radical call to independence suggests that Christians can carry out their own agenda and not have it set by philosophers with fundamentally different presuppositions. The Christian's calling is primarily to be faithful to the believing community and not to the problematic set by the programs of the secular university, which often are diametrically opposed to Christian belief. As Plantinga writes, "they fit in badly with a Christian or theistic way of looking at the world." The Christian has as much right to start from Christian assumptions as secular thinkers have to start from the assumption of naturalism. The Christian need not always be on the defensive, and may start with Christian beliefs and theorize on the basis of them.

The philosophical and Christian boldness of Plantinga's address engendered an immense flowering of Christian philosophy in the subsequent decade. Significant and acclaimed work has been done on such diverse topics as prayer, God's suffering, the problem of evil, the Incarnation and atonement, the Trinity, Scripture studies, emotions and virtues, social theory, forgiveness, religious pluralism, the doctrines of heaven and hell, God and time, the nature of probability and mathematics, and the rationality of religious belief. Christian philosophers, no longer constrained merely to defend their use of religious language or to prove the existence of God, have boldly and powerfully expanded into significant areas of deeply Christian concern unfettered by the constraints of modern secular thought. Let me consider in some detail the accomplishments of three of the contributors: Basil Mitchell, Richard Swinburne and Alvin Plantinga.

Mitchell's philosophical career can be seen as a constant struggle against the reigning orthodoxy of logical positivism and linguistic analysis. Both of these philosophies limited themselves to the empirical world and considered meaningless any talk of worlds outside of the senses. Thus ethical talk, such as "Murder is wrong," and religious talk, such as "God loves us," were considered simply absurd or mere expressions of feelings. Logical positivism finds its roots in the philosophy of the great empiricist and skeptic, David Hume. Hume contended that all knowledge was limited to what can be learned either directly from the senses or by reflection on this sensory input. So if something cannot be sensed—like God—it cannot be known. Logical positivism goes beyond this by setting limits on what can be sensibly *said*, not merely on what can be *known*; it takes a position on what makes language meaningful. A statement is meaningful, the logical positivist claims, only if it can be verified by immediate sense experience. This, as one might imagine, greatly restricts the domain of meaningful assertions. Since God is by definition intangible, assertions about God cannot be verified by immediate sense experience and, therefore, are considered absurd utterances.

Logical positivism began in the early 1920s in an informal discussion group in Austria called the Vienna Circle. The original members, led by physicist Moritz Schlick, included mathematicians, physicists, sociologists and economists but no professional philosophers. United by their passionate dislike of the metaphysical—the realm beyond the experienceable, physical world—the group developed a unified philosophy that embraced science and attempted to destroy philosophy. Although there was a great deal of disagreement, there was an initial impulse to accept the verification theory of meaning, that a statement is meaningful only if it can be verified conclusively by immediate experience. This pivotal principle was simply unjustifiable philosophical imperialism that, in the end, could not survive critical scrutiny.

Although logical positivism would die a well-deserved death in the sixties and seventies, it swept Anglo-American philosophy and theology; indeed theologians capitalized upon the "discoveries" of logical positivism in the infamous Death of God movement (in reality, at least among philosophers, it was really logical positivism that was dead). It would be difficult to imagine an intellectual atmosphere more hostile to belief in God than that found at Oxford in the forties and fifties. And that is where Mitchell was trained and taught. His response was the courageous (because unfashionable) publication of *The Justification of Religious Belief*—a novel approach to the rational justification of belief in God. Mitchell argued that belief in God ought to be justified more like the accumulation of a variety of evidence when making a judgment about the meaning of a literary text or determining an event of history. Such "cumulative case" arguments are more like the judgments that we typically make in our lives—we carefully study the preponderance of available evidence and then make our best judgment concerning the best explanation of the evidence. This commonsensical yet rational approach to the justification of belief in God has influenced countless students of philosophy.

Richard Swinburne, the premier rational apologist of our era, developed, in a very formal fashion, a cumulative case argument for the existence of God. He felt it his calling to respond rationally and not retreat in unreason from the logical positivist attack on theism. Logical positivism was doomed from the outset. Its proponents proved incapable of stating the verification principle in any way that made itself meaningful. If the verification principle itself were true, for it to be meaningful it must be verifiable through sense experience. But it is a philosophical claim of the sort that it was intended to eliminate, and it cannot be verified by experience. By its own standard, then, it is a piece of gibberish; the verification principle is self-referentially inconsistent.

It also had a further troubling defect: it could not justify the essential claims of science that it so cherished. Think about those scientific entities that are central to science but cannot be conclusively verified by experience—protons, neutrons, quarks, the centers of stars, the DNA molecule and so forth. None of these theoretical entities can be observed. Thus, the verification principle would render meaningless any assertions concerning these entities.

Swinburne contends that a more tenable version of verificationism is possible—one that does not depend on conclusive verification by immediate observation. Rather, the proper method of rational inquiry is to support beliefs with evidence or arguments. This is the method of both science and metaphysics, according to Swinburne. Swinburne's unique contribution to the rational defense of theism is his attempt to bring the canons of scientific rationality to bear on religious belief. If belief in God is an explanatory hypothesis, then it can be justified rationally in much the same way as one would justify belief in electrons or gravity. Swinburne contends that science is incapable of explaining the existence and design of the universe, hence it is appropriate to seek a personal explanation—one in terms of the goals and powers of a person. Since God desires an arena for the significant moral and spiritual development of free human beings, he provides a perfectly adequate and rational (but not infallible) explanation of the existence and design of the universe. The existence of God is a simple hypothesis that leads us to expect these otherwise infinitely unexpected phenomena. Swinburne has also used his powerful intellect in much-discussed defenses of Scripture, the atonement, the nature of God and the existence of the soul.

Alvin Plantinga is perhaps best known among philosophers for his penetrating analyses of the problem of evil and the rationality of religious belief. From the time of the Ancients it has been alleged that there is an incompatibility between an omniscient, omnipotent and wholly good God and the fact of evil. Plantinga's "free will defense" demonstrates that this contradiction is only apparent and that the existence of evil does not logically disprove the existence of God. This project is virtually universally acknowledged as successful by theist and nontheist alike.

Plantinga constructs an argument from evil *for* the existence of God as well. Naturalism is the reigning philosophy that denies the existence of anything supernatural or beyond nature; all that exists is matter and energy in their many manifestations. In a naturalistic worldview there are no deep moral values; indeed the natural world (matter in motion) is the world of *facts*, and is indifferent to morality. Hence, the simple judgment that there is evil implies that there is some deep value that is being violated; but naturalism cannot countenance such values. If there is evil, Plantinga argues, there is an ultimate source of value. If the main alternative worldviews under consideration are theism and naturalism, evil weighs heavily in the direction of theism.

With respect to belief in God, Plantinga contends that one does not need arguments or evidence for that belief to be rational. You can imagine what a ruckus such a view has caused among philosophers who prize arguments above all else. Indeed, the reigning orthodoxy since the Enlightenment has been that in order for belief in God to be rational it must be supported by arguments or evidence. This demand for evidence, which Plantinga calls "evidentialism," has developed into the evidentialist objection to belief in God—the claim that belief in God must be supported by evidence to be rational and that there is not sufficient evidence for the existence of God. Plantinga rejects the evidentialist objection for four reasons. First, there *is* evidence for the existence of God. Second, this demand for evidence presumes a misguided theory of rationality that is self-referentially inconsistent (if one accepts it, one is irrational by its own standards) and that excludes cases of clearly rational beliefs. Third, belief in God is more like belief in other persons than belief in a scientific theory (for which there is clearly a demand for evidence). Finally, he has developed his own theory of rationality, or warrant, which is better suited to how human beings actually acquire beliefs. He recognizes how little we would be able to believe if we were under the tyranny of the demand for evidence; but since we have so many clearly justified beliefs, they must be acquired in some other manner. Plantinga argues that they are most often acquired by cognitive faculties that produce beliefs immediately, that is, without recourse to or need of arguments or evidence.[4]

All of the thinkers in this volume have made impressive contributions to their disciplines. Few graduate students in this country have not worked carefully through Suppe's history of the philosophy of science of the past century; Suppe's current work on scientific theories will be recounted in the history of the next century of philosophy of science. John Rist has focused on the long-neglected late Ancient and early Medieval periods of philosophy; Rist's writings have helped bring this important era, scorned and ignored because of its love of metaphysics, back into the modern era. Mortimer Adler's voluminous writings and tireless efforts on behalf of a classical education have helped revive the emphasis on the "Great Books" in higher education; his philosophical work is perhaps surpassed by his involvement in The Paideia Project, an educational reform program for the restoration of general liberal education in our schools and universities. Linda Zagzebski is a young philosopher whose recent work on divine foreknowledge and human freedom has been much discussed of late.

The work of Stephen Davis ranges from philosophy to theology. He has written on such diverse topics as the nature of God, the resurrection, hell and the inspiration of Scripture. Terence Penelhum's acclaimed writings in many ways parallel his journey toward faith; his research on skepticism, religious belief and faith in the Enlightenment and post-Enlightenment eras reveals a passionate struggle for rational faith. As a writer and an editor, Nicholas Rescher has made an indelible mark on philosophy; in addition to his many and diverse books on virtually every major area of philosophy, Rescher has long edited prestigious scholarly journals. Nicholas Wolterstorff is known for his uncanny ability to master a new discipline in a very short period of time and then to write about and make a genuine contribution to the discipline. His innovative work on philosophical theology has led to invitations to deliver the distinguished Wilde Lectures at Oxford and Gifford Lectures at the major universities of Scotland.

The grapplings with faith and reason in an accessible manner by people of prodigious intellect provide encouragement for those struggling with their faith—these intelligent people have struggled with belief in God and come out on the side of God. Given the general hostility to theism within academic philosophy, there is a tremendous opportunity for important witness by esteemed Christian philosophers. Within departments where there are Christian members, a different climate has been created wherein students who were repressing or hiding spiritual struggles, questions or concerns are welcome to discuss matters of faith with someone they respect. As Suppe notes in his essay, both students and professional philosophers have asked contributors to this volume: "Tell me about your faith. Since I respect you as a philosopher I have to treat very seriously the fact that you are a believer."

Although Christian philosophers have attained to the highest scholarly level in their discipline, little attention has been paid to the actual generation, development and sustenance of their beliefs. Philosophers are often considered calculating devices, devoid of a psychology, sociology or personal story; yet psychological and sociological factors have played crucial roles in the faith development of professional philosophers. I know of a young philosopher who did his graduate work at a university well known for its hostility to theism; indeed, he wrote his dissertation under a professor who was a self-professed evangelist for atheism. This atmosphere had a negative effect on this person's faith. Shortly after graduate school he attended an American Philosophical Association meeting and noticed Alvin Plantinga walking down a hall; he desperately wanted to speak with him and be told (or just feel) that his Christian beliefs were acceptable, but he was afraid to approach him. Eventually he did meet and speak with Plantinga, which was crucial to reestablishing his faith. It is important to many Christians that they be part of a believing community that includes respected intellectuals.

I recently spoke with a friend who was moved by a comment that William Alston had made in an article on religious experience; Alston indicated that he prayed to God on his knees and that God had spoken to him and told him to work in Christian philosophy. Ostensibly the article was a sophisticated and complicated defense of the view that such experiences do not require philosophical justification for their rational acceptance. But the person with whom I spoke was astonished—not by the philosophical arguments but by the fact that a famous philosopher prayed on his knees. Having felt uneasy about his own devotion, the comment was liberating. Respected Christian philosophers are not only models of Christian philosophy, they are models of how thinkers can be Christians.

The Literature of Confession

"Thou hast made us for thyself and our hearts are restless until they find their rest in Thee." So exclaims St. Augustine in the most famous quotation from *The Confessions*, the greatest of all spiritual autobiographies. The topic of his spiritual autobiography is set from the beginning: finding rest in God. More deeply it is about the *God* in whom St. Augustine finds rest. He writes of this extended prayer that it

praise[s] the righteous and good God as [it] speaks either of my evil or good, and [it is] meant to excite men's minds and affections toward him. At least as far as I am concerned, this is what [it] did for me when [it was] being written and [it still does] this when read. What some people think of [it] is their own affair; but I do know that [it has] given pleasure to many of my brethren and still does so.[5]

Spiritual autobiography produces a salutary effect both in its author and in its readers. Self-reflection provides an occasion for becoming aware of God's mysterious and providential grace in the details of one's life; what at the time may have seemed serendipitous happenstance, in recollection through the eyes of faith is recognized as divine providence.

What then is a confession but a profession of the goodness and mercy of God? The dual meaning of *confess* includes admitting one's moral and spiritual deficiencies as well as acknowledging the grace of God. The occasion of recounting one's sins therefore becomes an opportunity to praise and give thanks to God for his compassion. Confession, as opposed to a boastful recounting of one's experiences, involves a loathing of one's past and a sense of need and gratitude toward God for divine forgiveness; it is the publican giving voice to his plaintive cry: "God be merciful to me, a sinner." Rather than making sin seem exciting and glorifying it, confessional writers describe its odious effects—both the degradation of character as vice eclipses virtue as well as the dehumanization caused by others through willful abuse and neglect.

Although writers of spiritual autobiographies have been deeply involved in sins, both in the giving and receiving, the details are typically spared. One need only include that which makes a necessary contribution to the spiritual dynamics, and the details may be safely excised. Tolstoy in his spiritual autobiography, *Confession*, reduces an extremely sordid past into a single, powerful paragraph:

I cannot recall those years without horror, loathing and heart-rend-ing pain. I killed people in war, challenged men to duels with the purpose of killing them, and lost at cards; I squandered the fruits of the peasants' toil and then had them executed; I was a fornicator and a cheat. Lying, stealing, promiscuity of every kind, drunkenness, violence, murder—there was not a crime I did not commit; yet in spite of it all I was praised, and my colleagues considered me and still do consider me a relatively moral man.[6]

While he includes every kind of sin, he rightly omits the specifics.

One may observe in the literature of confession that the authors have known every sin and temptation common to humankind. This makes their experiences universal and manifests the universal nature of temptation; the power of good confessional literature is that it speaks for every person. St. Paul writes of his mysterious thorn in the flesh and thereby allows each of us to fill in the thorn-in-the-flesh blank for our own life. St. Augustine speaks for all when he prays, "Grant me chastity . . . but not yet." St. Augustine and St. Paul have written confessions that could be mine; I understand their need for redemption precisely because they are speaking for me.

Of course the literature of confession has power only if it is honest, even about the lifelong battle with wickedness and doubt. One may be rightly suspicious of spiritual writings that facilely turn famous Christians into saints. C. S. Lewis often lamented that people considered him better than he really was because they viewed him through the lenses of his (triumphalist) writings. Lewis was so clever that he could make it seem totally contrary to reason to doubt the existence of both heaven and Narnia. The misleading impression of Lewis's personal virtues could have been easily remedied if his spiritual autobiography had extended beyond his conversion. Only his brutally honest confessions of doubt and anger with God upon the suffering and death of his wife in *A Grief Observed* reveal Lewis for the moral and spiritual mortal that he really was. No glib theodicies suffice when Lewis becomes the sufferer; he curses God, calling him a cosmic sadist and divine vivisectionist. Curiously *A Grief Observed*, his most authentic writing, was published under a pseudonym. One most fully understands the Christian Lewis in this book, not in his earlier autobiography or his other writings.

Although a novel, Frederick Buechner's *Godric*, a compelling spiritual biography of an English pirate who converted to Christianity and was later declared a saint (this much of the story is true), is an honest confession of the lingering power of sin. Buechner's imaginative genius is displayed in his attempt to understand what it must have been like to be transformed from lascivious pirate to reluctant saint. In those days, as Kierkegaard writes, faith was a project for a lifetime. How is one actually set free from one's lusts to genuine and willing obedience to God? For Godric, it was not without a lifetime of kicking and screaming. Godric does not characterize the Christian life as a single dying with resurrection to new life once and for all, but rather he exclaims: "As a man dies many times before he's dead, so does he wend from birth to birth until, by grace, he comes alive at last."[7] As a very old man Godric wistfully reflects on the power of the old self over the new self: unable even to lust, he *wishes* that he still could. He describes his state:

> How I rage at times to smite with these same fists I scarce can clench! How I long, when woods are green, to lark and leap on shanks grown dry as sticks! Let a maid but pass my way with sport in her eye and her braid a-swinging, and I burn for her although my wick's long since burnt out. . . . So ever and again young Godric's dreams well up to flood old Godric's prayers, or prayers and dreams reach God in such a snarl he has to comb the tangle out, and who knows which he counts more dear.[8]

Confession is the story of the old self being made new, again and again, by the grace of God.

The Bible itself is a treasure trove of confessional literature. Job, for example, in the midst of his anger with God—his intense desire to have his day in court with God as defendant and Job as prosecuting attorney—can still proclaim: "For I know that my Redeemer lives, and at last he will stand upon the earth; and tho worms destroy my body, yet in my flesh shall I see God."[9] The Psalms contain confession of every variety: pious profession of faith, anger that God seems unjust and absent, confession of sin, expressions of gratitude toward God for being steadfast in love and slow to anger, praise of God for his mighty works, pleadings with and cajolings of God, false praise, and so forth. In the painfully honest Psalms we see into the very heart of the authentic religious believer. "Why dost thou hide thy face? Why dost thou forget our affliction and oppression?" (Ps 44:24 KJV). Wake up, God, the psalmist screams, and come to our rescue. Although Jeremiah, the weary prophet, confesses his anger with God ("O, Lord, thou hast deceived me, and I was deceived; thou art stronger than I, and thou has prevailed"—20:7), he returns to God and places his trust in him. Yet Jeremiah chafes against the divine inscrutability and curses the day he was born. And it is in St. Paul's sober yet fleeting confessions that we see him as a fellow pilgrim, and not merely a divine vehicle of doctrine, struggling as we along the way.

It takes more than honesty to construct a powerful and enduring spiritual autobiography. The story and the life remembered must be interesting. It must appeal to universal sins, temptations, needs, desires and struggles. And in order to avoid egotism and interest only to its author, its subject matter must ultimately be God. In the best, there is an intermingling of the personal and the intellectual. While reflecting on what makes life worth living, Tolstoy wanders about in the "forest of human knowledge," discussing with alacrity and clarity the worldviews of the great philosophers and the Wisdom literature of the Bible. There is an ease with which great autobiography engages the most compelling and profound human questions in an insightful and illuminating manner.

In this collection, Plantinga moves from the mentioning of specific tragedies to people he has known to a discussion of the problem of evil. After recording the effect of the cries of the oppressed in South Africa and Palestine, Wolterstorff discusses the notion that the Bible is a book about justice. Penelhum laments being in the Christian minority among philosophers as well as being painfully cognizant of apparently rational alternatives to theism. And Swinburne's essay is primarily intellectual—recounting the chief influences on his development as the premier rational apologist for the Christian faith of our era.

The content of each essay is both personal and philosophical (no writer was to present a philosophical treatise). Indeed, the essays are primarily personal. Let me mention a few examples. Fred Suppe discusses his struggles growing up under the tyranny of a sadistic father. Alvin Plantinga reminisces about the church camps that he attended as a youth and about Sunday school, and he admits to being an insufficiently attentive husband. Nicholas Rescher mentions his doubts about God's existence. Terence Penelhum discusses the struggles he faces being both a philosopher and a Christian. John Rist traces his childhood development. Basil Mitchell wistfully remembers how, a young man, he unexpectedly wept on the eve of a world war. Nick Wolterstorff describes the impact of losing a son in a mountain-climbing accident.

The reader is invited to enjoy the confessions contained within this collection. May each reader treat them as St. Augustine treated his—a prayer of thanksgiving to God who manifests his providential care in the various circumstances of our lives. May you find in each essay some reflection of your life as seeker, Christian, pilgrim, questioner, thinker, struggler, doubter and most important as a sinner in need of grace. May the prayers of these philosophers prod you to cry out: "Lord, hear *my* prayer." As Augustine urges of his confessions, may we see the depths from which we cry to God: "For nothing comes nearer to your ears than a confessing heart, and a life grounded in faith."[10]

War and Friendship

BASIL MITCHELL

Basil Mitchell was for many years the Nolloth Professor of the Christian Religion at Oxford University. For twenty years he was fellow and tutor in philosophy at Keble College at Oxford. He moved to Oriel College, Oxford, during the tenure of his chair from 1968 until 1984. His professional work is marked by originality, clarity and accessibility to laypeople. His major works include The Justification of Religious Belief, Morality: Religious and Secular *and* How to Play Theological Ping-Pong.

I was born in Bath, Somerset, on April 9, 1917, and narrowly survived the influenza epidemic of 1918. After a number of moves my parents settled in Southampton when I was eleven and my sister nine. My father was by that time an established quantity surveyor, having worked his way up by his own efforts from modest beginnings. My mother was a small, lively, highly intelligent woman who had trained as an elementary-school teacher and shared with my father a passion for amateur dramatics. As a producer of Gilbert and Sullivan opera my father was later to achieve something like a professional standard.

When I was twelve, not long after we had moved to Southampton, an event occurred that irreversibly transformed our lives. My mother, who had recently given birth to another daughter, was suddenly struck down by rheumatoid arthritis in a particularly virulent form. She retired to bed and stayed there, almost entirely helpless, for the remaining twenty years of her life. After an initial period of intense pain she attained a sort of equilibrium, but was unable ever again to feed herself. The most she could do in the way of physical activity was to turn the pages of a book. We kept a housekeeper and a maid, which was within the means of a middle-class family in those days, and my sister increasingly took over the task of nursing her.

From then on the focus of life in the household became my mother's room. She was moved into the sitting room, from which she could get a view of the street, and there she received a growing number of visitors who came in the first instance out of pity or neighborliness and stayed because she was good company. As time went on and my sister and I grew into adolescence, it was chiefly our own friends who congregated in my mother's room. The talk was lively and unstuffy, and there was constant laughter. My mother turned out to be a remarkable catalyst, and the group of boys and girls from our own and neighboring schools who were always dropping in felt demonstrably at ease in her company, and with one another. We soon took the situation so much for granted that my sister and I would say to some new acquaintance, "You must come along and meet my mother," without seeing any need to explain that they would find her bedridden. I was the chief beneficiary of the stimulus she provided and, more indirectly, of my sister's devoted care of her.

The Sufi Days
I do not remember how it was that we first encountered the Sufi movement. Since orthodox medicine could do nothing for my mother it is not surprising that she came in touch with the varieties of alternative medicine and philosophy that flourished as much then as they do today. The Sufis held a regular service of Universal Worship in Southampton at which selections were read from the sacred writings of the major world religions—Jewish, Christian, Islamic, Hindu, Buddhist and Zoroastrian. The underlying idea was that essentially the same truth was to be found in all religions, above all in their mystical writings and practices. It was an accepted principle that Sufism was not in itself an alternative religion and that its adherents could and should maintain the practice of their own religion. As children my mother and

father had both attended their parish church—my father singing in the choir—but as a family our links with the church had been only intermittent. My sister and I were duly confirmed, but I felt unhappy at the exclusive claims of Christianity and at the particular, historical basis of the Christian gospel, which seemed at odds with the mystical essence of religions emphasized by the Sufis.

By the time I went to Oxford as an undergraduate in 1935 the Sufi influence was very strong, and it remained so until the outbreak of war in 1939. In 1937 we took my mother to Suresnes, a suburb of Paris, where the movement had its European headquarters. There we encountered the family of Hazarat Inayat Khan, who had brought the Sufi message from India a generation before and was revered as the founder of the movement. In a secluded garden on the outskirts of Paris there was a sort of ashram, and Vilayat and his sisters Noorunnissa and Chaironnissa presided over a kind of court in which Vilayat was heir apparent. He was a young man of striking good looks, of which he seemed well aware, and very considerable charm, and there was a good deal of devotion to him among the many middle-aged ladies assembled there. It was only partly shared by my family, who had been used to a more spontaneous and less reverential atmosphere. Yet there was apparent a genuine strain of gentle spirituality that I had found also among our Sufi friends in Southampton. What it could effect in a person of rare integrity was shown later in the life and death of Noorunnissa, who was executed in Ravensbruck after being parachuted into France by SOE in 1940, a story movingly told by Jean Overton Fuller in her book *Madeleine*.

My own spiritual experience at this time was less deliberately contemplative in its character than spontaneously Wordsworthian. It was while reading, when still at school, T. R. Glover's *The Conflict of Religions in the Early Roman Empire* that I found quoted there the lines from "Tintern Abbey":

> And I have felt
> A presence that disturbs me with the joy
> Of elevated thoughts; a sense sublime
> Of something far more deeply interfused,
> Whose dwelling is the light of settling suns,

And the round ocean and the living air,
And the blue sky, and in the mind of man:
A motion and a spirit, that impels
All thinking things, all objects of all thought,
And rolls through all things.

I was deeply moved and recognized, as I thought, the sense that I often had, when walking alone in the countryside near Southampton, that some intense reality was just on the point of breaking through the surface of things and revealing itself to me.

When at Oxford I eventually started to study philosophy, I was deeply disappointed. I had expected that I should be encouraged to ask questions about the nature of ultimate reality and the place of human beings in relation to it, but even when, as with Plato's *Republic*, the text plainly demanded it, these issues were systematically avoided, and we discussed only those questions which readily offered themselves to philosophical analysis in the mode of Moore and Russell. "The trouble with you, Basil," my tutor despairingly exclaimed, "is that you are interested in the great rolling themes of philosophy."

War and Duty

In consequence I rapidly learned, as I suppose many bright undergraduates do, to separate the technical study of philosophy from what most deeply concerned me, with the result that my own working philosophy of life remained immature, undeveloped and quite inadequate to cope with the crisis that was soon to overtake all of us.

I had had some inkling of what was in store when in the autumn of 1938 I had been invited by a Sufi friend to go with her from Suresnes to her home in Rotterdam. I was there at the time of the Munich crisis, and we found ourselves standing outside radio shops and listening almost against our will to Hitler's staccato speeches and the barbaric cries of "Sieg Heil; Sieg Heil!" I returned from Rotterdam to Southampton in the liner *Statendam;* as I went on deck the first morning at sea, we were in the Straits of Dover in brilliant sunshine, which intensified the whiteness of the cliffs, the green of the fields above them and the blue-black clouds beyond. In face of this dramatic spectacle I suddenly found myself sobbing uncontrollably as it became apparent to me what that narrow stretch of water might mean.

The war found me, like many of my student generation, still unprepared for the decisions that needed to be made. In my attitudes I was vaguely cosmopolitan and regarded patriotism as an outdated concept. Hence my tears on the *Statendam* took me entirely unawares. To the political situation my response was contradictory. I was strongly inclined to pacifism, as were many of my contemporaries, but nevertheless I believed that Munich was a disgrace and that we ought to have gone to war to save Czechoslovakia. When the time came and I had to decide whether to allow myself to be called up for military service or to seek exemption as a conscientious objector, I was in a state of painful and not very creditable indecision.

Not only did I not know what were the right answers to the right questions, but I was by no means sure what the right questions were. I was, I think, at the time young for my age and still had a good measure of adolescent self-absorption. It was not chiefly for me a question of what a man situated like myself ought to do in these circumstances and what principles he ought to act upon, but rather a matter of what I should do, I with my particular gifts and aspirations. I had already been given a scholarship to study Indian philosophy under Radhakrishnan, then a professor at Oxford, and I thought that this was valuable work that I was uniquely fitted to do. I didn't want to waste years of my life on military activities that I was unsuited to undertake and the very idea of which filled me with distaste. I was even sorry for myself and others like me because we had been constrained by events to make a decision that there was no means of evading, but that we were too young and uninformed to make responsibly.

As I now attempt to relive my spiritual history, there is no doubt that the summer of 1940 was the most critical point in it, because it compelled me to draw upon and eventually to call in question the religious philosophy I had endeavored to live by until then, and initiated, as I can now see, a fundamental change.

But one other formative influence needs to be mentioned. In 1937, as I began to read philosophy, I was introduced to a woman, a fellow student, who was every bit as able academically as myself but who was quite remarkably talented also as a poet, a musician and a painter. For a blissful summer and autumn we walked in the hills around Oxford, idled on the river and talked interminably. During summer vacation we hired a skiff with friends and paddled up the Thames to Lechlade and back, where in the evenings we would go for walks along the river bank among the meadowsweet, the willowherb and the loosestrife—names I learned from her—while she recited from memory a sequel she had composed to *Twelfth Night*. It was pure magic. I had experienced "the marriage of true minds," and there was nothing I wanted to do about it but let it continue indefinitely, as it was surely destined to do. I just assumed that we were meant for one another, and it did not occur to me that any physical gesture was needed to make that plain. In any case I doubt that there was anything I could have done about it. I was a lively, sensitive and reflective boy with a lot of growing up still to do; she had all these qualities in abundance but was already a mature woman. I needed to be ten years older.

We agreed to "remain friends," and for once this commonplace solution became a reality. I spent the next ten years falling in and out of love with her, managing almost always to be out of phase with her own attachments to other men, but during that time, as will become apparent, there developed between us a deep and enduring affection.

In early 1940, still very uncertain of my attitude toward fighting, I was registered as a conscientious objector and waited to be called up for ambulance service. I had persuaded myself—and indeed still believe—that in time of war some individuals and groups have a vocation to display in their lives the spirit of nonviolence. But was I such a person? In May of that year, as the German tanks rolled through the Low Countries and then through France, the question became ever more insistent. In that crisis it would need a very sure conviction to justify my refraining from doing what I could toward stopping this palpable evil. Moreover, my motives were mixed. I still had the feeling, absurd as it now seems, that I was someone special, whose specific talents were not to be wasted. This was a vocation of a sort, but it was not of the kind that I needed to justify my refusal to fight, and I felt myself failing miserably to distinguish the two.

In this dilemma my Sufi friends urged me to turn to the Bhagavad Gita, which I was at the time reading in Sanskrit. The entire burden of that work was the inability of the warrior, Arjuna, as he viewed the army drawn up against him, to decide whether he should fight. The poem is a dialogue between him and his charioteer, the god Kṛiṣṇa in disguise, and in it Kṛiṣṇa expounds the principles that ought to guide anyone in a similar predicament. So I turned to the Gita and searched it earnestly for guidance. I was impressed, as who could fail to be, by the majesty of that noble poem, but found to my distress that it had no message for me—or rather that it had a message, but one that I could not accept. Kṛiṣṇa tells Arjuna that it is not the action itself that matters; it is the spirit in which it is done.

> He who in work sees no-work, and in no-work work, he is the man of judgement among men; he the controlled, doing work perfectly. That man whose every enterprise is without desire or motive, whose work is burnt up in the fire of knowledge, the wise call learned. Having cast off attachment to the fruit of work, contented ever and on none dependent, though he engage himself in work, yet works he not at all.[1]

> Hold equal pleasure and pain, gain and loss, victory and defeat; then gird thyself for the battle; thus shalt thou not gather to thee guilt.[2]

What, then, was Arjuna to do? How was he to find the duty appropriate to himself? The answer was that he was a Kṣatriya, a member of the warrior caste, and the duty of such a man is to fight: "Again if thou considerest thy duty, thou shouldst not waver; for than a fight decreed by duty is naught better for a Kṣatriya."[3] "Better a man's own duty, though ill done, than another's duty ill-performed."[4]

I found that I just could not view the matter in these terms. Not only was the concept of duty deriving from one's social status totally irrelevant to my situation, but the underlying philosophy was one I could not accept. I felt profoundly that what was at stake in Europe was (when all the necessary qualifications had been made) a fight of good against evil and that the outcome was of momentous importance.

From that time on, although I did not clearly perceive it, the Sufi influence began to lose its hold on me. I had been compelled to deny, under the pressure of practical decision, that the same truth was to be found in all religions. The Gita, impressive though it was, represented a view of the world and of our place in it that was not only different from but incompatible with any that I could bring myself to believe or live by.

Meanwhile I was recalled to sober good sense by the woman whose friendship now showed its worth: "It is impossible," she wrote,

> to estimate the precise value of what we have to give the world but we must keep a sense of proportion. Supposing you became as distinguished a philosopher as, say, Bradley, and I as distinguished a painter as Dame Laura Knight—no mean achievement either of them—how can we estimate how much that degree of competence justifies us in setting ourselves apart—I choose these two because they are well above the average, yet certainly nothing like in the top class. . . .

> Please don't think I am urging you to go and fight. Far be it from me. All I am doing is querying whether this inner voice demanding better things of you is not felt by a great number of people; and whether, if this is so, one has not to try and see oneself for the time being as a contributing part of a great entity working for an aim which we both agree is infinitely worth while, rather than as a unit working out one's own salvation.

The Naval Life

In the end this counsel prevailed, and in November 1940 I joined the Royal Navy. The next six years were spent in naval service: in the North Atlantic and the Mediterranean for a short time as a rating, in the North and South Atlantic and the Indian Ocean as an officer in a corvette, and toward the end of the war in a training establishment ashore. How, in terms of my "spiritual development," can I describe those years?

Like the innumerable others who underwent the experience of wartime service in the armed forces I lived several lives, which only partly overlapped. There was the life at sea or in harbor entirely bounded by the Navy; there was, at occasional and almost invariably unpredictable intervals, life at home or with friends during brief periods of leave; and there were the letters that for most of the time were all that served to keep these different lives together.

Perhaps the most surprising thing, in retrospect, is that I came increasingly to respect the Navy itself as an institution. My life as a student had been intensely individualistic. I was quite unaware of the college or the university as performing any function but that of providing a necessary social and academic background for myself and my friends. I was, of course, aware of the kindly concern shown for me by my tutors and by other teachers who had occasion to help me. I was, I hope, genuinely grateful, but I had no conception that in so doing they were, among other things, performing a role within the institution that they served. And if I had realized this, I should have thought their concern to that extent less authentic.

In the Navy I quickly became aware of this extra institutional dimension. I had known in advance that I would be subject to military discipline and that a warship must be strictly governed by firm regulations and a clear structure of command. I had assumed that I should find this wholly repugnant, the necessary condition, indeed, of an ultimate good to be achieved—or rather evil to be avoided—but without any value in itself. I had expected the regime to be, if not brutal, then at least insensitive. The reality was quite different. I wrote, while still an ordinary seaman in a battleship:

> One thing that impresses me more and more as a result of this semi-totalitarian existence is how absolutely awful such a life must be when not ruled, as in the Navy it so obviously is, by a genuine solicitude for the welfare of the people. The higher ranks have such complete power which could so easily be abused by a very slight relapse from honesty and kindliness. Where these standards are openly denied, there are no limits to the cruelty of those above and the frustration and misery of those below.

Before being sent to the battleship I had had a brief experience of what it might be like when discipline had largely broken down. The naval barracks at Portsmouth had been badly damaged in air raids and were used as a temporary transit camp for sailors who were waiting for draft to seagoing ships. The Navy, understandably, did not appoint its best officers or petty officers to serve in such an establishment, and, in consequence, all sorts of rackets and corruption flourished there. Having neither the resources nor the desire to bribe myself out of it, I went quickly to the head of the queue for drafting and was soon at sea again. I have always remembered the experience as approximating closely

Hobbes's state of nature as "a war of every man against every man."

Together with this sense of the Navy as an institution went a lively appreciation of qualities in people that I had simply taken for granted before and had not particularly valued. At Oxford what had mattered was that people should be clever, sensitive and interesting. One relished what differentiated people, not what they had in common. In the Navy it mattered supremely that men should be solid and reliable—that they would know their job, whatever it was, and do it well. My admiration for this quality as I found it especially in the petty officers and other long-service ratings was accentuated by the difficulty I had in developing it myself. I had constantly to be taking thought to anticipate problems that might arise, and devise strategies to deal with them, knowing always that this was an inadequate substitute for the trained capacities and the ingrained character that would lead them in an emergency to act spontaneously as the situation demanded.

While an ordinary seaman in the battleship *Queen Elizabeth* I became subject once again to the ministrations of the Church of England. The chaplain, Launcelot Fleming, was a man of rare spiritual discernment; he quickly realized that above all things I longed for times when I could be quiet and alone. In a ship you can never get away from people, and wherever you go there are mechanical noises of one sort or another. He offered me the use of his cabin from time to time and lent me books.

On Sundays in harbor Divisions and Prayers were held on the quarterdeck. Both were at that time compulsory—a military parade in full uniform followed by a religious service. Although many will find it hard to believe, these services made a deep impression upon me, and I do not think I was alone in this. Fleming was a man with a strong pastoral sense to whom the ship's company were devoted, and he was able to set a tone for these occasions in which the timeless language of the Book of Common Prayer released one for a while from the "changes and chances of this mortal life."

I was moved especially by the prayer prescribed in the Prayer Book to be used in the Navy at sea, with which I was later to become familiar:

O Eternal Lord God who alone spreadest out the heavens, and rulest the raging of the sea; who hast compassed the waters with bounds until day and night come to an end; Be pleased to receive into thy

almighty and most gracious protection the persons of us thy ser-
vants and the Fleet in which we serve. Preserve us from the dangers
of the sea and from the violence of the enemy; that we may be a
safeguard unto our most gracious Sovereign King George and his
dominions, and a security to such as pass on the seas upon their
lawful occasions; that the inhabitants of our Island may in peace and
quietness serve thee our God; and that we may return in safety to
enjoy the blessings of the land with the fruits of our labours, and
with a thankful remembrance of thy mercies to praise and glorify
thy Holy Name; through Jesus Christ our Lord. Amen.

With extraordinary perceptiveness this said all that a sailor wants to
say in language as splendid as it is memorable.

Later on when I was an officer in a small ship I noticed once again
how the ethos of identical ships could vary with the personality and
principles of officers and petty officers in key positions. The greatest
difference, however, from life in a battleship was how much closer one
was to the sea. Corvettes had been designed on the model of whalers
to ride the Atlantic swell, which they did superbly but with no regard
for the comfort of those on board. The worst storms we endured were
those off the southern point of Africa, Cape Agulhas, where strong
intersecting currents reinforced the fury of the winds. I was surprised
to find either that I was not afraid at all or that my fear was altogether
eclipsed by awe at the natural forces that were being unleashed. It has
often been remarked that sailors are rarely irreligious, and it is perhaps
not surprising that I still had on occasion those Wordsworthian moments when the veil seemed on the point of being withdrawn and the
underlying truth revealed. I do not think I ever doubted the creative
and sustaining power of God, although I cannot now remember if I
prayed or not.

So much for my naval life. The other two lives—of occasional, usually short, periods of leave and of letters written and received at irreg-
ular intervals—were inextricably intertwined. As with all men at sea,
my life was lived for the most part in and for letters. They were more
significant almost than the rare and abbreviated meetings with family
and friends that the circumstances of the time allowed. The effect was
to intensify self-consciousness and other-consciousness to an unusual

degree. My friend was now employed as a senior civil servant in the Air Ministry in London, where she endured the blitz and later the flying bombs and was continuously overworked at serious risk to her health. Her war was in many respects worse than mine.

We invariably met when I was on leave—it would have been unthinkable for either of us not to do so—and the unbroken flow of letters, often on her part written in the early hours of the morning when desperately tired, bore witness to deep affection and a prevailing level of mutual understanding. There was nothing I could do but be at hand to offer consolation when that was possible and to hope that, when the war came to an end and normal life was resumed, the underlying affinity between us would finally assert itself.

Endings

The war did eventually come to an end, but I was kept in the Navy until August 1946. I was lucky enough to be able to return to Oxford the next term as a research fellow to continue my study of Sanskrit and my research in Indian philosophy. But, truth to tell, the heart had gone out of it; I no longer possessed the conviction that had propelled me into it. Indeed, the further I pursued my research into the Vedanta, the more it seemed to me that there were very fundamental differences between the worldview it represented and that of Christianity. So when the opportunity arose of applying for a tutorial fellowship in philosophy at Keble College in 1947, I embraced it without hesitation and, having been elected, began my career as a mainline teacher of philosophy.

So far what I have written is more obviously autobiography than it is *spiritual* autobiography. What elements of spiritual development are to be found in it? I cannot answer this question with any degree of honesty without first completing the straight autobiography, because the two were inextricably linked. By the end of the war things in our family had changed. My father had left my mother to live with, and eventually to marry, his business partner. They had remained in Southampton to continue the business while my mother and sisters had been evacuated to Oxford; and the outcome was, perhaps, not surprising. In 1945 my younger sister, by then aged twenty-one and a woman of vivid, sky-blue temperament, was killed while riding pillion on Vilayat's motor-cycle. It was a devastating blow to our already divided family, which shocked Vilayat deeply. It inevitably tended to distance him somewhat from us and ourselves from the Sufi movement. My mother's care then devolved upon myself and my other sister, who was by that time married to an army chaplain. On Good Friday 1947 my mother died after a brief illness. The doctors were astonished that her emaciated frame not only had allowed her to survive for twenty years, but had permitted her to display to the end such extraordinary energy and spirit. When the time came, with her surviving daughter married and her son securely set upon the career he wanted, it seems that she simply declined to make the effort to stay alive any longer.

My friend and I were now both over thirty. She had returned to painting as I had to philosophy, and the difficulties for her were, if anything, even greater than mine. It was not easy to recover the practical skills involved and to become in effect a student again after so many years as an administrator. It was becoming increasingly clear, too, that she was beginning to encounter the kind of problems that feminist writers were to identify ten or twenty years later. How was she to secure the independence necessary to her development as an artist within the framework of a conventional marriage? She deeply loved children and knew that if she had any of her own they would inevitably come first. She was, moreover, the youngest member of a large and awesomely intellectual family, whose authority she respected but from which she needed desperately to obtain freedom. She experienced in her own person a sometimes violent struggle between the analytical and intuitive elements in her nature. Plato, she always insisted, was right about the conflict between art and philosophy.

It was clear to me and, indeed, to both of us that we could no longer sustain the old comradely relationship that had been possible only because of my long absences. A decision had to be made. I could not go on living indefinitely in the kind of uncertainty that had been tolerable during the war, when all things were uncertain. The outcome was, as I had feared, that she was not ready to marry me. She doubted if she was ready to marry anyone, and the trouble with me, in contrast to her other men friends, was that it was clearly marriage or nothing. A plainly eligible suitor, no matter how patiently he waited—indeed the more patiently he waited—was something that in her predicament she could not cope with, and she said so. My appearance in that role raised so many problems for her that it put our long friendship itself at risk. So the break took place, on my instigation, and it was attended by much distress on both sides.

Two years later I was married to my present wife, and there began for me an era of settled happiness that falls outside the scope of the present narrative. The old relationship did not end but was transmuted into a less intense but still secure friendship, the tone of which is heard in a letter I received just before my wedding: "If we don't meet much now, and I suppose we shan't, it has been worth it, hasn't it? I hope for you it will be a jumping off point for better things, not a mill stone. I can't say in a letter all I want to say, but I hope and believe life will give you of its best, because you give it so much of yours." Three years later, in September 1953, after spending a week's holiday with us as godmother to our second child, she was drowned while sailing with two friends in circumstances that were never fully explained.

Means of Grace
It is only in retrospect that the account I have given can be read as a spiritual autobiography at all. When I began my teaching career at Oxford and endeavored to make coherent sense of what had happened to me in my adult life till then—and I could not disentangle this personal problem from the professional task that lay ahead of me—I met for the first time Christian thinkers who were imaginative and articulate and also philosophically sophisticated.

What had increasingly led me to be dissatisfied with the essentially monistic philosophy of my Sufi mentors was its failure, as I now saw it, to attach enduring importance to individual persons; to the institutions that molded them and enabled them to flourish; to the historical processes that had formed them; and to the natural world that nourished them. My native cast of thought was idealistic, and, left to myself, I was liable to rest satisfied with abstractions. But I had been compelled by circumstances to attend to particulars—in the Navy to the needs of particular individuals acting out a particular role in a particular historical situation through involvement in a particular institution; and, in my personal life, in responding to the demands of a person of very acute observation who had a sharp sense of truth in respect of feelings and their expression. Hence what had initially, in my Sufi days, repelled me in Christianity—its insistence upon the embodiment of the divine in a particular figure who had entered the world at a particular time and place—now seemed to me congruous with what I had learned about the nature and development of human beings. The destiny of individual souls was such that it could be realized only in a community, both in this life and beyond, a community in which they could be known and loved. The ultimate love that expressed and reflected the love of God in Christ was of worth in itself and unaffected by change.

I recognized now that I had been the object of this love, preeminently in the two closest relationships of my life up to that point, with my mother and my friend, but also, as I could now see, with many others who had shown their regard for me. I believed also that I had myself, however inadequately and incompletely, got some inkling of it, not least in the latter days of that protracted, eventually frustrated, but deeply enriching love affair. It had become apparent that, however intractable the problems we encountered as a man and a woman of only partly overlapping vocations, involved in the complexities of a specific social situation, we had nevertheless been enabled to see each other clearly and to recognize and respond to each other's aspirations with a certain kind of disinterested love. I had found that, above all, I wanted her to resolve her tensions, fulfill her varied capacities and flourish as a human being, if possible with, if necessary without, my own participation. And this flourishing was not a matter simply of some satisfactory accommodation between her conflicting desires, but of her becoming fully what she was meant to be. And it had become abundantly clear that this was also her wish for me, whatever role I might subsequently play in her life. It took time for these thoughts to sort themselves out, but they began to take shape quite early in my academic career.

So I came back into the Church of England with a curious sense that I had never left it. This is something hard to explain to anyone whose Christian formation has been different. The church had always been there in the background of my life, patiently waiting, but never obtrusive, never insistent. On the *Queen Elizabeth* Launcelot Fleming, as far as I can remember, never pressed me to take Communion or engaged me in theological discussion. He offered me a place to be quiet in and books to read, because these were what I most needed at the time. The formal Prayer Book services I attended in the Navy made no attempt to work upon my feelings or to persuade me into the further practice of religion, so that I was scarcely aware of the long-term effect they were having on me. But when I returned to Oxford and found myself in the company of committed Anglicans, I felt entirely and immediately at home. I had, in effect, undergone a prolonged *praeparatio evangelica*. The human lessons I had been schooled to accept during the war years and immediately afterward asked to be understood in Christian categories—grace, charity, vocation, the church as the body of Christ. From then on I became a regular churchgoer, and my intellectual and spiritual lives became increasingly intertwined. I underwent a process that in theological writing is often supposed not to happen, in which my attempts, philosophically, to achieve a coherent view of the world went hand in hand with my efforts to live a Christian life. I went to church and said my prayers because to do those things followed from what I was coming to believe about the nature of God, humankind and the world.

Hence I was then, and have since always been, puzzled by the insistence of many Reformed theologians that there is and has to be a sharp dichotomy between the acceptance of the gospel and the findings of natural reason. That this is how faith presents itself to many devout Christians I do not doubt, but it was not so in my experience, and in my slowly deepening understanding of the Christian revelation what struck me was the way in which it explained and complemented what I had already learned in the course of experiences that were deeply felt but were not at the time explicitly religious.

If there was a moment in my new life at Oxford at which I experienced a conversion, or rather realized that a conversion had occurred, it was while listening to Austin Farrer's Bampton Lectures, given in St. Mary's Church in Michaelmas term 1948 and published under the title *The Glass of Vision*. The restrained delivery, the precision of utterance, the controlled imagination, together with the capacity, without apparent alteration of pace or emphasis, to raise the discourse to the most intense level of religious contemplation without loss of philosophical substance, were unlike anything I have ever experienced before or since. And I responded at once to the confession he made in the first lecture:

> I would no longer attempt, with the psalmist, "to set God before my face." I would see him as the underlying cause of my thinking, especially of those thoughts in which I tried to think of him. I would dare to hope that sometimes my thought would become diaphanous, so that there should be some perception of the divine cause shining through the created effect, as a deep pool, settling into a clear tranquillity, permits us to see the spring in the bottom of it from which its waters rise. I would dare to hope that through a second cause the First Cause might be felt, when the second cause in question was itself a spirit, made in the image of the divine Spirit, and perpetually welling up out of his creative act. (*Glass of Vision*, p. 8)

Here at last was the mystical vision to which Sufi teaching at its best had inclined me, but a vision that acknowledged and enhanced the reality of the created order and the significance of human history and was intimately involved in the lives and loves of individual persons.

Christianity and Philosophy

From this point on the problems I encountered were of an entirely different order from those that had gone before. In the place of continual uncertainty I experienced a way of life that was ordered and predictable. I was no longer required to adapt myself to an organization to which I was fundamentally unsuited or to undertake a job that had been imposed on me by forces beyond my control. I was doing work I had always wanted to do in an institution in which I was thoroughly at home. I did not have to exert all my energies to try to occupy a role in someone else's life that I could not adequately fill, and perhaps at the time no one could have. Instead I enjoyed the trust and support of a wife whose talents and temperament were complementary to my own and whose commitment to the marriage was never in doubt. There was, in short, nothing now in my situation except my own limitations to prevent me making of my life what I wanted to make of it. I had always taken it for granted that, when the time came, I should have the capacity to teach philosophy and make some contribution to the subject, but I had very little idea of what that would involve.

I was, of course, absurdly ill prepared. I had done no Western philosophy since the end of my undergraduate career in 1939, and my Indian studies had virtually no relevance to what I was now required to teach. There was, also, an even more serious handicap that had remained with me since my undergraduate days—my preoccupation with "the great rolling themes of philosophy." When I was an undergraduate there had been a tacit consensus among my teachers (with the conspicuous exception of Professor H. H. Price) to the effect that questions of theology and metaphysics were not important. By the time I returned to Oxford this had been replaced by the dogmatic assertion that metaphysics was impossible. It is hard to convey the impact upon me of postwar Oxford philosophy. It was severely analytical, and there was a well-nigh universal suspicion of broad questions or comprehensive answers. To someone of my temperament it was bound to appear arid and constricting, but to most of my colleagues it was the "revolution in philosophy"—a marvelously new and liberating experience. If I was to teach philosophy, there was no escaping the dilemma presented to me. I would have to come to grips with philosophy as currently practiced and learn its techniques as far as I was able; and if I felt that its boundaries were arbitrary and unsatisfactory, I should have to vindicate this conviction in terms that my colleagues would understand and respect.

It was, to all appearance, a straightforwardly intellectual task, but it was one that made exacting spiritual demands of a kind that is not always appreciated by those whose spiritual battlefields lie elsewhere. It was necessary to hold on to one's Christian belief and practice, tentative and undeveloped though they were, while endeavoring to ensure that the criticisms to which they were being subjected were fairly and honestly faced. This would have been difficult enough if one could have been fully confident in one's own ability to assess the issues competently, but there was every reason to be doubtful of this. Moreover, the pressures were by no means purely intellectual. Reputations were a factor to be reckoned with, and the prevailing orthodoxy was reinforced by gestures, tones of voice and figures of speech that served to define the boundaries of what it was acceptable to think. That these devices were employed quite unconsciously in an atmosphere of personal friendliness made them all the more difficult to resist.

In retrospect the movement was less monolithic than it appeared at the time. Some of the most lasting work of the period represented an attempt to break out from the constraints of logical positivism: Ryle in philosophy of mind, Strawson in philosophical logic, Hart in jurisprudence, Hare and Foot in moral philosophy were venturing large-scale theories—or, at any rate, theories with large-scale implications—that only masqueraded as logical analysis. Differences were beginning to appear that were, ultimately, metaphysical.

I was not myself perceptive enough at the time to be aware of this, and for the first few years I was in effect pursuing my undergraduate strategy of going through the motions in the accepted way, while remaining skeptical as to the value of the exercise. So far as my university lecturing commitments were concerned, I had recourse once again to Plato and took over the standard course of thirty-six lectures on *The Republic*. I enjoyed these lectures almost more than anything I have done since. For one thing they were "bread and butter" lectures, and I had a reasonably constant audience (something not easily to be had in Oxford). For another *The Republic* is inexhaustible, and there was never any difficulty in finding fresh, topical illustrations of Plato's argument. And there was also, of course, the factor that had so attracted me as an undergraduate, that Plato provided an ideal opportunity to venture confidently into fields that were currently out of bounds.

It would be wrong to give the impression that in the university at large no voices were raised in defense of Christianity. C. S. Lewis's Socratic Club was a lively forum for the discussion of Christian apologetics and attracted numbers of able undergraduates. Lewis himself addressed a national, indeed an international, audience and was a figure to be reckoned with. But his philosophical roots were in an earlier generation, and he was not equipped, and did not feel himself to be equipped, to engage with the highly technical arguments of contemporary Oxford philosophers.

I have referred earlier to the experience of encountering for the first time, on my return to Oxford, Christian thinkers who were trained philosophers, and in particular the impact made upon me by Austin Farrer's Bampton Lectures in 1948. Around that time Eric Mascall, who was then teaching at Christ Church, decided to gather together a group of philosophers and theologians who were unhappy with the antimetaphysical tenor of Oxford philosophy and wanted to explore issues that were currently under suspicion. Their aim was to reestablish the claims of metaphysics; he called them "the Metaphysicals." The group was destined to persist, with changing membership, for forty years, meeting two or three times a term. The first meeting, held in Mascall's rooms in Christ Church, was attended, so far as I can remember, by Ian Crombie, Austin Farrer, Michael Foster, Richard Hare and Iris Murdoch in addition to Mascall and myself. There is no doubt that, among the rest of us, an important object of this exercise was to prevent Austin Farrer's abandoning philosophy to devote all his energies, less fruitfully as we thought, to biblical exegesis. In this we were successful, and Farrer was conspicuous among us for actually doing the sort of philosophical theology whose possibility we wished to vindicate.

The Metaphysicals did not attempt to form a common mind, let alone to initiate a philosophical movement, but certain characteristic themes began to emerge. One was the use of metaphor and analogy in language generally and especially in religious language. This was preeminently the province of Austin Farrer. In *The Glass of Vision* I found a treatment of divine inspiration that, for the first time in my life, brought together the two things that mattered most to me, an abiding sense of the divine presence and a recognition of the inexhaustibility of human personality, and exemplified a way of talking and thinking about them that allowed, to an appropriate degree, of rational criticism.

Another theme was that of informal reasoning. Much of the antimetaphysical bias of the time proceeded from the assumption that only a limited number of types of reasoning could be exhaustively expressed in rules. Ian Crombie first proposed to me a distinction between canonical and noncanonical reasoning (which John Lucas later developed). Connected with this was the thought that when one had elicited the assumptions underlying various uses of language, one did not face a mere arbitrary choice between them but could form a rational assessment of their comparative claims.

By the mid-1950s the membership of the Metaphysicals had changed somewhat. Iris Murdoch had dropped out, because so far as the church was concerned, she now felt "more of a fellow traveller than a party member." We were joined by Christopher Stead, John Lucas and Ian Ramsey. After some years of lively but unorganized discussion we began to think that some kind of public manifesto was called for to show that theism was not philosophically a lost cause. The result was *Faith and Logic*.

The most perceptive chapter, as I now think (though I did not recognize it at the time), was Michael Foster's " 'We' in Modern Philosophy," in which he detected unerringly the underlying weakness in the "linguistic philosophy" of the period. The "ordinary language" that philosophers purported to analyze and interpret in a supposedly neutral fashion was in fact deeply theory-laden, and the theories themselves involved substantive claims that it was the task of philosophy to articulate and subject to criticism. It followed that critics of theism were not, as they liked to think, disposing of it from a position of unchallengeable neutrality, but proposing an alternative metaphysics of some kind or other which it was incumbent upon them to acknowledge and defend.

My own contribution to the volume was entitled "The Grace of God," and the choice of subject did to some extent reflect the spiritual history I have outlined here. The sense of a divine presence was something I had never been entirely without, and my Sufi upbringing had helped to nurture it. What made me a Christian, or brought me back to Christianity, was above all the crisis of the war and the requirement it imposed upon me to decide how I was to act in a crucial moment of human history. The recognition that it was crucial implied a judgment upon the importance of events in time and space that was incompatible with the kind of mystical philosophy I had hitherto embraced. The experience of the war years with the constant separations, transitory meetings and reliance upon letters for spiritual sustenance taught me, as it taught many people, that love was the one thing necessary. This lesson, once learned, had been confirmed by the very different disciplines of family life and undergraduate teaching, depending as they both did on valuing people for their own sakes. But what must men and women be like if they are to be capable of love and appropriate objects of it, and what kind of love is needed? It was in answering this question that a metaphysic must be judged, and I found an answer, once again in the Book of Common Prayer. This time the answer was in the General Thanksgiving: "We bless thee for our creation, preservation, and all the blessings of this life; but above all, for thine inestimable love in the redemption of the world by our Lord Jesus Christ; for the means of grace and for the hope of glory." Men and women are to be loved as those whom God has loved—created, redeemed and destined to eternal life. They are to be loved by us with that same love, and it is through his grace that in spite of our weakness and our limitations, we are able to love and be loved in that way.

A Christian Life Partly Lived

ALVIN PLANTINGA

Alvin Plantinga holds the John A. O'Brien Chair of Philosophy and is director of the Center for Philosophy of Religion at the University of Notre Dame. Prior to his Notre Dame appointment he taught at the universities of Yale, Wayne State, Harvard, Chicago, Michigan, Boston, Indiana, UCLA, Syracuse and Arizona and, for twenty years, at Calvin College. Called by Richard Swinburne "the leading philosopher of God," Plantinga has led the revival in Christian philosophy for the past thirty years. He has delivered the prestigious Gifford and Wilde lectures and was granted an honorary doctorate from Glasgow University. He has also been elected president of the Society of Christian Philosophers and the American Philosophical Association. His influential works include over ninety articles; among his many books are God and Other Minds, The Nature of Necessity, God, Freedom and Evil, *and* Warrant.

When Kelly Clark asked me to write a spiritual autobiography, my first impulse was to decline. That was also my second impulse, and my third. For I have at least three good reasons not to do such a thing. First, I have already written something called an "intellectual autobiography";[1] the rule "At most one to a customer" seems to me an excellent one for autobiographies—more than one is unseemly. Second, my spiritual life and its history isn't striking or of general interest: no dramatic conversions, no spiritual heroism, no internal life of great depth and power, not much spiritual sophistication or subtlety, little grasp of the various depths and nuances and shading and peculiar unexplored corners of the spiritual life. It is very much an ordinary meat-and-potatoes kind of life. (It is also, I regret to say, a life that hasn't progressed nearly as much as, by my age and given my opportunities, it should have.)

Third, writing any kind of autobiography has its perils; but writing a spiritual autobiography is particularly perilous.[2] The main problem has to do with truthfulness and honesty: there are powerful temptations toward self-deception and hypocrisy. According to Psalm 51, the Lord desires truth in our innermost being; but according to Jeremiah, "the human heart is deceitful above all things; it is desperately sick; who can understand it?" Truth in our innermost being is not easy to achieve. It is hard to see what the truth *is*; it is also hard to *tell* the truth, to say what you see without imposing some kind of self-justificatory and distorting framework. (For example, you find good or at least coherent motives where in fact there was really no discernible motive at all, or perhaps a confusing welter of motives you can't really sort out, or don't *want* to sort out; or maybe you subtly slant and shift things for no better reason than that it makes a better tale.)

Still further, there are elements of my life before the Lord that might be of interest and of use to others, and where I might even be able both to see and to say what is at least fairly close to the truth, that I don't propose to make public. For most of us, I'd guess, the whole truth about ourselves would be (from one perspective, anyway) a sorry spectacle we wouldn't want completely known even by our best friends—who in any event wouldn't particularly want to know. (Jeremiah is right, even if there is more to the story.) For most of us also, I suspect, there are sides of our lives with respect to which complete and public candor would cause others considerable pain. This is certainly so with me.

I shall therefore make a compromise. Much of what follows is taken from my "intellectual autobiography" in the Profiles volume; I am interpolating comments here and there of a more personal nature. I do not propose to say everything that may be of possible interest, yet I shall try (but probably fail) to be honest about what I do say. What follows, accordingly, is certain selections from the Profiles autobiography, along with some additions.

Roots and Early Days
I was born November 15, 1932, in Ann Arbor, Michigan, where my

father, Cornelius A. Plantinga, was then a graduate student in philosophy at the University of Michigan. My mother, Lettie Plantinga (née Bossenbroek), was born near Alto, Wisconsin. On her mother's side her family had come to the United States about the time of the Civil War; her father's family came some twenty years later. Both groups came from the villages of Elspeet and Nunspeet in the province of Gelderland in the Netherlands, then distinguished for prosperous dairy farms and now also for the Kröller-Muller Museum. My father was born in Garijp, a small village in Friesland. The Dutch think of Friesland as their northwesternmost province. Frisians, however, know better. Friesland has its own culture, its own flag, and its own language closer to Old English than to Dutch (in fact, of all the Germanic languages, Frisian is closest to English).

Both sets of my grandparents—Andrew and Tietje Plantinga and Christian and Lena Bossenbroek—were reared in Calvinist churches originating in the so-called Afscheiding or secession of 1834. During the 1830s there was a religious reawakening ("The Reveille") in the Netherlands, as in much of the rest of Europe. Thoroughly disgusted with the theological liberalism, empty formalism and absence of genuine piety in the Dutch state church (the Hervormde Kerk), many congregations seceded from it to create the Gereformeerde Kerken, dedicated to the practice of historic Calvinism. The Seceders underwent a good deal of punishment and persecution at the hands of the established authorities; they were ready to risk their livelihoods and even their freedom for what they believed to be right worship of God.

Participating in the life of the seceding churches was a strenuous matter. The idea that religion is relevant just to one's private life or to what one does on Sunday was foreign to these people. For them religion was the central reality of life; all aspects of life, they thought, should be lived in the light of Christianity. They also held (rightly, I think) that *education* is essentially religious; there is such a thing as *secular* education but no such thing as an education that is both reasonably full-orbed and religiously *neutral*. They therefore established separate grade schools and high schools that were explicitly Christian, schools in which the bearing of Christianity on the various disciplines could be carefully and explicitly spelled out. Later, under the leadership of the

47

great theologian and statesman Abraham Kuyper (premier of the Netherlands from 1901 to 1905), they established a Calvinist university in Amsterdam: the Free University—so called not, as one might expect, because it is free from the state, but because it is free from ecclesiastical control.

My mother's parents owned a farm in Wisconsin, between Waupun and Alto, and as a small boy I spent most of my summers there. Going to church, of course, was an extremely important part of life; there were two services on Sunday, one in the morning and one in the afternoon, and in those days the afternoon service was in Dutch. Some of my earliest memories are of long, hot Sunday afternoons in church, dressed in my sweltering Sunday best, listening to the minister drone on in a language I could barely understand, counting the tiles in the ceiling, while all along the cicadas outside were setting up their characteristic summertime din. As I saw it then, just getting outside would have been heaven enough. After church, the main topic was often the minister's sermon; and woe unto the preacher who got his doctrine wrong or was guilty of a "wrong emphasis"! Although most of the members of the church were rural folk who hadn't had the benefit of much formal education (my grandfather was lucky to finish the sixth grade), there was an astonishing amount of theological sophistication about. Many had read their Kuyper and Bavinck, and a few were considerably better at theology than some of the ministers in charge of the church.

What was preached, of course, was historic Calvinism. When I was eight or nine I began to understand and think seriously about some of the so-called five points of Calvinism[3] enshrined in the TULIP acronym: Total depravity, Unconditional election, Limited atonement, Irresistible grace and the Perseverance of the saints. I remember wondering in particular about total depravity. I do indeed subscribe to that doctrine, which, as I understand it, quite properly points out that for most or all of us, every important area of our lives is distorted and compromised by sin. When I first began to think about it, however, I took it to mean that everyone was completely wicked, wholly bad, no better than a Hitler or a Judas. That seemed to me a bit confusing and hard to credit; was my grandmother (in fact a saintly woman) really completely wicked? Was there nothing good about her at all? That seemed a bit too much. True, I had heard her say "Shit" a couple of times: once when someone came stomping into the kitchen, causing three cakes in the oven to drop, and once when I threw a string of firecrackers into the fifty-gallon drum in which she was curing dried beef (they began exploding in rapid-fire succession just as she came to look into the drum). But was that really enough to make her a moral monster, particularly when so much else about her pointed in the opposite direction? I spent a good deal of time as a child thinking about these doctrines, and a couple of years later, when I was ten or eleven or so, I got involved in many very enthusiastic but undirected discussions of human freedom, determinism (theological or otherwise), divine foreknowledge, predestination and allied topics.

During junior-high and high-school days we lived in Jamestown, North Dakota, where my father was a professor of philosophy, psychology, Latin and Greek (with an occasional foray into sociology and religion) at Jamestown College. We attended the Presbyterian church in Jamestown; but I heard about as many sermons from my father as from the minister of the church we belonged to. He often preached in churches in nearby villages that were without a minister, and I often accompanied him. I went to church, Sunday school, a weekly catechism class my father organized, and weekly "Young People's" meetings. I also remember a series of midweek Lenten services that were deeply moving and were for me a source of spiritual awakening. In addition, we young people also went to summer Bible camps sponsored by the church. I'm sure these were spiritually useful for many and perhaps for me; and we were certainly stirred up emotionally. By and large, however, I found the girls more interesting than the sermons, and for me (and others) the stimulation was by no means exclusively spiritual. As I remember those camps, there was a sort of fervid, febrile atmosphere, shimmering and throbbing with energy and excitement that was as much sexual as spiritual.

Apart from my parents, perhaps the most important influence in high school was my association with Robert McKenzie (now a Presbyterian minister in the San Francisco Bay area). Bob was a couple of years my senior, and we spent an enormous amount of time together.

One summer we spent twelve hours a day, six days a week (and eight hours on Sunday), working for a construction company, putting in a city water line in Westhope, North Dakota, a tiny village six miles or so from the Canadian border. Bob was (and is) enormously full of enthusiasm, idealism and energy; he laughed often, infectiously and loudly; he and I hatched a whole series of adolescent fantasies about how he would be a minister and I a professor in the same town and what great things we would accomplish. (At the same time we were also planning to run a construction company in the Colorado mountains; how this was supposed to mesh with our ministerial and professorial jobs is no longer clear to me.)

In the fall of 1949, a couple of months before my seventeenth birthday, I enrolled in Jamestown College. During that semester my father was invited to join the psychology department at Calvin College; he accepted the offer and took up his duties there in January of 1950. I reluctantly went along, having no desire at all to leave Jamestown and Jamestown College, where I had very strong attachments. During my first semester at Calvin I applied, just for the fun of it, for a scholarship at Harvard. To my considerable surprise I was awarded a nice fat scholarship; in the fall of 1950, therefore, I showed up in Cambridge.

I found Harvard enormously impressive and very much to my liking. I took an introductory philosophy course from Raphael Demos in the fall and a course in Plato from him in the spring. I still remember the sense of wonder with which I read *Gorgias*—its graceful language, absorbing argumentative intricacy and serious moral tone relieved now and then by gentle, almost rueful witticisms at the expense of the Sophists. I also took a splendid course from the classicist I. M. Finley, and in a large social science course (as it was called) my section leader was Bernard Bailyn, now a distinguished Harvard historian. I attended a Methodist church where the Sunday-school class for people my age was conducted by Peter Bertocci, the philosopher from Boston University. (He was the last of the series of three great Boston personalists whose names began with B: Edgar Sheffield Brightman, Bordon Parker Bowne and Bertocci.)

At Harvard I encountered serious non-Christian thought for the first time—for the first time in the flesh, that is; I had read animadversions on Christianity and theism by Bertrand Russell *(Why I Am Not a Christian)* and others. I was struck by the enormous variety of intellectual and spiritual opinion at Harvard, and spent a great deal of time arguing about whether there was such a person as God, whether Christianity as opposed to Judaism (my roommate Herbert Jacobs was the son of a St. Louis rabbi) was right and so on. I began to wonder whether what I had always believed could really be true. At Harvard, after all, there was such an enormous diversity of opinions about these matters, some of them held by highly intelligent and accomplished people who had little but contempt for what I believed. My attitude gradually became one of a mixture of doubt and bravado. On the one hand I began to think it questionable that what I had been taught and had always believed could be right, given that there were all these others who thought so differently (and were so much more intellectually accomplished than I). On the other hand, I thought to myself, what really is so great about these people? Why should I believe *them?* True, they know much more than I and have thought much longer: but what, precisely, is the *substance* of their objections to Christianity? Or to theism? Do these objections really *have* much by way of substance? And if, as I strongly suspected, *not,* why should their taking the views they did be relevant to what *I* thought? The doubts (in that form anyway) didn't last long, but something like the bravado, I suppose, has remained.

The two events that resolved these doubts and ambivalences for me occurred during my second semester. One gloomy evening (in January, perhaps) I was returning from dinner, walking past Widenar Library to my fifth-floor room in Thayer Middle (there weren't any elevators, and scholarship boys occupied the cheaper rooms at the top of the building). It was dark, windy, raining, nasty. But suddenly it was as if the heavens opened; I heard, so it seemed, music of overwhelming power and grandeur and sweetness; there was light of unimaginable splendor and beauty; it seemed I could see into heaven itself; and I suddenly saw or perhaps felt with great clarity and persuasion and conviction that the Lord was really there and was all I had thought. The effects of this experience lingered for a long time; I was still caught up in arguments about the existence of God, but they often seemed to me merely academic, of little existential concern, as if one were to argue about whether there has really been a past, for example, or whether there really were other people, as opposed to cleverly constructed robots.

Such events have not been common subsequently, and there has been only one other occasion on which I felt the presence of God with as much immediacy and strength. That was when I once foolishly went hiking alone off-trail in really rugged country south of Mt. Shuksan in the North Cascades, getting lost when rain, snow and fog obscured all the peaks and landmarks. That night, while shivering under a stunted tree in a cold mixture of snow and rain, I felt as close to God as I ever have, before or since. I wasn't clear as to his intentions for me, and I wasn't sure I approved of what I thought his intentions might be (the statistics on people lost alone in that area were not at all encouraging), but I felt very close to him; his presence was enormously palpable.

On many other occasions I have felt the presence of God, sometimes very powerfully: in the mountains (the overwhelming grandeur of the night sky from a slope at thirteen thousand feet), at prayer, in church, when reading the Bible, listening to music, seeing the beauty of the sunshine on the leaves of a tree or on a blade of grass, being in the woods on a snowy night, and on other kinds of occasions. In particular I have often been overwhelmed with a sense of *gratitude*—sometimes for something specific like a glorious morning, but often with no particular focus. What I *ought* to be most grateful for—the life and death and resurrection of Christ, with the accompanying offer of eternal life—is harder, simply because of its stupendous and incomprehensible magnitude. You can say "Thank you" for a glorious morning, and even for your children's turning out well; what do you say in response to the suffering and death and resurrection of the Son of God? Or to the offer of redemption from sin, and eternal life?

The second event that semester at Harvard was as follows. During spring recess I returned to Grand Rapids to visit my parents; since Calvin's spring recess did not coincide with Harvard's, I had the opportunity to attend some classes at Calvin. I had often heard my father speak of William Harry Jellema, who had been his philosophy professor at Calvin in the late twenties and early thirties. Accordingly I attended three of Jellema's classes that week—it was a course in ethics, I believe.

That was a fateful week for me.

Jellema was obviously in dead earnest about Christianity; he was also a magnificently thoughtful and reflective Christian. He was lecturing about modernity: its various departures from historic Christianity, the sorts of substitutes it proposes, how these substitutes are related to the real thing and the like. Clearly he was profoundly familiar with the doubts and objections and alternative ways of thought cast up by modernity; indeed, he seemed to me to understand them better than those who offered them. But (and this is what I found enormously impressive) he was totally unawed. What especially struck me then in what he said (partly because it put into words something I felt at Harvard but couldn't articulate) was the thought that much of the intellectual opposition to Christianity and theism was really a sort of intellectual imperialism with little real basis. We are told that humankind come of age has got beyond such primitive ways of thinking, that they are outmoded, or incompatible with a scientific mindset, or have been shown wanting by modern science, or made irrelevant by the march of history or maybe by something else lurking in the neighborhood. (In this age of the wireless, Bultmann quaintly asks, who can accept them?) But why should a Christian believe any of these things? Are they more than mere claims?

I found Jellema deeply impressive—so impressive that I decided then and there to leave Harvard, return to Calvin and study philosophy with him. That was as important a decision, and as good a decision, as I've ever made. Calvin College has been for me an enormously powerful spiritual influence and in some ways the center and focus of my intellectual life. Had I not returned to Calvin from Harvard, I doubt (humanly speaking, anyway) that I would have remained a Christian at all; certainly Christianity or theism would not have been the focal point of my adult intellectual life.

Calvin

What I got from Jellema that week and later on was the limning of a certain kind of stance to take in the face of these objections; one could take them seriously, see what underlies them, see them as in some ways profound, understand them at that level, sympathize with the

53

deeply human impulses they embody, and nonetheless note that they need have little or no real claim, either on a human being as such or on a Christian. All that chronological talk about "man come of age" and what modern science has shown is obviously, in the final analysis, little more than bluster. These claims and arguments are not the *source* of modern Enlightenment turning away from God; they are more like *symptoms* of it, or ex post facto justifications of it; at bottom they are really intellectual or philosophical developments of what is a fundamentally religious or spiritual commitment or stance. If so, of course, they don't come to much by way of objection to Christianity. They really proceed from a broadly religious commitment incompatible with Christian theism; taken as arguments against Christianity, therefore, they are wholly inconclusive, because they are clearly question begging.

Jellema's way of thinking about these matters (as he said) goes back to Abraham Kuyper and other Dutch Calvinists and ultimately back through the Franciscan tradition of the Middle Ages, back at least to Augustine. Jellema's thought was in many respects "postmodern" long before contemporary postmodernism announced itself with such cacophony and confusion (and foolishness); his thought was also incomparably deeper, more subtle, more mature than most of the current varieties.

Jellema was by all odds, I think, the most gifted teacher of philosophy I have ever encountered. When I studied with him in the early fifties, he was about sixty years old and at the height of his powers; and he was indeed impressive. First of all, he *looked* like a great man—iron gray hair, handsome, a vigorous, upright bearing bespeaking strength and confidence, a ready smile. Second, he *sounded* like a great man. Although he had grown up in the United States, there was a trace of European accent—Oxford, I thought, with perhaps a bit of the Continent thrown in. Jellema lectured in magisterial style, with the entire history of Western philosophy obviously at his fingertips. He seemed to display astonishing and profound insights into the inner dynamics of modern philosophy—the deep connections between the rationalists and the empiricists, for example, as well as the connections between them and Kant, and the contrast between their underlying presuppositions and those underlying earlier medieval and Christian thought. Although he was a man of razor-sharp intellect, Jellema wasn't first of all a close or exact thinker; his métier was the method of broad vistas, not that of the logical microscope. I came deeply under his spell; had he told me black was white I would have had a genuine intellectual struggle.

And of course I wasn't the only one. In the early days in particular, an extremely high proportion of the serious students at Calvin wound up either majoring or minoring in philosophy. This phenomenon was due in part to a widespread grassroots interest in theology and theological argumentation. Many Christian Reformed students in those days came to college with an already highly developed taste for theological disputation and a strong interest in philosophical questions. But much was due to the intellectual power and magnetism of Harry Jellema. Given the size of Calvin—three hundred students when my father was there as a student, thirteen hundred when I was—a remarkable number of graduates have gone on to careers in philosophy. Many had Frisian names ending in *a*: Bouwsma, Frankena, Hoitenga, Hoekema, Hoekstra, Mellema, Pauzenga, Plantinga, Postema, Strikwerda, Wierenga and more. This has given rise to the lawlike generalization that if an American philosopher's name ends in *a* and is not Castañeda, Cochiarella or Sosa, then that philosopher is a graduate of Calvin College.

Calvin was a splendid place for a serious student of philosophy. At Calvin then (as now) the life of the mind was a serious matter. There was no toleration of intellectual sloppiness and little interest in the mindless fads (deconstruction, Lacanian/Freudian literary theory) that regularly sweep academia; rigor and seriousness were the order of the day. What was genuinely distinctive about Calvin, however, was the combination of intellectual rigor with profound interest in the bearing of Christianity on scholarship. There was a serious and determined effort to ask and answer the question of the relation between scholarship, academic endeavor and the life of the mind, on the one hand, and the Christian faith on the other. We students were confronted regularly and often with such questions as what form a distinctively Christian philosophy would take, whether there could be a Christian novel, how Christianity bore on poetry, art, music, psychology, history and science. How would genuinely Christian literature differ from non-

Christian? Obviously Christianity is relevant to such disciplines as psychology and sociology; but how does it bear on physics and chemistry? And what about mathematics itself, that austere bastion of rationality? What difference (if any) does being a Christian make to the theory and practice of mathematics? There were general convictions that Christianity is indeed profoundly relevant to the whole of the intellectual life including the various sciences (although not much agreement as to just *how* it is relevant).

This conviction still animates Calvin College, and it is a conviction I share. Serious intellectual work and religious allegiance, I believe, are inevitably intertwined. There is no such thing as religiously neutral intellectual endeavor—or rather there is no such thing as serious, substantial and relatively complete intellectual endeavor that is religiously neutral. I endorse this claim, although it isn't easy to see how to establish it, or how to develop and articulate it in detail.

Harry Jellema (as well as Henry Stob, another gifted teacher of philosophy at Calvin) saw the history of philosophy as an arena for the articulation and interplay of commitments and allegiances fundamentally religious in nature; in this they were following Kuyper and Augustine. Jellema spoke of four "minds"— four fundamental perspectives or ways of viewing the world and assessing its significance, four fundamentally religious stances that have dominated Western intellectual and cultural life. These are the ancient mind, typified best by Plato; the medieval and Christian mind; the modern mind; and last and in his judgment certainly least, the contemporary mind, whose contours and lineaments, though not yet wholly clear, are fundamentally naturalistic. He therefore saw all philosophical endeavor—at any rate all serious and insightful philosophy—as at bottom an expression of religious commitment. This gave to philosophy, as we learned it from Jellema and Stob, a dimension of depth and seriousness. For them the history of philosophy was not a record of humanity's slow but inevitable approach to a truth now more or less firmly grasped by ourselves and our contemporaries, nor, certainly, a mere conversation with respect to which the question of truth does not seriously arise; for them the history of philosophy was at bottom an arena in which conflicting religious visions compete for human allegiance. Philosophy, as they saw it, was a matter of the greatest moment; for what it involved is both a struggle for human souls and a fundamental expression of basic religious perspectives.

Jellema and Stob were my main professors in philosophy; I also majored in psychology, taking some six courses in that subject from my father, from whom I learned an enormous amount inside the classroom as well as out. My father was trained as a philosopher, although at Calvin he taught only psychology courses. (True to his Dakota form, however, he taught a large number of different psychology courses, in fact all the courses offered except the introductory course.) The sort of psychology course he taught, however, had a strong philosophical component. He was wholly disdainful of contemporary reductionistic attempts to make psychology "scientific," to try to state laws of human behavior that more or less resembled those of physics, to study only that which can be quantified, to declare, with Watsonian behaviorists, that there really aren't any such things as consciousness or mental processes, on the grounds that if there were, it wouldn't be possible to study them scientifically. That was forty years ago; contemporary efforts along these lines don't do much better.

One prominent example: we all think that one's actions and behavior can be understood or explained in terms of one's beliefs and desires, and in particular in terms of the *content* of those beliefs and desires. (It is the fact that I believe my office is south of my house that explains why I go south when I want to go to my office; that content enters essentially into the answer to the question, Why did he go south?) But contemporary naturalistic philosophy of mind has enormous difficulty seeing, first, how it can be that my beliefs *have* content; how could that work, from a naturalistic perspective? How could a neural process of some kind wind up being the belief that the South won the Civil War? And second, there is if anything even greater difficulty in seeing how the content of a belief, or its having the content it does, should play some kind of causal or explanatory role in explaining behavior.[4]

There is another legacy of those days at Calvin, however, that isn't quite so beneficent. This was a sort of tendency to denigrate or devalue other forms of Christianity, other emphases within serious Christianity. For example, there was a bit of an inclination to ridicule pietists and "fundamentalists." We Calvinists, we thought, were much more rigorous about the life of the mind than were fundamentalists, and as a result we were inclined to look down our Reformed noses at them.[5]

This took many forms; I remember, for example, attending the first of Wheaton College's series of philosophy conferences with the late Dirk Jellema (son of Harry Jellema and for many years professor of history at Calvin); this was in the fall of 1954, nearly a year after I had left Calvin, when I was a graduate student at the University of Michigan. The conference seemed to us pretty weak tea after what we had been used to at Calvin (and in fact it wasn't anywhere nearly as good as the conferences later on, when they became an extremely distinguished and valuable part of the Christian philosophical community). Dirk and I found ourselves feeling smugly superior (that's really not the way to put it: we felt so smug and superior that we didn't know that we *were* feeling smug and superior); from our lofty heights we regarded these poor benighted fundamentalists with a certain amused but benevolent disdain. Further, Dirk and I were both smokers at the time; it was a point of honor among Calvinist types to sneer at fundamentalist prohibitions against smoking and drinking.[6] Smoking and drinking were forbidden on the Wheaton campus; every hour or so, therefore, Dirk and I had to dash over to his car, drive off the campus and smoke a cigarette. After the conference ended, we went barhopping in Chicago, listening to Dixieland jazz, amusing ourselves by sneering at fundamentalists and dreaming up various scurrilous fantasies about Wheaton and Wheatonians. Not our finest hour.

Since the Enlightenment, we Christians have had *real* enemies to fight and real battles to win; why then do we expend so much time and energy despising or fighting each other? Why don't we treat each other like the brothers and sisters in Christ we are? This is something the Christian community will have to answer for, and it is not going to be pleasant. Indeed, the whole of modern apostasy in the West is due (so I think) in considerable part to the unedifying and indeed appalling spectacle of Christians at each other's throats in the sixteenth and seventeenth centuries. We aren't now literally at each other's throats, but we still have nothing to boast of along these lines. Evangelicals in South and Central America claim that Catholics aren't really Christians at all; some Catholics return the favor. Many fundamentalist Christians deeply disapprove of those Christians who accept some form of theistic evolution and propose to read them out of the whole Christian community; those on the other side return the favor by joining the secular scientific establishment in declaring those of the first part ignorant, stupid, dishonest or all of the above.[7] Not a pretty picture.

Family Life

In the fall of 1953 I met Kathleen DeBoer. She was then a Calvin senior and had grown up on a farm near Lynden, Washington, a village fifteen miles from Puget Sound and just four miles south of the Canadian border. Her family, like mine, was of Dutch Christian Reformed immigrant stock, having come to northwest Washington in the early days of the twentieth century. I'm not sure what she saw in me, but I was captivated by her generous spirit and mischievous, elfin sense of humor. We were engaged the following spring and married in June 1955. She has had need of that sense of humor. Over the years she has had to put up with my idiosyncrasies (and worse) and also with a rather nomadic lifestyle: during the thirty-six years of our married life we have moved more than twenty times. She has also had to bear a great deal of the burden of rearing our four children,[8] particularly when they were small; my idea of a marriage in those days, I regret to say, involved *my* having a career and spending what I now see as an inordinate amount of time on my work, and *her* taking care of the children and family.[9] (But that isn't exactly right either, although it contains a lot of truth; this is another of those places where it is hard to see the truth straight. I also loved [and love] the children with a passion, and did spend a lot of time caring for them; and I immensely enjoyed playing, talking, arguing, wrestling, singing, hiking and just being with them. Our dinnertimes were often a kind of rich but wacky discussion of ideas ranging over theology, philosophy, psychology, physics, mathematics, literature and what dumb thing someone's teacher had said today. [Since all of our children took courses from me at Calvin, the teacher in question was sometimes me.])

Kathleen has been a wonderful mother, a wonderful wife and a wonderful ally and support. Some will see this as a monumentally banal sentiment, a conventional cliché; furthermore, of course, in many quarters being a wonderful wife and mother is not a recommendation but a condemnation, something she should perhaps confess shamefacedly, with the earnest intention of doing better. I say they are dead wrong. I was myself dead wrong in assuming early in our marriage that men had careers outside the home and women were to stay home and be housewives; that was unjust and unfair. Nevertheless, being a housewife (or househusband) is as important and honorable a career as there is. Can anything we do really be more important, more weighty, than rearing our children?

Kathleen has gone willingly with me to all sorts of places she had no real interest in, often with several small children. During the decade of the 1960s, for example, I taught at Wayne State University in Detroit, Calvin, Harvard and the University of Illinois; I also spent a year at the Center for Advanced Study in the Behavioral Sciences in Palo Alto, California. A couple of years later we spent the academic year 1971-72 in Los Angeles, while I was a visitor at UCLA. All of these moves were for my benefit, or for the benefit of my career, or at any rate for doing something I thought I needed to do. All of this was also despite her sometimes being less than overwhelmed with the worth of some of my philosophical projects. (I remember that on first hearing she thought the thesis of *God and Other Minds*—which might be summarized as the idea that belief in God and belief in other minds are in the same epistemological boat—was one of the sillier things she had heard.)

She has also had to put up with my relationship with mountains and mountaineering. In the summer of 1954 I accompanied her and her parents to Lynden, Washington, where her parents lived. I had never been west of Minot, North Dakota, and my first sight of the mountains—the Big Horns of Wyoming, the Montana Rockies, the Washington Cascades—struck me with the force of a revelation from on high. Splendidly beautiful, mysterious, awe-inspiring, tinged with peril and more than a hint of menace—there was nothing I had ever seen to compare with them. Thus began a lifelong love affair with mountains. Mountains have been an important part of my life ever since. I've climbed in many of the main ranges of the United States, perhaps concentrating on the Tetons and the Cascades and Sierras; I've also climbed a bit in Europe (the Matterhorn, Mt. Blanc, a bit of rock climbing in Great Britain). The last few years I have turned more to rock climbing, which is less prodigal of time and energy than mountaineering, and in each of the last few summers have climbed with my friend Ric Otte in Yosemite. Among my favorite rock climbs would be the Black Quacker on Mt. Lemmon (just north of Tucson), the Exum route on the Grand Teton and Guide's Wall, also in the Tetons; in Yosemite my favorites are the Nutcracker, a beginner's set piece; Snake Dike, the easiest (5.7) technical route on Half Dome; and Crest Jewel, a long (ten pitches or so) and splendid moderately difficult route on North Dome.

Mountains have been a blessing: for many years anyway, the *Sensus Divinitatis* seemed to work most strongly for me in the mountains. I mentioned above the time I was lost in the mountains; but on dozens of other occasions I have strongly felt the presence of God in the mountains—although on some occasions what I also felt was guilt and divine disapproval. For if mountains were a blessing for me, they were also a bane. The problem was that (particularly during the first couple of decades of our marriage) I was positively obsessed with mountains. At home in Grand Rapids during the close, humid Michigan summer, I would think of the dry, cool, delicious air of the Tetons; that marvelously blue sky pierced by those splendid towers; the wind, the rough feel of Teton granite, the sweep of a steep, exposed ridge below my feet—and I would almost weep. *Why* was I in Grand Rapids rather than in the mountains? I would be overcome with a sort of yearning, a desperate longing, a *Sehnsucht* for which the only remedy was going to the mountains. So to the mountains I went. Kathleen had two choices: she could stay home in Grand Rapids and take care of the children alone, or she and the children could come along. The only accommodation we could afford in the Tetons (or for that matter anywhere else away from home) was camping: so she and the children camped in a tent while I assaulted the heights. This was not her idea of a good time; and once more, it was wholly unfair. Her reaction to all this was one of Christian grace; but my part would have to be judged as self-centered. Fortunately, this sort of thing no longer happens; but it isn't as if I can take much credit for it. With the passage of the years (and the cooling of the hot blood of youth) my obsession with the mountains has gradually dissipated, leaving behind a more reasonable if less fierce love for them.

Michigan and Yale

In January of 1954 I left Calvin for graduate work at the University of Michigan, where I studied with William P. Alston, Richard Cartwright and William K. Frankena. The first semester I enrolled in a seminar in the philosophy of Whitehead and a course in philosophy of religion, both taught by Alston; his careful, clear and painstaking course became a model for the courses I was later to teach in the same subject. Coming from Calvin, however, I was struck and puzzled by the diffidence he displayed toward the essential elements of the Christian faith.[10] I also learned much from William Frankena—much at the time and much later on. I admired his patient, thoughtful and considerate way of dealing with students almost as much as his analytical powers. Again, however, I was puzzled by the extremely low profile of his faith.

At Michigan, as earlier on, I was very much interested in the sorts of philosophical attacks mounted against traditional theism—the ancient claim that it was incompatible with the existence of evil, the Freudian claim that it arose out of wish fulfillment, the positivistic claim that talk about God was literally meaningless, the Bultmannian claim that traditional belief in God was an outmoded relic of a prescientific age and the like. These objections (except for evil) seemed to me not merely specious but deceptive, deceitful, in a way: they paraded themselves as something like discoveries, something we moderns (or at any rate the more perceptive among us) had finally seen, after all those centuries of darkness. All but the first, I thought, were totally question begging if taken as arguments against theism.

I conceived a particular dislike for the dreaded Verifiability Criterion of Meaning; it seemed to me that many believers in God paid entirely too much attention to it. Although I wasn't then aware of the enormous difficulties in stating that criterion,[11] I could never see the slightest reason for accepting it. The positivists seemed to trumpet it as a *discovery* of some sort; at long last we had learned that the sorts of things theists had been saying for centuries were entirely without sense. We had all been the victims, it seems, of a cruel hoax—perpetrated, perhaps, by ambitious priests or foisted upon us by our own credulous natures; they had somehow got us to think that what we believed was in sober fact sheer nonsense. At the same time, however, the positivists seemed to regard their criterion as a *definition*—in which case, apparently, it was either a proposal to use the term *meaningful* in a certain way, or else an account of how that term is in fact used. Taken the second way, the Verifiability Criterion of Meaning was clearly wide of the mark; none of the people I knew, anyway, used the term in question in accord with it. And taken the first way it seemed even less successful. Clearly the positivists had the right to use the term *meaningful* in any way they chose; but how could their using it in some way or other show anything so momentous as that all those who took themselves to be believers in God were fundamentally deluded? If I proposed to use *positivist* to mean "unmitigated scoundrel," would it follow that positivists everywhere ought to hang their heads in shame? I still find it hard to see how the positivists could have thought their criterion would be of any *polemical* use. It might have a sort of *pastoral* use; it might be useful for bucking up a formerly committed but now flagging empiricist; but what sort of claim would the verifiability criterion have on anyone who had no inclination to accept it in the first place?

This interest continued at Yale, to which I went from Michigan because I wanted to study metaphysics in the grand style. I have little to add to what I say in the Profiles volume about life at Yale, except that already then some of the habits of mind that led to the demise of that department were evident.[12] Already there was that sort of paranoia with respect to the rest of the philosophical world, coupled with the self-serving idea that Yale was the last bastion of proper diversity; and already there were the beginnings of the sorts of personal animosities and the turning of all of one's energies to internecine warfare that eventually destroyed the department.

Wayne Days

I left Yale, shiny new Ph.D. in hand (or nearly in hand), in the fall of 1957 for Wayne State University in Detroit. The philosophy department at Wayne in the late 1950s and early 1960s was a real phenomenon and for me enormously valuable; I have already said most of what

I have to say about it in the Profiles volume. Here I add a couple of further reflections. At Wayne, the late Hector Castañeda, George Nakhnikian and Edmund Gettier confronted me with antitheistic arguments of a depth and philosophical sophistication and persistence I had never encountered before. Both Gettier and Nakhnikian were sons of the clergy; both had resolutely turned their backs upon Christianity; and both attacked my Christianity with great verve and power. They were joined by Castañeda, who was raised as a Catholic in Guatemala but had long since given up the religion of his youth (and indeed displayed a sort of bitter resentment against it). Nakhnikian was our chairman; he thought well of my powers as a budding young philosopher, but also thought that no intelligent person could possibly be a Christian. He would announce this sentiment in his usual stentorian tones, whereupon Robert Sleigh would say, "But what about Al, George? Don't you think he's an intelligent person?" George would have to admit, reluctantly, that he thought I probably was, but he still thought there had to be a screw loose in there somewhere.

This sort of atmosphere at Wayne was in one way extremely good for me. My colleagues were people I loved and for whom I had enormous respect; there was among us a close and happy camaraderie unmatched in my experience of philosophy departments. It was us against the world, and the world was in real trouble. We worked closely together, forging a kind of common mind. My Christianity, however, didn't fit into this common mind at all. As a result, my thought was influenced in two ways. On the one hand, I encountered antitheistic argument at a level and of a caliber unequaled by anything I've seen published (with the possible exception of parts of the late John Mackie's *The Miracle of Theism*); this was a great stimulus to rigor and penetration in my own work. In those days I was writing *God and Other Minds*; I still remember the winter evening in a dingy parking lot at Wayne when the central idea of the free will defense—that even if God is omnipotent, there are nonetheless possible worlds he could not have actualized—struck me. (It literally *struck* me; it felt like a blow.) I also remember the first seminar in which I presented this idea; it was subjected to merciless criticism by Larry Powers, then the most philosophically gifted sophomore (or maybe junior) I have ever seen. (As an undergraduate Powers was regularly the best student in our graduate seminars.)

This stimulation was enormously valuable; on the other hand, however, I was never able to get beyond a sort of defensive posture. I concentrated on arguing (contrary to my colleagues' claims) that theism was not wholly irrational—that, for example, there wasn't, contrary to received philosophical opinion, any contradiction in the propositions "God is omnipotent, omniscient and wholly good" and "There is evil." I often felt beleaguered and, with respect only to my Christianity, alone, isolated, nonstandard, a bit peculiar or weird, a somewhat strange specimen in which my colleagues displayed an interest that was friendly, and for the most part uncensorious, but also incredulous and uncomprehending. It wasn't that this atmosphere induced doubt about the central elements of Christianity; it was more that my philosophical horizons were heavily formed by my colleagues and friends at Wayne. It was hard indeed to go beyond interests that we shared; it seemed out of the question, for example, to take it for granted that Christianity or theism is true and proceed from there. That requires the support of a Christian philosophical community; and that, for all the benefits I received from the Old Wayne department, was something wholly unavailable there.

In 1963, at the age of seventy, Harry Jellema retired from Calvin's philosophy department. I was invited to replace him. I was flattered to be asked to be his successor but timorous at stepping into shoes as large as his; after considerable agony I decided to leave Wayne for Calvin. Many of my non-Calvin friends found it hard to see this as a rational decision. Wayne had a splendid philosophy department; I had found it educational and stimulating *in excelsis;* I immensely liked the department and my place in it and had rejected several attractive offers in order to stay there. Why, then, was I now proposing to leave it for a small college in western Michigan? In point of fact, however, that decision, from my point of view, was eminently sensible. I was and had been since childhood a Christian; I endorsed the Calvinist contention that neither scholarship nor education is religiously neutral; I was therefore convinced of the importance of Christian colleges and universities. I wanted to contribute to that enterprise, and Calvin seemed an excellent place to do so. Calvin, furthermore, is the college of the Christian

Reformed Church, a church of which I am a committed member; so there was an element of ecclesiastical loyalty at work. Most important, perhaps, I realized that scholarship in general and philosophy in particular is in large part a communal enterprise: promising insights, interesting connections, subtle difficulties—these come more easily and rapidly in a group of like-minded people than for the solitary thinker. The topics I wanted to work on were the topics to which I'd been introduced in college: the connection between the Christian faith and philosophy (as well as the other disciplines) and the question how best to be a Christian in philosophy. Calvin was the best place I knew to work on these questions; nowhere else, so far as I knew, were they as central a focus of interest, and nowhere else were they pursued with the same persistent tenacity. I therefore went to Calvin.

Apart from frequent leaves, I spent the next nineteen years at Calvin. There is much to be said about Calvin and about the marvelously stimulating and formative years I spent as a faculty member there, and the people, in particular Paul Zwier and Nicholas Wolterstorff, from whom I learned. I went to Calvin in part because of a long-term interest in Christian scholarship and Christian philosophy, the sorts of topics and questions raised at Calvin when I was a student there. And at Calvin, in one way, I found the very sort of communal Christian scholarship I was hoping for, as I say in the Profiles volume. In another way, though, what I say there is much too rosy; we certainly didn't make nearly as much progress, for example, on the question how in fact to be a Christian philosopher, as could reasonably be hoped. Partly this was due, of course, to the fact that this question of how to be a Christian philosopher, the question of the bearing of one's Christianity on one's philosophy, is extraordinarily difficult, and there isn't much by way of guidance or precedent or (recent) tradition with respect to it.

In my own case, furthermore, during most of the first decade of my stay at Calvin, I was working on the metaphysics of modality, writing parts and versions and drafts of *The Nature of Necessity*. After finishing that I returned to the topics and concerns of *God and Other Minds* (although that isn't how I thought of the matter then); if there aren't strong arguments either for belief in God or for belief in other minds, how is it that we are justified in believing as we do? My answer was that both are properly basic (which in a way isn't much of an answer: it is simply the declaration that one doesn't need propositional evidence in order to be justified in believing propositions of this sort). This project culminated in "Reason and Belief in God";[13] it occupied much of my time during the second decade of my time at Calvin. (I wish to remark parenthetically that I regret having referred to this project, half in jest, as "Reformed Epistemology" or "Calvinist Epistemology"; some didn't realize this was supposed to be just a clever title, not a gauntlet thrown at the feet of Catholic philosophers.)

Calvin Again and Notre Dame

In 1982 we left Calvin for Notre Dame (and it is at this point that the Profiles "intellectual autobiography" stops). And what can I say about my spiritual life since leaving Calvin? For me as, I suppose, for most others, spiritual life is an up and down proposition, with what one hopes are the consolidation of small but genuine gains. Sometimes I wake in the wee hours of the morning and find myself wondering: Can all this really be true? Can this whole wonderful Christian story really be more than a wonderful fairy tale? At other times I find myself as convinced of its main lineaments as that I live in South Bend.

For me, church and Sunday school play a very important role in the life of faith. Again, this is no doubt insipid, boring, banal, bourgeois and conventional; I wish I could report something more exciting. When I was in college, the idea that at some future time (at any rate prior to complete senility) Sunday school and church would be the high point of my week (even the spiritual high point) would have seemed laughable; but there it is: what can I say? When I was growing up, Sunday school was the sort of thing one did only because one's elders insisted on it. I remember almost nothing about any Sunday school from my childhood and youth, except that I once had a teacher whose name was Ethel; with typically incisive fifth-grade wit we called her "High Test," which in those days was the way one referred to premium gasoline. As an adult, on the other hand, I was astonished, one year, to find Sunday school a genuine occasion for learning and spiritual growth; this was an adult Sunday-school class in the Christian Reformed Church in Palo Alto, California (where in 1968-69 I was a fellow in the Center for Advanced

Study in the Behavioral Sciences). This class was led by Glen vander Sluis, whose decision to become an architect deprived the world of a terrific theologian. More recently, Sunday school in our present church (the South Bend Christian Reformed Church), often led by John Van Engen, a professor of medieval history at Notre Dame, has played the same role for me—as it did, not so surprisingly, the years I led it myself.

I've gone on at length, oddly enough, about Sunday school; but I have also benefited enormously from the rest of what goes on in our church. First, from regular church services and wonderful preaching. Preaching has always been a matter of paramount importance in Reformed Christianity. This emphasis has its downside: what do you do when you have a really poor preacher? the kind who, like one of the preachers I heard as a child in Waupun, spends about fifteen minutes explaining that the blind man Christ healed could not, as a matter of fact, see? By the same token, however, excellent preaching can be, and at my church has been and is, of absolutely enormous value.

And second, I must mention, of course, people: the people in my church and more generally other Christians I know—colleagues, friends, students—who in a thousand ways, ways far too numerous to tell, have offered spiritual support and upbuilding. Here I must also mention especially my mother, from whom in some ways I have learned as much recently as when I was a child. My father has suffered from manic-depressive psychosis[14] for fifty years and more; and of course this has placed enormous burden on my mother, who has cared for him and helped him with magnificent generosity and unstinting devotion. She has done this day after day, year after year, decade after decade; and she has done so, furthermore, with (for the most part) a sort of cheerful courage that is wonderful to behold. And I must also mention especially my youngest brother (fourteen years younger), Neal. As we all know, relationships with parents constantly change; eventually the parent becomes the child and the child the parent. Something similar can go on with relationships between siblings; and in recent years I am sure I have learned more from Neal than he from me.

God and Evil
One of my chief interests over the years has been in philosophical

theology and apologetics: the attempt to defend Christianity (or more broadly, theism) against the various sorts of attacks brought against it. Christian apologetics, of course, has a long history, going back at least to the Patristics of the second century A.D.; perhaps the main function of apologetics is to show that, from a philosophical point of view, Christians and other theists have nothing whatever for which to apologize. I can scarcely remember a time when I wasn't aware of and interested in objections to Christianity and arguments against it. Christianity, for me, has always involved a substantial intellectual element. I can't claim to have had a great deal by way of unusual religious experience (although on a fair number of occasions I have had a profound sense of God's presence), but for nearly my entire life I have been convinced of the *truth* of Christianity.

Of course the contemporary world contains much that is hostile to Christian faith: according to much of the intellectual establishment of the Western world, Christianity is intellectually bankrupt, not worthy of a rational person's credence. Many of these claims strike me as merely fatuous—the claim, for example, that "man come of age" can no longer accept supernaturalism, or Bultmann's suggestion (mentioned above) to the effect that traditional Christian belief is impossible in this age of "electric light and the wireless." (One can imagine an earlier village skeptic taking a similarly altitudinous view of, say, the tallow candle and the printing press.)

Three sorts of considerations, however, with respect to belief in God, have troubled me and have been a source of genuine perplexity: the existence of certain kinds of evil, the fact that many people for whom I have deep respect do not accept belief in God, and the fact that it is difficult to find much by way of noncircular argument or evidence for the existence of God. The last, I think, is least impressive and no longer disturbed me after I had worked out the main line of argument of *God and Other Minds*. The second has remained mildly disquieting; its force is mitigated, however, by the fact that there are many issues of profound importance—profound *practical* as well as theoretical importance—where such disagreement abounds.

But the first remains deeply baffling, and has remained a focus of my thought after moving to Notre Dame.[15] Evil comes in many kinds; and some are particularly perplexing. A talented young woman is invaded by a slow and horrifying disease—so long-lasting that she gets to explore each step down in excruciating detail; a young man of twenty-five, in the flood tide of vigor and full of bright promise, is killed in a senseless climbing accident; a radiant young wife and mother, loved and needed by her family, is attacked by a deadly cancer; a sparkling and lovely child is struck down by leukemia and dies a painful and lingering death: what could be the point of these things? As I said, my father has suffered from manic-depressive psychosis for the last fifty years; in his case the manic but not the depressive phase is satisfactorily controlled by drugs—yet the suffering involved in serious clinical depression is almost beyond belief. What is supposed to be the good in that? Why does God permit these things? The sheer *extent* of suffering and evil in the world is appalling. In one extended battle during the Chinese Civil War, six million people were killed. What about Hitler and Stalin and Pol Pot and a thousand lesser villains? Why does God permit so *much* evil in his world?

Sometimes evil displays a cruelly ironic twist. I recall a story in the local paper a few years ago about a man who drove a cement mixer truck. He came home one day for lunch; his three-year-old daughter was playing in the yard. After lunch, when he jumped into his truck and backed out, he failed to notice that she was playing behind it; she was killed beneath the great dual wheels. One can imagine this man's brokenhearted anguish. And if he was a believer in God, he may have become furiously angry with God—who, after all, could have forestalled this calamity in a thousand different ways. So why *didn't* he? And sometimes we get a sense of the demonic—of evil naked and pure. Those with power over others may derive great pleasure from devising exquisite tortures for their victims: a woman in a Nazi concentration camp is forced to choose which of her children shall be sent to the ovens and which preserved. Why does God permit all this evil, and evil of these horrifying kinds, in his world? How can it be seen as fitting in with his loving and providential care for his creatures?

Christians must concede that we don't know. That is, we don't know in any detail. On a quite general level, we may know that God permits evil because he can achieve a world he sees as better by permitting evil than by preventing it; and what God sees as better is, of course, better. But we cannot see *why* our world with all its ills would be better than others we think we can conceive, or *what*, in any detail, is God's reason for permitting a given specific and appalling evil. Not only can we not see this, we often can't think of any very good possibilities. Christians must therefore admit that we don't know why God permits the evils this world displays. This can be deeply perplexing, and deeply disturbing. It can lead believers to take toward God an attitude they themselves deplore; it can tempt us to be angry with God, to mistrust God, like Job, to accuse him of injustice, to adopt an attitude of bitterness and rebellion. No doubt there isn't any logical incompatibility between God's power and knowledge and goodness, on the one hand, and the existence of the evils we see on the other; and no doubt the latter doesn't provide a good probabilistic argument against the former. No doubt; but this is cold and abstract comfort when faced with the shocking concreteness of a particularly appalling exemplification of evil. What the believer in the grip of this sort of spiritual perplexity needs, of course, is not philosophy, but comfort and spiritual counsel. There is much to be said here, and it is neither my place nor within my competence to say it.

I should like, however, to mention two points that I believe are of special significance. First, as the Christian sees things, God does not stand idly by, coolly observing the suffering of his creatures. He enters into and shares our suffering. He endures the anguish of seeing his Son, the second person of the Trinity, consigned to the bitterly cruel and shameful death of the cross. Some theologians claim that God cannot suffer. I believe they are wrong. God's capacity for suffering, I believe, is proportional to his greatness; it exceeds our capacity for suffering in the same measure as his capacity for knowledge exceeds ours. Christ was prepared to endure the agonies of hell itself; and God, the first being and Lord of the universe, was prepared to endure the suffering consequent upon his Son's humiliation and death. He was prepared to accept this suffering in order to overcome sin and death and the evils that afflict our world, and to confer on us a life more glorious than we can imagine. So we don't know why God permits evil; we do know, however, that he was prepared to suffer on our behalf, to accept suffering of which we can form no conception.

The chief difference between Christianity and the other theistic religions lies just here: according to the Christian gospel, God is willing to enter into and share the sufferings of his creatures, in order to redeem them and his world. Of course this doesn't answer the question, Why does God permit evil? But it helps the Christian trust God as a loving father, no matter what ills befall him. Otherwise it would be easy to see God as remote and detached, permitting all these evils, himself untouched, in order to achieve ends that are no doubt exalted but have little to do with us, and little power to assuage our griefs. It would be easy to see him as cold and unfeeling—or if loving, then such that his love for us has little to do with our perception of our own welfare. But God, as Christians see him, is neither remote nor detached. His aims and goals may be beyond our ken and may require our suffering; but he is himself prepared to accept much greater suffering in the pursuit of those ends. In this regard Christianity contains a resource for dealing with this existential problem of evil—a resource denied the other theistic religions.

Second, it is indeed true that suffering and evil can occasion spiritual perplexity and discouragement; and of all the antitheistic arguments, only the argument from evil deserves to be taken really seriously. But I also believe, paradoxically enough, that there is a *theistic* argument *from* evil, and it is at least as strong as the *antitheistic* argument from evil. (Here I can only sketch the argument and leave it at an intuitive level.) What is so deeply disturbing about horrifying kinds of evil? The most appalling kinds of evil involve human cruelty and wickedness: Stalin and Pol Pot, Hitler and his henchmen, and the thousands of small vignettes of evil that make up such a whole. What is genuinely abhorrent is the callousness and perversion and cruelty of the concentration camp guard taking pleasure in the sufferings of others; what is really odious is taking advantage of one's position of trust (as a parent or counselor, perhaps) in order to betray and corrupt someone. What is genuinely appalling, in other words, is not really human suffering as such so much as human wickedness. This wickedness strikes us as deeply perverse, wholly wrong, warranting not just quarantine and the attempt to overcome it, but blame and punishment.

But could there really be any such thing as horrifying wickedness if naturalism were true? I don't see how. A naturalistic way of looking at the world, so it seems to me, has no place for genuine moral obligation of any sort; a fortiori, then, it has no place for such a category as horrifying wickedness. It is hard enough, from a naturalistic perspective, to see how it could be that we human beings can be so related to propositions (contents) that we believe them; and harder yet, as I said above, to explain how that content could enter into a causal explanation of someone's actions. But these difficulties are as nothing compared with seeing how, in a naturalistic universe, there could be such a thing as genuine and appalling wickedness. There can be such a thing only if there is a way rational creatures are *supposed* to live, *obliged* to live; and the *force* of that normativity—its strength, so to speak—is such that the appalling and horrifying nature of genuine wickedness is its inverse. But naturalism cannot make room for that kind of normativity; that requires a divine lawgiver, one whose very nature it is to abhor wickedness. Naturalism can perhaps accommodate foolishness and irrationality, acting contrary to what are or what you take to be your own interests; it can't accommodate appalling wickedness. Accordingly, if you think there really *is* such a thing as horrifying wickedness (that our sense that there is, is not a mere illusion of some sort), and if you also think the main options are theism and naturalism, then you have a powerful theistic argument from evil.

Evidence and Theistic Belief
One focus of my thought since moving to Notre Dame has been evil; a second has been continued concern with the issues surrounding the evidentialist objection to theistic belief—the issues that were the focus of *God and Other Minds*. The atheologian claims that belief in God is *irrational*—because he thinks it conflicts with such obvious facts as the existence of evil, perhaps, or because there is evidence against it or because there is no evidence for it. When he makes this claim, just what property is it that he is ascribing to theistic belief? What is rationality and what is rational justification? What does it mean to say that a belief is irrational? The central topic of *God and Other Minds* is "the rational justification of belief in the existence of God as he is conceived in the

Hebrew-Christian tradition" (p. vii). I was really considering the evidential objection to theistic belief, without explicitly considering or formulating it. I argued, in brief, that belief in God and belief in other minds are in the same epistemological boat; since belief in other minds is clearly rational, the same goes for belief in God. What I wrote there still seems to me to be substantially true, although now I see the issues in a broader context and (I hope) more clearly. But even though the topic of the book is the rational justification of theistic belief, there is almost no consideration of the protean, confusing, many-sided notion of rationality.

In *God and Other Minds* I assumed that the proper way to approach the question of the rationality of theistic belief is in terms of argument for and against the existence of God. Following contemporary fashion, furthermore, I thought a *good* argument (either theistic or antitheistic) would have to be more or less conclusive, appealing to premises and procedures hardly any sensible person could reject. This assumption is part of a larger picture, total way of thinking of the main questions of epistemology, which has come to be called "classical foundationalism." Like everyone else, I imbibed this picture with my mother's milk; and the conclusion of *God and Other Minds* is really that from the perspective of classical foundationalism, belief in God and belief in other minds are in the same epistemological boat.

Returning to the topics of *God and Other Minds* after an excursis into the topics of *The Nature of Necessity*, I began to consider more explicitly the evidentialist objection to theistic belief—the objection that theistic belief is irrational just because there is no evidence or at any rate insufficient evidence for it. (This objection, of course, has been enormously influential. In the 1950s and 1960s I heard it a thousand times.) In 1974 I argued in "Is It Rational to Believe in God?" that belief in God can be perfectly rational even if none of the theistic arguments works and even if there is no noncircular evidence for it; my main aim was to argue that it is perfectly rational to take belief in God as *basic*—to accept it, that is, without accepting it on the basis of argument or evidence from other propositions one believes.

Again, I didn't look at all deeply into the question of what this notion of rationality *is*. Just what is it that one is objecting to when one claims that belief in God is irrational? This question had and has received little attention, either from the detractors or the defenders of theism. But by the time I wrote "Reason and Belief in God" (see n. 13) in 1979-80 it was becoming clear that the evidentialist objector should be construed as holding that the theist who believes without evidence thereby violates an intellectual *obligation*, flouts some epistemic *duty* and is unjustified in the core sense of having done something one has no right to do. This, once more, is just another facet of classical foundationalism; for according to this picture one has an intellectual obligation, of some sort, to believe a proposition only if it is at least probable with respect to what is certain for you (and according to the [modern] classical foundationalist, the propositions that are certain for you are those that are self-evident or incorrigible for you).[16]

Once one sees clearly that this is really the issue—that is, the issue is really whether the theist without propositional evidence is violating an intellectual duty or obligation—the evidentialist objection no longer looks at all formidable; for why suppose there is any such obligation, an obligation to believe such propositions only on the basis of evidence from other propositions?

In *God and Other Minds* and "Is It Rational to Believe in God?" I failed to distinguish rationality in the sense of justification—being within one's intellectual rights, flouting no intellectual duties or obligations—from rationality in the sense of *warrant:* that property, whatever precisely it is, that distinguishes knowledge from mere true belief;[17] and in "Rationality and Belief in God" I was groping for this distinction. (It is one of the achievements of contemporary epistemology to rediscover a clear distinction between justification and warrant—a distinction known to some of the medievals but lost later on in the triumph of modern classical foundationalism.) If we take rationality as warrant, an entirely different galaxy of considerations becomes relevant to the question whether belief in God is rational. Indeed, so taken, this epistemological question is not ontologically or theologically neutral; pursued far enough, it transforms itself into an ontological or theological question.

Reformed thinkers such as John Calvin have held that God has implanted in us a tendency or nisus toward accepting belief in God under certain widely realized conditions. Calvin speaks, in this connection, of a "sense of deity inscribed in the hearts of all." Just as we have a natural tendency to form perceptual beliefs under certain conditions, so, says Calvin, we have a natural tendency to form such beliefs as "God is speaking to me" or "God has created all this" or "God disapproves of what I've done" under certain widely realized conditions. And a person who in these conditions forms one of these beliefs is (typically) within her epistemic rights (justified) and also is such that the belief has warrant for her; indeed, Calvin thinks (and I agree) that such a person may *know* the proposition in question. In sum, on the Reformed or Calvinist way of looking at the matter, those who accept belief in God as basic may be entirely within their epistemic rights, may thereby display no defect or blemish in their noetic structure and, indeed, under those conditions may *know* that God exists.

This still seems to me to be correct; over the last few years, I have been thinking about the same question, but trying to put it into the framework of a broader theory of justification, rationality and warrant. I began to explore these matters in the Gifford Lectures given at the University of Aberdeen in 1987.[18] Since then I have been working on the written version of these lectures, and have now just finished the first two volumes of what looks like a three-volume project.[19]

Christian Philosophy

In 1982 I left Calvin College for the University of Notre Dame. In the Profiles volume, I say the following:

> Notre Dame, paradoxically enough, has a large concentration of orthodox or conservative Protestant graduate students in philosophy—the largest concentration in the United States and for all I know the largest concentration in the world. During my nineteen years at Calvin perhaps my central concern has been with the question how best to be a Christian in philosophy; and during that time my colleagues and I have learned at least something about that topic. I hope to be able to pass on some of what we've learned to the students at Notre Dame.

This is another case where it is hard *in excelsis* to determine what your motives for a given action really are and the ambiguity and difficulty of seeing and speaking the truth on such matters (didn't that fat salary have anything to do with it?). However, I should like to think that passage describes my motives; and if, as Robert Nozick suggests, one can choose which motives to act from (or in this case to *have* acted from), then I choose these. But part of this passage is seriously misleading: it isn't really true (as became clear to me when rereading and rethinking the Profiles autobiography) that my central concern at Calvin was "with the question how best to be a Christian in philosophy." I spent the bulk of my time at Calvin thinking about the metaphysics of modality, the problem of evil and "Reformed epistemology." True, my colleagues and I learned *something* about being a Christian philosopher; how little, however, became apparent to me when at Notre Dame I began to teach a course entitled (immodestly enough) "How to Be a Christian Philosopher." This topic wasn't often something we thought about explicitly and in a focused way at Calvin; it was more like a constant background condition. In fact we didn't make a lot of progress with it, although we did make *some* progress, and were able at least to figure out some of the right questions. However, there is nothing like teaching a course or seminar in an area as a stimulus to learning something about it; I have, I think, made a bit of progress in this area since teaching courses in it at Notre Dame. (I also taught a course on this topic at Calvin, some seven years or so after I left there for Notre Dame; neither I nor anyone else taught a course of that sort at Calvin during the nineteen years I was there as a faculty member.)

This question has come to assume an increasingly large proportion of my time and attention. At Calvin we learned from Jellema and others that the popular contemporary myth of science as a cool, reasoned, wholly dispassionate attempt to figure out the truth about ourselves and our world entirely independent of religion, or ideology, or moral convictions, or theological commitments is just that: a myth. And since the term *myth* is often used in such a way as not to imply falsehood, let me add that this myth is also deeply mistaken. Following Augustine (and Abraham Kuyper, Herman Dooyeweerd, Harry Jellema and many others), I believe that there is indeed a conflict, a battle between the *civitas Dei*, the city of God, and *civitas mundi*, the city of the world.

As a matter of fact, what we have, I think, is a three-way contest.

On the one hand is perennial naturalism, a view going back to the ancient world, according to which there is no God, nature is all there is, and humankind is to be understood as a part of nature. Second, there is what I shall call "Enlightenment humanism"; we could also call it "Enlightenment subjectivism" or "Enlightenment antirealism." This way of thinking goes back substantially to Immanuel Kant. According to its central tenet, it is really we human beings, we men and women, who structure the world, who are responsible for its fundamental outline and lineaments—its fundamental structure and value. Of course I don't have the space here to go into this matter properly; my point, however, is this: serious intellectual endeavor—including science—is by no means neutral with respect to this conflict. Science, philosophy and intellectual endeavor generally—the attempt to understand ourselves and our world—enters into this conflict in a thousand ways. And the closer the science in question is to what is distinctively human, the deeper the involvement.[20]

If Augustine is right about the conflict between the *civitas Dei* and the *civitas mundi*, and about the involvement of philosophy and scholarship generally in this conflict, then that is a matter of considerable importance, something very much worth knowing. As a matter of fact, his diagnosis has important implications for the question of how Christian philosophers should carry out their business. I've said most of what I have to say about these matters in the pieces mentioned in note 20; here I want only to emphasize one point together with a corollary. Christian philosophers are members of *several* communities: the Christian community, a local church community, the community of Christian scholars, the professional community of philosophers, the modern Western intellectual community and of course many others. The point I want to make is that Christian philosophers should *explicitly* and *self-consciously* think of themselves as belonging to the Christian community (and the community of Christian intellectuals); perhaps they should think of themselves *primarily* or *first of all* as members of the Christian community, and only secondarily as members of, say, the philosophical community at large, or the contemporary academic community. Our first responsibility is to the Lord and to the Christian community, not first of all to the philosophical community at large—although of course that is also a very serious responsibility, and a serious responsibility in part because of its connection with the first responsibility.

In some cases this orientation may require a certain courage, or Christian boldness or confidence;[21] in the philosophical and academic world at large there is a good deal of disapproval and disdain for Christianity and Christians, in particular for those who publicly identify themselves as Christians (private Christianity is more likely to be indulgently regarded as a relatively harmless peccadillo or weakness, like being addicted to television or computer games) and propose to practice their scholarly craft in the light of their faith.

The corollary is this. A *successful* Christian philosopher is not first of all one who has won the approval and acclaim of the philosophical world generally, not someone who is "distinguished"; it is rather one who has faithfully served the Lord in the ways put before her. We philosophers are brought up to practice our craft in a sort of individualistic, competitive, even egotistical style; there is enormous interest among philosophers in ranking each other with respect to dialectical and philosophical ability, deciding who is really terrific, who is pretty good, who is OK, who is really lousy and so on. (Those who do well in this derby sometimes remind me of Daniel 8:8, "And the he-goat magnified himself exceedingly.") Your worth, at any rate *qua* philosopher, tends to depend on your ranking, as if your main job is to try to achieve as high a ranking as possible. (Just as a politician's main job, obviously, is to get reelected.) There is a corresponding tendency to value students in proportion to their philosophical ability, thinking that our best efforts ought to be reserved for our ablest students, and that weaker students aren't really worthy or as worthy of our attention. It is as if we were training a stable of would-be professional boxers, or potential Olympic competitors.

But all this is flummery, a snare and delusion. Philosophy is not an athletic competition; and success as a Christian philosopher is not an individualistic matter of doing well in the intellectual equivalent of a tennis tournament. This is not to say that a Christian philosopher ought not to hope to gain the respect of other philosophers; of course not. Recognition for one's work is a blessing to be enjoyed, and may furthermore be useful in doing the job Christian philosophers need to do. But reputation and recognition are a mixed blessing, one which contains real spiritual pitfalls and traps; it is no measure of the success of a Christian philosopher, and the quest for it is vain foolishness. Christian philosophers are successful, not when they achieve a "reputation" but when they properly play their role in the Christian community.

This is of course a multifaceted role, but what I want to emphasize here is its *communal* side. Christian philosophers are engaged in a *common* project: a project they have in common with other Christian philosophers, but also and more generally with other Christian intellectuals and academics. This project has several different sides: apologetics, both positive and negative; philosophical theology; what we might call philosophical consciousness-raising, where the aim is to see how current cultural products (contemporary science, philosophy, literature and so forth) look from a Christian perspective; working at the sorts of questions philosophers ask and answer; and working at these questions from a Christian perspective, where that perspective is relevant (and it is relevant in more places than one might think). All of this and more constitutes the task of the Christian philosophical community. Part of the ground of this task (its justification, we might say) lies in the fact that it is necessary for the spiritual and intellectual health and flourishing of that community. Another part of its justification, however, is just that it is part of the task of developing a community of persons in which the image of God is communally displayed. This multisided project, then, is a communal project in which the whole Christian philosophical community must be engaged.

Of course this means thinking of other philosophers not as competitors for a scarce or limited commodity, but as colleagues, or teammates, or cooperators, or perhaps coconspirators joined in a common task. (The main idea isn't always to see what's *wrong* with someone's paper, but to see how you can help.) But then the attitude that what really counts—in institutions, as well as people—is philosophical excellence (whatever precisely that is) or, worse, prestige and reputation, is foolish and shortsighted; what really counts, of course, is the performance of the function Christian philosophers must fulfill in and out of the Christian community. (That involves philosophical excellence, but it involves much more.) Then success is to be measured in terms of contribution to the proper performance of those functions. You carry out this project by way of teaching, writing, conversation and many other ways; it is a complex, multifarious task, and it is by no means clear that you contribute to it in proportion to the strength of your curriculum vita.

Another part of the corollary is that teaching must be taken really seriously. Teaching, for a Christian philosopher, isn't just a meal ticket, a tradeoff whereby you give up some of your time so that you can spend the rest of it doing "your own work"; it is a central and essential part of the task. At the undergraduate level, where students will not for the most part become professional philosophers, the teacher can contribute directly to the common task I mentioned. At the graduate level the aim is to help train our successors, those who will carry on the task in the next generation. It is hard to think of anything more important (or more baffling!) than bringing up your children properly; it is also hard to think of any task more important, for a Christian philosopher, than doing what one can to train and equip the next generation of Christian philosophers. This means seeing younger philosophers, fledgling philosophers and graduate students as of immense value. Their well-being and development as members of the community of Christian philosophers is a source of real concern: it requires our best efforts and any encouragement and help we can give. For it is they, after all, who will carry on this task of Christian philosophy after the current generation has left the scene.

When I left graduate school in 1957, there were few Christian philosophers in the United States, and even fewer Christian philosophers willing to identify themselves as such. Had there been such a thing as the Society of Christian Philosophers, it would have had few members. Positivism was very much in the ascendancy, and the general attitude among professional philosophers was something like George Nakhnikian's: an intelligent and serious philosopher couldn't possibly be a Christian. It looked as if Christianity would have an increasingly smaller part to play in the academy generally and in philosophy specifically; perhaps it would dwindle away altogether. This was of course discouraging. One does one's best and leaves the results to the Lord;

but the demise of Christian philosophy is not a happy prospect for someone who hopes to devote himself to it.

Now, some thirty-five years later, things look different indeed. There are hundreds of young Christian philosophers in the United States, many of them people of great philosophical power; much first-rate work is going on in Christian or theistic philosophy and allied topics; many have accepted the challenge to try to see precisely what being a Christian means for being a philosopher, who have tried to see what the Christian community must do in philosophy, and then tried to do precisely that. (A fair number of these people are or have been graduate students at Notre Dame, and I consider it a privilege to be involved in their growth and development.) Many of them are not only philosophers of real ability; they are also absolutely first-rate people—people with a deep loyalty to the Christian faith, who know how to treat each other with Christian love. Of course one never knows what the future will bring; but it looks as if Christian philosophy, for the next generation or two, will be in good hands indeed. For me personally this is a source of amazement, delight and gratitude.

Where Else?

JOHN RIST

John Rist is professor of classics and philosophy at the University of Toronto and is a life member of Clare Hall in the University of Cambridge. He has also taught at St. Michael's College in the University of Toronto and was Regius Professor of Classics at the University of Aberdeen. Rist is a historian of philosophy of the Ancient and Patristics periods with over sixty articles to his credit. His books include Eros and Psyche; The Stoics; Human Value: A Study in Ancient Philosophical Ethics; Platonism and Its Christian Heritage; Plotinus: The Road to Reality; *and* The Mind of Aristotle. *He is currently working on the foundations of ethics. He once served as president of the Coalition for Life (Canada).*

Witness Newman and Augustine. Not only the senile write spiritual autobiography, though spiritual autobiography is often written by the senile. Looking back on one's past brings several benefits: one is the sense of astonishment that much of what once seemed true is now so obviously false. Yet it is as hard for an intellectual convert to pass as a devotee of the blood of the martyrs as it is for a revolutionary theorist to pass as an authentic freedom fighter. It has been said, behind my back, that I am no true Catholic. I must leave my readers—and my Maker—to judge as to that.

Ancestry

My mother's parents were English peasants, though my grandfather preferred to spend much of his time as a soldier in various parts of

Africa. He was almost illiterate, fond of large quantities of food and drink, and superstitious. He feared that if he were buried without a headstone his spirit would "walk." My grandmother was down-to-earth and kind, and would always take in stray animals. Dogs were devoted to her, though she was rough with them. She often sang "The Old Rugged Cross" but never went near the village church or the "parson," whom she considered high-falutin', aloof and a bit effete. During World War II she developed a strong antipathy toward conscientious objectors ("conchies"), especially those who refused nonmilitary tasks, in particular the Jehovah's Witnesses. They were willing to eat food brought to the country at the risk of other men's lives, she observed, and if one of them failed to remove himself quickly from her property she would offer to set the dog on him. These grandparents were both nominal members of the Church of England.

My father's family was respectable and Congregationalist, though I never knew my grandfather, whom I inferred to have been a harmless alcoholic. The family's religion was based on the chapel that they attended and the Bible that I never saw them read. They were proud of the Empire, enjoyed cricket and distrusted foreigners. My father and his brother became officers in the Boys' Brigade, a plebeian, decidedly Protestant organization. They ate rice pudding (as he said) virtually every day, and my father went to a fairly good school where, however, he seems to have learned little: no languages, no science, no history, even no mathematics, though when he grew up he became an able accountant and company director.

My parents married in the Church of England, of which my father, without applying for admission, became and remained for the rest of his life a communicant member. When I was a boy, he became a "sidesman," but he never spoke of Christianity (he was not much given to speaking about anything) except as a moral code: proper Christians did not lie, steal or indulge in overt sexual behavior. Kissing in public was foreign at best. I never noticed any kissing at home, either of each other or of me. As a young man he had occasionally visited the music hall in London, but he disapproved of shows put on to entertain the soldiers in World War II. Two doors away from us in our dreary Romford street—just outside the East End of London—lived a dancer who performed in such shows: "Just an excuse to show all she's got."

Foreigners were not popular at home in World War II: the French were cowards, the Italians clowns, the Germans—more understandably—thugs. Catholicism was associated with such people, or with the Irish, who were "too close" to the Nazis; the Church of England was Protestant and British. A great-aunt was an admirer of Stalin now that he was on our side, but in our family that was highly eccentric, and the reactions were for me a source of entertainment.

My mother had been a teacher mainly of "infants" in tough London schools. She had once toyed with the left, at least as far as being interested in Wells, Shaw and country-dancing under the aegis of the communist vicar of Thaxted Church in Essex. It was only dabbling, and she later began to dabble in religion too, sometimes taking me along to weary chapels where the preachers offended her either by talking of God as "just like a kind old uncle" or by giving the impression that they were a bit more moral than their congregations; she had a keen nose for humbug. She always preferred the Church of England, though with diminishing enthusiasm as she grew older: it stood for an earlier England with woods and hedgerows and clean water, with the red splashes of the British Empire on the map beyond. My father never accompanied us on the chapel-crawling; he stuck with the Church of England and the Reverend Elvin, though he deemed the latter's activities on the stock market to be dubious and his sermons to be unduly centered on the iniquities of children.

School Days

I was an only child, and my parents were ambitious for me. My mother wanted me to be a diplomat; she dreamed of an ambassadorship or some other "establishment" position—though those who know me best would probably agree that diplomacy is a line for which I have peculiarly little aptitude! My father had no specific ideas; he wanted great, but honest, success. Accordingly, for secondary schooling I was sent to Brentwood School, where a year later I gained a scholarship. The school had been founded by Sir Anthony Browne, a Tudor profiteer, nominally to honor the memory of William Hunter, who had been burned at the stake under Queen Mary for distributing English Bibles. Its traditions were Church of England Protestant, and Foxe's *Book of Martyrs* was on prominent display in the Bean Library to recall the bad old Catholic days. Quite a number of the boys enjoyed reading of tortures duly recorded in the *Book*.

The former headmaster, Jimmy Hough, had been efficient and popular, but in his latter days things had deteriorated, and when his successor, C. Ralph (pronounced Rafe) Allison, took over, he had to pull together something not unlike the "anarchy tempered by despotism" of the unreformed Eton. In this he had a certain success, but many of the vices of the old system remained, while Allison himself was largely responsible for a strong new element of snobbery and place-seeking. Beatings with various instruments (canes, slippers, rubber tubing) were common and administered by senior boys as well as masters; many of these "prefects" much enjoyed the chance to beat. Homosexuality was frequent and at least tacitly encouraged by some of the masters. In many of the "houses" into which the boys were divided (including my own) there was a cult of sports extreme even by the standards of British "public" schools. These were supposed to encourage manliness, and boys who tried to avoid them by skulking in the changing-rooms were liable to be stripped and sometimes forcibly masturbated. Those whose pubic hair grew late were particularly at risk, especially if they were academically or artistically inclined.

There were some very good teachers, especially of history, English and classics, but not of modern languages and certainly not of religion: this subject and its purveyors were a joke. Of the three clergymen who taught religious education, one (who, after enlisting without identifying his profession, had been shell-shocked at Alamein) used to get into blind rages, accompanied by violence, if anyone mentioned (and especially if anyone attempted to defend) New Testament miracles—a subject which therefore came up regularly and pointlessly in almost every class. Another, who doubled as a chemist, for some mysterious reason would talk endlessly about Dagon the Tyrian fish-god. We learned to amuse ourselves by playing the alphabet game: getting him to say words that began with each letter of the alphabet in turn; hence frequent questions about when missionaries first went to Quebec or Zululand!

Nevertheless, I was confirmed into the Anglican Church at the age of thirteen and for a brief while became an enthusiastic communicant, though part of my motivation was that the Communion service included no sermon by the Reverend Elvin. My preparation for confirmation was sparse: avoiding masturbation seemed to be the main point in the religious program. Such was the assumed limit of licentiousness in a boys' school; the occasional but popular sessions of strip poker with the girls from the neighboring Ursuline Convent with which our school had formed some links (its being Catholic was of less moment than the fact that it was more establishment than County High) remained unknown, at least officially.

Having entered the "arts" side of the school at about twelve, I had to choose between Greek and German a year later. I was already devoted to Latin, and I recall the moment when, traveling on the train to school, I made up my mind to opt for Greek. It was an important decision. Even beginning to see the Greco-Roman world in its entirety was a stupendous revelation. I soaked in all I could find, both learning the languages with enthusiasm and immersing myself in the history. When ill, I read endlessly in North's translation of Plutarch's *Lives*. By fifteen I had devoured Gibbon's *Decline and Fall*, by sixteen Syme's *Roman Revolution*. My reading was encouraged by a lack of social activity at home: no parties and few outings during the school term. Moving naturally and easily from Rome to the Renaissance, I took in Machiavelli's *Prince* in English, and by seventeen had begun to learn Italian under the guidance of one of the classics teachers and his Venetian wife. Humanism was what mattered, and Christianity looked increasingly alien, obscurantist and hypocritical.

For several years I had found that the unintelligibility of the notion of a Trinity seemed only to reinforce my fear of death; now the problem was historical evidence, in two major areas: the origins of the Church of England and the origins of Christianity itself. Frazer's *Golden Bough* helped persuade me that Christianity was "really" an overblown fertility cult tied to the seasons, while religious instruction informed me that Mark was the earliest Gospel, and that it contained no reference to the resurrection and only a few (presumed interpolated) miracles. Matthew and Luke were later and corrupted, partly by a "sayings-source" (Q), of which no independent traces remained, and partly by the simplemindedness and credulousness, if not fraudulence, of their authors. I never believed in Q, but the notion of fraudulence was attractive: either Jesus was a megalomaniac or, more probably, his followers had persuaded too many of the credulous that he himself had claimed to be divine.

So much for Christianity in general. As for the Church of England in particular, and its dubious historical origins, my mother brought in a well-meaning and good-natured clergyman—the Reverend Elvin having gone to his reward—to persuade me that King Henry VIII was peripheral and that the Church of England was just a local part of the church universal going back to the apostles. Even then I could not understand how he could genuinely believe this to be true. I had no doubt that More and Fisher knew better, and somewhere I came across an Irish rhyme (later quoted by Brendan Behan in *Borstal Boy*) that pithily summed up for me the historical realities.

Pay no heed to the alien preacher
Or his Church without meaning or faith
'Cause the foundation-stone of his temple
Is the bollocks of Henry the Eighth.

Though I always had a few friends (some of whom were interested in religious discussions), what really excited me was what I could find in books. I loved what I saw as the clear light of the ancient world. I was not astute enough to see that "the Glory that was Greece and the Grandeur that was Rome" was itself something of a nineteenth-century myth and that somehow the brutalities and squalidness of much of antiquity had evaded the eyes of the scholars who were my guides. I also failed to see that clarity itself can be a form of reductionism, as it is in a book that I and my contemporaries were regularly inclined to overestimate: Bertrand Russell's *History of Western Philosophy*, with its simplistic and sophistic misinterpretations of most Western ethics and metaphysics. Later, when in Cambridge, I was interested in a woman who had covered a large portion of one wall of her room with Russell's portrait.

Thus by the time I won a scholarship to Trinity College, Cambridge, and well before I spent two years in the Air Force doing National

Service prior to becoming an undergraduate, religion had virtually disappeared. I was in the habit of saying that Christianity had got only one thing right: its doctrine of original sin. I applied this doctrine selectively, along partly Marxist, partly "liberal" lines: the colonized, the poor and the repressed were free of it, or would be if they were liberated from foreign oppression and supplied with better education, better medical services and so on.

The Military and College Life: First Brushes with Catholicism

Such views were confirmed by my experience of the military. I declined the chance of a commission, but they taught me Russian and sent me off to Iraq. I continued reading voraciously and became interested in Islam—not least because it seemed to have little time for the fate of the individual—and among the Iraqi soldiers and the general populace, for the first time I noticed people who seemed to like killing. On returning to Britain and proceeding to Cambridge (at just the time of the Suez adventure), I received a timely lesson in politics by reading the lies in British papers (of all levels of respectability) about recent activity in the Middle East. Machiavelli, as also Plato's "tyrannical man," seemed alive and well and living in Britain.

I enjoyed Trinity College and Cambridge, though in unexpected ways. In almost all the lectures and a high percentage of the "supervisions," the teaching of classics was of shamefully poor standard. The faculty took full advantage of the preparedness and intelligence of the majority of the undergraduates, knowing that they would do reasonably well however badly they were taught. Many of the dons were very learned, but some of them could just as well have collected and classified matchbox-tops, except that the prestige of doing so was less. The study of literature was largely resolved into source hunting and textual criticism, in neither of which I had much interest. The first part of the degree program, however, had in those days virtually no syllabus, and provided we could read (and to some extent compose) in Greek and Latin, we were free to read whatever we wanted once the most obvious "central" authors had been "covered." I read widely and more or less indiscriminately among all kinds of texts, with a certain special fondness for comedy and satire.

The real excitement of the place was the students, many of whom were more intelligent than anyone I had met before. One of them, Denis O'Brien, was a Catholic from Cardinal Vaughan's School with serious interests in classical philosophy. Like me, he had little time for the way the subject had degenerated into a form of cultural anthropology or into the customary pointless erudition. Substantive problems were sidestepped: for example, though book one of Aristotle's *Metaphysics* was one of our set books for finals, we studied it largely as source material for philological work on the pre-Socratics. Just as the archaeologists—as I was fond of observing—seemed more interested in Praxiteles' chisel than his Hermes, so the "ancient philosophers" normally treated their subject matter as cultural phenomena with no particular reference to contemporary problems, whether in the world of ideas generally or in technical philosophy. There was a course on Ancient and Modern Philosophy along the lines of Plato and Wittgenstein, but it was deeply obscure and seemed to find Plato of interest only insofar as he was supposed to have anticipated contemporary developments and "refinements." There was no attempt to understand Plato or Aristotle as philosophers who might have something valuable to say that had not appeared better subsequently. And in any case metaphysics was normally reduced to the philosophy of language, though no one explained the "necessity" of that; it was supposed to be obvious to intelligent people.

I was tempted to move out of classics into straight philosophy (still called "Moral Sciences," though it was neither moral nor scientific), but there the situation looked equally unattractive. It was still the era of the "dissolving away" of philosophical problems, of Ryle and Hare and the belief that a mere polishing of the epistemological lens—as Alan Ker put it to me as a warning—would lead to the disappearance of the old substantive difficulties about free will or the foundations of ethics or the existence of God. There was a premium once again—the phenomenon is already well portrayed in Platonic dialogues—on calmly overbearing sleight-of-hand, and I had by now lost confidence that much of philosophical (as distinct from scientific) worth could be obtained from the current inhabitants of the FDR (Fenland Don Reserve, as some of my acquaintance called Cambridge). I assumed that the portentousness, self-importance and sherry-party cleverness of the practitioners of wisdom could guarantee only that specialized contempt for one's own subject that arises when it is treated largely as a means to self-glorification.

Arguing with contemporaries was another matter, and in the case of Denis O'Brien I became acquainted, perhaps for the first time, with a Christian who was both highly intelligent and interested in philosophical (though not historical) ideas for their own sake. Meeting O'Brien and some of his friends drew Catholicism to my attention. Of course I knew of it historically, but almost entirely of its more vicious side: the Inquisition, the Index of Prohibited Books, the gross anti-intellectualism of much of its post-Tridentine life. I had *never* considered it hypocritical, merely tyrannical and obscurantist, and I had early swallowed the notion that a Catholic (or even a Christian) philosopher is a contradiction in terms. Such a person would never dare "think things through"; there would be conflicts between "free" thought and faith, and either truth or religion would have to be sacrificed. With most of my contemporaries and teachers, I believed it possible to think "dispassionately," from a totally uncommitted standpoint. I failed to see that "Cartesian tolerance" can be as much a hindrance to thought as Christianity or any other tradition, not least that of the Greeks, as Aristotle—I later came to see—had frankly admitted. I failed to see that first principles equally or more bizarre and unproven might lie at the base of the acceptable dogmatism that purported to have replaced Christianity in what we now call a "post-Christian" age; moreover, that conclusions were worth no more than the axioms and first principles from which they were somehow derived, and that, for example, the liberal assumption of the secular perfectibility of the individual or of one's natural goodness is no less a dogma—and perhaps a less plausible one—than the belief in original sin, the authority of the pope or the resurrection itself.

Denis and I translated, or rather adapted into an English version fashionably entitled *Angry Young Women,* one of Aristophanes' comedies for a "May Week" production. While auditioning people for parts in the performance, I met Anna Vogler, a refugee from the philistinism of the Classics Department to English, and also, as I later discovered, in the process of moving from agnosticism to the Catholicism in which she had been baptized but not brought up. For both of us it was a *coup de foudre* that led to courtship and eventually to marriage, though the idyll almost foundered over my hostility to her intended religion, which she, like O'Brien, found as satisfying to the intellect as to the emotions.

It was through Anna that I first met an intellectual and artistic Catholic of an earlier generation. Through the good offices of Monsignor Gilbey, the university chaplain, Anna was sent for instruction to the even then apparently ageless and visibly ascetic Dominican Father Kenelm Foster, who was also reader in Italian studies in the university. Later, when we decided to marry, Father Kenelm gave us marriage instruction, though I hardly remember him talking about marriage. Rather, he would wander from Dante through Aquinas and Averroës to Manzoni, with literal wanderings around his bookshelves to check references.

Though antecedently deeply suspicious of Kenelm, I liked him immediately, and he seemed to like me. He was an internationally recognized scholar who had written much on Dante and Leopardi, translated some Aquinas and was later to publish a book on Petrarch. He claimed to know little about philosophy and regretted a poor acquaintance with Greek. Many years later he commented wryly that in his early days as a Dominican he had probably had to spend too much time on Aquinas, yet it seemed rather a misfortune that some of his confrères (it was the late sixties) appeared not to know who Aquinas was! His knowledge of Dante was formidable and fascinating. I remember him looking up into the night sky and remarking that Dante was right to see the moon like a bucket.

Unlike many of my Cambridge mentors, he was always willing to talk about what interested him, and to raise sharp questions when inquiring about some current enthusiasms of my own. He was genuinely puzzled by human (and especially academic) stupidity; he could not understand why so many academics published abstruse and wholly foolish comment. My explanation that they were out for mere prestige always seemed to him implausible, partaking perhaps of the "mystery of iniquity." But his intellectual integrity was transparent. He found it difficult to tolerate learned, and particularly clerical, fools, but he seemed remarkably patient with arrogant young men. Once many years later (though before I was a Catholic), he asked me what I thought of the work of Heidegger. I said I knew little of it but what little I knew I found needlessly obscure, a decadent form of metaphysics. "That's very interesting," he replied. "Some of my confrères tell me that he is to be the St. Thomas of contemporary Catholicism."

I got a good degree at Cambridge, but had no wish to stay. The senior tutor at Trinity told me that if I waited around awhile I could probably get a fellowship, and when I said I wanted to move on, he remarked uncomprehendingly that if I left at this stage I would never get back: which proved to be correct. Instead I looked for a job. I had come to hold that if there was a God, he was probably the Christian God, and that given Christianity, then Catholicism would be its truest form. But though I had learned that Catholics (and even a few other Christians) could be intellectually honest, I was hardly nearer to their faith.

Early Career: The Search for Truth

I applied for jobs at random: on the BBC and, on the basis of pure chutzpah, with an economic forecasting unit. I applied to teach philosophy in Khartoum, but my application was never acknowledged. Then, at almost the same time, I was offered a position in Nigeria and a one-year job teaching classics, especially ancient philosophy, at the University of Toronto; they had fired someone late in the year and were in need of a replacement. My Cambridge supervisor gave them to understand that I was worth risking for a year—though he later told me that he had entered on my college notes that I was unsuited for an academic career. I borrowed money from my father for a steamship passage and, having failed to persuade Anna, who had a teaching position, that we should be married immediately, said sad farewells on the quayside, knowing that we both needed the job.

I soon realized that if I taught as badly as I had been taught at Cambridge, I would be fired as quickly as I had been hired; I also realized that to survive I had to publish, and the need for a first subject proved another turning point in my intellectual life. As an undergraduate I had admired and enjoyed Dodds's *The Greeks and the Irrational*, which had helped to deepen and darken my idealistic view of classical antiquity. Dodds develops a picture of the Greeks as steadily progressing in rationality until the fourth century B.C., after which comes what he calls a "failure of nerve"; he makes a comparison with a horseman approaching a jump: if the horse backs off, Dodds asks, which of the two has failed, the horse or the rider? He hopes it was the horse, and that Man, now approaching such a jump again, as he supposes, will not fail a second time; that first time, on Dodds's view, was a protracted failure. As the ancient world lurched on, the "irrational" returned, ultimately in the form of religion—the Christian religion in particular.

The question interested me for many reasons. Why did the ancient world "fail"? Was the spirit of Greek rational inquiry swallowed up by Christian irrationalism? And is the role of Christianity similar in the twentieth century? In the third century A.D., the period of ancient thought in which the balance of power between Hellenism and Christianity seemed to swing decisively in favor of the latter, there appeared Plotinus, the last great philosopher of pagan antiquity. At that time Dodds was one of the very few in the English-speaking world who had any interest in him, seeing him as the final representative of what was best in the Greek rational tradition.

At least until recently, English-speaking philosophers interested in the history of philosophy have been largely the victims and perpetrators of the prejudice that ancient philosophy ended with Aristotle— though they might make a bow in the direction of Stoic logic—and that the subject began again with Descartes. The intervening centuries were dismissed as "religious," though rather casual reference might be made to Augustine's political ideas, or to Aquinas, or more particularly to Anselm's "ontological" argument for the existence of God. The reasons for this included the tyranny of the undergraduate curriculum, which did not allow time for "lesser figures," and more fundamentally the "Protestant" suspicion that metaphysics and metaphysicians were a breeding ground for Popery. Plato, if one concentrated on the *Theaetetus*, could be read for epistemology, Aristotle for ethics, rational psychology and theories of causation. Plotinus, though, was a hard-core metaphysician: a metaphysician concerned above all with the primacy of a One God from which all things are derived and on which all things depend, and with a theory that a person is a soul whose goal (often despite oneself) is to return and unite with the One who is one's origin, while the power that drives one ever upward is Eros.

I had been introduced to philosophy at a time when in Britain many of the most intelligent students were driven away from the subject because it had been rendered banal. In Plotinus, however, I met a philosopher who never trivialized, who had not been trivialized by his contemporary interpreters, and who seemed to offer at least a coherent view of the world. Furthermore—and here I found myself face to face with the bad faith of many of the pundits—his work seemed to be at least a legitimate development of the thought of Plato. I had always assumed that Plato's thought was a development of that of Socrates, and that it was impossible to know exactly where Socrates ends and Plato begins. Plotinus, for his part, always claimed (perhaps somewhat disingenuously) that he was doing little more than clarifying Plato's principles and insights, and that the Platonic account of the Forms and of the relationship of the soul to the body, if rigorously pursued, would lead to the conclusion that the Forms are eternal realities somehow identical with a divine mind, and that the First Principle itself, if it is to be a genuine first principle, must transcend them both.

Reading and writing about Plotinus affected me in many ways. I was convinced that here was a great mind whose views were disregarded, among English-speakers, though not on the Continent, because people feared to consider the possibility that they might have truth in them. It seemed to me that if a sense of and a desire for justice were to be anything more than an indulging of a feeling that I did not like certain kinds of behavior—that there is nothing *intrinsically* wrong, for example, in anything Hitler had done—then there must exist something like a Platonic Form, for we surely did not merely *agree* or *contract* that genocide should be avoided. Yet if there is something like a Platonic Form of Justice, it must, as Plotinus held, exist in a mind—which was assuredly not my (or our) mind. I began to put my ideas together into a book, posting them across the Atlantic for Anna to correct and type. It was she who suggested the title *Eros and Psyche,* and in 1964 it was published by the University of Toronto Press.

The Search for Justice

By the end of the academic year 1959-60 my appointment was extended, but I returned to England, where Anna and I were married—what was then called a "mixed" marriage—in the Catholic Church. Father Kenelm, who had to attest to my suitability for such a marriage, told Anna that he had given as grounds the possibility (which he was at pains to caution her he considered remote) that I would eventually become a Catholic. As I continued work on what was later to become *Plotinus: The Road to Reality* (published by the Cambridge University Press in 1967), I began to reflect that since the "wise" seemed so willing to admit distortion in the case of theoretical issues in metaphysics, and in the evaluation of a philosopher whom I read with continuing admiration, I should not be surprised when I found a corresponding bad faith in some practical implications of the problem of justice. I had not as yet read Sartre on the subject of *mauvaise foi*, but I later found his notion of great value, not least in evaluating academic orthodoxies and Sartre himself.

The problem of justice which from the mid-sixties came increasingly to attract my attention was that of abortion, an issue which in my younger days of growing radicalism I had ignored, following the stream of fashion. I cannot remember how it first came to my attention, but the process was gradual. Anna held instinctively that abortion was wrong, but personal events made the matter more vivid. She herself suffered two miscarriages, and in believing that we had lost two children, she understood the significance of the fact that others were killing similar unknowns simply because they wanted to be rid of them. In the old maternity hospital in Cambridge, where we spent a few summers, she noticed a visiting vicar chatting with a woman in the ward who had been taken in for what was then an illegal "termination"; the woman was prosperous and cheerful and explained to Anna that she regarded her childbearing days as over. A Catholic aunt of Anna's used to maintain that the one institution that had consistently stood up for the rights of the unborn child was the Roman Catholic Church, and that that, if nothing else, would validate it in her eyes.

Abortion did not concern me first as a religious matter, an issue concerned with the sanctity of life. Indeed, a person who does not believe in God can hardly be expected to take the "sanctity" of life seriously. For me, abortion was a simple question of justice, of unjust killing. One was not allowed (rightly) to "terminate" the lives of one's infants or teenagers because they were too expensive or troublesome; on the same grounds one should not therefore be allowed to kill one's unborn child either. What mattered was simply whether or not the child is a human being. Once I had satisfied myself that it is—and later scientific findings have only confirmed that view, confirming also that those who deny it deny it merely because it is inconvenient, that is, because they *choose* to deny it—then if any "unjust" killing is wrong, abortion is wrong. It is the killing of the innocent and the defenseless for no other reason than that one wants them out of the way.

Note that this is not an argument against all killing; I am not and have never been a pacifist. This argument against abortion does not depend on a claim that *all* killing is wrong; it is a claim that no one should be killed simply because someone wishes them dead and they are unable to defend themselves. It is important to recognize that the unborn are not only innocent; they are incapable of intending evil or doing anything by their own deliberate action which is in any way harmful or dangerous to anyone. To kill them is to kill them because they happen—inconveniently—to exist.

I became disturbed that many of those opposed to other political and social injustices seemed to favor abortion; it made me suspect that their reasons for opposing other injustices might not be as firmly grounded as they and I had assumed. I also worried about the attitudes of some other "prolifers," as we began to be called when the political process to allow the legal killing of the unborn built up in the sixties. Some of them seemed curiously oblivious to other injunctions to assist their fellow human beings, even when they might have regarded these injunctions as divinely sanctioned. Again, it seemed that the explanation lay in the false ethical view that if I do not admit something (such as exploitation of the poor or disadvantaged) to be wrong, then it is not wrong; it can be explained away as, for example, a merely *unfortunate* function of the laws of economics. There is no obligation to do more than allow other people to come into existence and compete, however unfair the conditions.

In the main, however, I was still content to hold ethical views based on what increasingly seemed different, indeed contradictory, first principles—a not unusual phenomenon. The question facing me was, If there is a Justice which governs the abortion issue, where is the Plotinian Divine Mind? Ought I perhaps to believe in some sort of God after all? Was it inconsistent not to do so?

My Return to Christianity

But habits are hard to change, and I was habituated to agnosticism. The conviction that theism is a more reasonable position required time; even more time was needed before I was prepared to accept its emotional implications. As Newman said, "I find my mind in a new place. . . . The whole man moves; paper logic is but the record of it." In any case, the Plotinian version of Platonism, unlike the Platonism of Plato himself, is underdeveloped in ethics: emphasis on the transcendence of the One has left more mundane considerations of human life behind. Not that Plotinus does not demand high standards of personal conduct, but these are necessary conditions for the love for God rather than, as Christianity holds, parts of the love for (and of) God itself. Furthermore, even the Platonism of Plato himself inclines, at least in theory, to undervalue human individuality. This is best seen if we consider the question of human worth. For Plato, one can forfeit any claim or "right" to decent treatment if one's transgressions are serious enough. For the criminal there can be no legitimate complaint against degrading treatment or torture; some people have forfeited their immunity and can be treated as the victorious and punishing virtuous see fit. For the Christian, on the other hand, human dignity derives, and can only derive, from the dignity of God and from our being made in God's image. This also entails that where belief in God has declined, respect for humanity becomes a mere charade or at best a mere choice: a survival of a metaphysic or theology long discarded, as Dostoyevski and others have regularly pointed out. Hence a permissive attitude toward abortion and other forms of unjust killing and exploitation.

If we compare the Christian and the neo-Platonic frames of reference, it is clear that where neo-Platonism emphasizes a timeless God who provides an escape for the individual from one's temporal individuality, which is viewed as something to outgrow, Christianity emphasizes the intervention of God in history, the privileged position of humanity—which may indeed be a necessary condition for the establishment of solid ethical foundations—and one's individuality as a unique mark of the omnipresence of divine providence. Spurred on especially by the problem of abortion, I began to see that the metaphysics of neo-Platonism is an excellent halfway house, an intelligible structure, but it is not enough. For God to be a moral substance, he must intervene in history. How he would do that we could not possibly predict, but if he himself has shown us, we may be able to see.

Christianity is above all others the religion that speaks of God's presence in history, not only in the past, as in creation and in the incarnation, but continuously into the present and, according to a theory of the development of doctrine akin to that of Newman, through the Church into the future. Of course that does not mean that all religious and ethical advances will be made by Christians, let alone by theologians or bishops; God needs no such limitations. What it means is that Christians *must* claim that the Church will, at least eventually, be able to accept all that is best among such advances, whatever their origin.

Thus Christianity began to look not only coherent but plausible. Yet if Christianity, why Roman Catholicism rather than Protestantism, Anglicanism or (perhaps better) Orthodoxy, which might appear to have a better claim than these? Essentially because though half a loaf is better than no bread, and three-quarters is better still, a whole loaf is best—best not least because the most coherent both philosophically and historically. To be coherent and plausible, however, is not necessarily to be true. God, I concluded, must have revealed himself to us if we are to know much about him. That is what Christians had always claimed. But earlier I had supposed that the historical origins of Christianity were so obscure, so liable to misrepresentation by various interested parties right back to the beginning, that we could not accept even as a reasonable hypothesis that the Gospel accounts are true. In the seventies I picked up again the problem of Christian origins which had troubled me as a teenager, publishing as a result a brief (and to some an infuriating) monograph, On the Originality of Matthew and Mark. What reopened my interest in the matter specifically was that I noticed that in the euphoria surrounding and especially succeeding Vatican II, a number of Catholic biblical scholars were making the same mistakes as earlier generations of Protestants had done, just at the time when some of the better Protestant scholars were repenting of them. They seemed like children let out of school, entranced with an exciting but dangerous new toy. The new toy was redaction criticism or form criticism. There seemed no sense of the limitations of such methods, no grasp of how to distinguish between their use and their abuse.

I had long realized that many of the earlier claims for Markan priority were question-begging and time-serving, designed to rationalize and justify a more or less "demythologized" account of Jesus' life and claims: a secularized, antimiraculous, ultimately antimetaphysical account of "God" and the Incarnation. I knew enough Patristic scholarship to be aware that our Gospel canon was not, and could not have been, authenticated and stabilized by its authors, but only by acceptance by the Church, as happened in the second century. Examination of the early evidence and of the Gospels themselves convinced me that Matthew's Gospel could not depend on Mark's and was more or less equally early (certainly before A.D. 70). My conclusions were similar to those others later established in much more detail, especially the work of J. A. T. Robinson, the more or less repentant author of *Honest to God*.

Thus the full range of Christian claims must go back to the very earliest followers of Jesus, and in all probability to Jesus himself. The solution that either Jesus was a lunatic or his earliest followers were all blatant liars again seemed the only alternative possibility if their claims were false. I could no longer delude myself that "real" scholarship told us that we have no evidence that Jesus himself, as well as the earliest generation of his followers, made claims for his divinity. The attempt of the biblical critics to show that such claims grew up (or were fabricated) within the Church seemed to be a tissue of bad argument, unhistorical treatment of the sources and wishful thinking: the wish being to make Christianity acceptable to the conventional "liberal" orthodoxy, with its characteristic bad faith, of the nineteenth and twentieth centuries. The resulting "scholarship" was defective to a degree that would not be acceptable in other philological disciplines. When I saw this clearly, biblical scholarship no longer stood in the way of my return to Christianity. I had to decide only whether the totality of Jesus' recorded behavior looked like that of a madman; it was not difficult to see that it did not.

In my undergraduate days (as I have said) I used to hold that all that could be salvaged of Christianity was something like the doctrine of original sin. That doctrine raised its head again when I considered the weak points of neo-Platonism and its possible completion within Christianity. For along with neo-Platonism's failure to comprehend the uniqueness of the individual went its inability (which it shared with most ancient thought, and indeed with most modern) to take seriously not only the human capacity for good but also the capacity for evil. Few have seen this more clearly than Augustine, a man greatly helped in his return to Christianity by his readings in the "Platonic books," that is, above all, in Plotinus's *Enneads*. I first became interested in Augustine in the late sixties, when I wrote a paper (some of which I still believe to be correct) on his account of free will and predestination, and another—more relevant to the present context—on his views of evil in comparison with those of Plotinus. The more I thought about the neo-Platonic (not to speak of the modern) accounts, the more obviously grotesque it became to suppose that Hitler, Stalin, Pol Pot and Idi Amin, not to speak of countless smaller-scale murderers and torturers, would all have been like Socrates or St. Francis if they had had a better education or if their parents had not been divorced, as the current orthodoxy seemed to hold. I became convinced that God's grace—I would not have so referred to it at the time—is needed for right action, let alone for human perfection, and I strongly reaffirmed that human perfection is not attainable in the present life.

By the late seventies I was a convinced Catholic, but I had not joined the Church and felt no urgency to do so, though I realized that the time had come. Anna—who always joked that she benefited from my not being a Catholic since I could look after the children when she was at Mass—mentioned my lack of a convert's enthusiasm to a priest, Father James Sheridan, who had been her boss when she taught classics at St. Michael's College and remained a friend and mentor when she gave up teaching on the birth of our third child. Father Sheridan's view was that feeling is unimportant and that if I believed I should join the Church "in cold blood," as it were. I was received by Father Charles Leland, CSB, a much-loved friend for twenty years, in June 1980, shortly before leaving Canada for what proved to be an abortive appointment as Regius Professor of Greek at the University of Aberdeen. Father Sheridan was my godfather. I was not conditionally baptized, my Anglican baptism being accepted.

The Church

I regard the outstanding benefits of membership in the Church as being able to receive Communion and the understanding of marriage as a sacrament; these, and all the sacraments, enable us to persevere to the end. Otherwise, my life as a Catholic has been more or less as I expected: there is always more to learn, more to understand. Scandals inside the Church are hurtful rather than worrying, as they were before, since I expect them. They are inevitable in our fallen race, and the Platonic-Augustinian thesis that "the corruption of the best is the worst" should not be strange to Christians. I had little experience of the characteristic vices of pre-Vatican II Catholicism. Those of the later period are largely similar to those of the secular world but in an ecclesiastical setting: the continuing abuse of power, moral laziness dressed up as "openness," anti-intellectualism (which in a clerical context can easily be presented as simple piety), malice exacerbated by an identity crisis among many of the clergy and a tendency in Rome to write off the contemporary West in favor of overly romantic notions of "Christendom" or of the "unspoilt" Third World. Nor can one neglect an abuse of the notion of "dialogue" as a search for the lowest common denominator; in practice this often means a willingness to adopt someone else's point of view for supposedly charitable reasons, whether that point of view is right or wrong. Opponents of Christianity are supposed to understand and respect such soft-headedness. In fact they often rightly regard it with contempt.

Augustine knew the proper antidote to such things: *Fecisti nos ad te et inquietum est cor nostrum donec requiescat in te* ("You made us for you, and our heart is restless until it rests in you"). To be a Catholic in a modern university requires a modicum of courage, but happily not that of the martyrs. Augustine's words are no recipe for withdrawal into a neo-

Platonic otherworldliness. They are a comfort and a source of hope in the "dark wood" of our present challenge.

Looking back, it seems to be a matter of a curious pattern of chance encounters and chance readings, but chance, as Aristotle knew, is no explanation of anything. My mother, I now see, was tormented by the difficulty of believing in the form of Christian faith that was on offer to her, attractive though Anglicanism was to her in some respects. My father, though stoically silent, was equally uncomprehending. And there have been countless like them. To a great extent they were the victims of the particular history of Britain and the perceived interests of its ruling classes. When I first met Anna, I remarked that she might convert my mother to Catholicism, but it is easy to see that that was an overly facile estimate, and that had she tried (as she did not) the dice would have been heavily loaded against her. Yet I think that my parents even half-welcomed my change of heart, which happened toward the end of their lives, and that they are now in a state in which they can rest in understanding.[1]

Passing the Baton

STEPHEN T. DAVIS

Stephen T. Davis is professor of philosophy and religion at Claremont McKenna College in Claremont, California. He is also a member of the faculty of the Claremont Graduate School in both philosophy and religion. He has taught at Pomona College, the University of California at Riverside, Fuller Theological Seminary and Southern Theological Seminary. He is the author of over forty articles and seven books, including Faith, Skepticism, and Evidence; Encountering Evil; Logic and the Nature of God; Encountering Jesus; *and* Risen Indeed: A Christian Philosophy of Resurrection.

*M*y favorite track and field event is the four-by-100-meter relay. It is a team event. You can have the fastest sprinters and still lose the race if you drop the baton or pass it poorly.

Each of the contributors to this book is a Christian because certain people in our history passed the baton. Perhaps they included a parent, a friend, a writer, a member of the clergy, even a stranger. In fact, countless Christians—our spiritual forebears from the time of Jesus until today—are to be thanked. We are Christians because of their faithfulness. They ran the race and passed the baton. Jesus gave this mission of baton-passing to his disciples; they turned it over to the people and generations who followed them; and because of their trustworthiness we are Christians today. For myself, it is easy to think of several people who passed the baton to me. Had they dropped it, so far as I can tell I would not be a Christian today.

Restless Youth

As a teenage boy in the San Fernando Valley of Southern California, I was restless and desperately unhappy.[1] One problem was that I did not know who I was. Because my parents divorced when I was a baby, I had two families rather than one. Both treated me well, but both also (perhaps unintentionally) treated me as if I were odd or out of the ordinary. So I often found myself wondering: Which was my true home? Or did I even *have* a true home? One was a military family that moved frequently, the other a cattle-ranching family in the Sand Hills of western Nebraska. One family was lower-middle-class, the other wealthy. One was nominally Protestant, the other Catholic. One was my family during the school year, the other occasionally during summer vacations. To whom did I belong? Who *was* I?

The other problem was that things were going badly in my life. At home, in my custodial family, things were in a state of disaster. The marriage between my mother and my stepfather was disintegrating. The oldest of six children, I occasionally had to act in parental roles, dealing as best I could with screaming arguments, weeklong silences, unprepared meals and younger brothers in trouble.

Academically things were going poorly as well. Teachers kept telling me that I had ability, but I could never muster the interest in my classes to try hard, and the problems of my dysfunctional family provided too many distractions. I earned B's and C's, taking mainly nonacademic subjects. I got by on natural ability rather than hard work; I cannot remember ever once doing homework during my high-school years. I was frustrated because I knew I should be doing better, but somehow I couldn't work up the initiative to excel.

Although I was a good athlete, competitive sports were a constant trial because years earlier I had skipped a grade; this, together with the fact that I matured late anyway, ensured that I was always much smaller than my classmates. Not till age seventeen did I catch up. Even relations with the opposite sex were going poorly. The beautiful and popular girls whom I admired liked me only as a friend and conversationalist. The only girls who were romantically interested in me seemed to me to be, well, not particularly attractive.

One Sunday night I was invited to the North Hollywood Presbyterian Church to hear two UCLA football players speak. My athletic interests ensured that I would accept the invitation. I have always remembered with gratitude the names of the two athletes: Bob Heydenfeldt and Terry Debay. Although I remember little of what they said, I distinctly recall the weird sense that they were speaking directly to me and to no one else in the congregation. Actually, the feeling was more eerie than that—I remember the sense that *God* was speaking to me that night. This is the only disproof of deism that I would ever need: God was somehow picking me out and calling me by name. When the two football players invited people to commit their lives to Christ, this teenager had no defense or resistance. It seemed to me the only decision I could possibly make.

Jesus said, "Come to me, all you that are weary and are carrying heavy burdens, and I will give you rest" (Mt 11:28 NRSV). That night I accepted Jesus' invitation and became a new person (2 Cor 5:17). I found in Christ rest for my soul—a place to stop, a person to be, a family to which to belong, a true home in which to live. Soon I sensed a new motivation and direction in my life, one that has been with me ever since.

After my conversion, I zealously read the Bible, listened to sermons, read religious books and talked with other Christians. The figure of Jesus intrigued, fascinated and overwhelmed me. I formed the impression that Jesus must have been an extraordinary person. Let me mention some reasons for this impression.

First, I remember thinking that Jesus must have been an attractive person who had a flair for leadership and an aura of charisma. Like most strong leaders, he was a great polarizer of people—they seem in the Gospels either to love him and follow him loyally or else to hate him and plot against him. He was not the sort to inspire neutrality.

Second, I remember thinking that Jesus must have been an enigma to his contemporaries. He struck people as being strangely different from other folk; they couldn't figure him out or place him in a category. Once, when hardened temple officers were sent by the authorities to arrest him, they were dumbfounded by his words. They returned to their superiors, saying, "No one ever spoke like this man" (Jn 7:32-46).

Third, I remember noticing that Jesus was a loving, concerned, compassionate person. The story of Jesus and Zacchaeus (Lk 19:1-10) is one of the earliest that I remember hearing about Jesus, and it made a deep impression on me, even as a child, that the Son of God would make friends with an ostracized tax collector. Jesus' love extended to all sorts of people, rich and poor, educated and ignorant, righteous and sinful, sophisticated and crude. The people with whom Jesus dealt in the New Testament formed a motley crew of outcasts and crackpots and odd-balls and sinners. How strange this seemed to me—you would expect a great religious teacher like Jesus to limit his contacts to religious people. After all, the Pope doesn't pal around with prostitutes; the clergy don't befriend terrorists. I remember feeling how wonderfully odd and unexpected it was that the Lord seemed to love and accept all the people he met, even his enemies (Lk 23:34).

Fourth, I remember being impressed with Jesus' power to change people. Almost nobody met Jesus and remained the same as before. Some changed for the better: Peter, an ignorant fisherman, became the courageous leader of the church. Saul, a persecutor of Christianity, met Jesus in a vision on the road to Damascus and became Paul, the greatest missionary and theologian the church has known. Others changed for the worse: the man we call the rich young ruler came to Jesus anxiously seeking salvation, but left Jesus rejecting salvation when he learned how dearly it would cost (Mt 19:16-22). An obscure Jew named Judas, of whom otherwise no one today would ever have heard, met Jesus, made a decision, and became infamous for an act of betrayal that history will never forget.

The set of people who have been changed by Jesus is a set that includes me. I was once on a wrong path that was leading nowhere but to sloth, inertia, self-pity, self-centeredness, self-indulgence and destruction. In Christ, I found the right path. I have a strong sense of having been created, guided, forgiven and redeemed by God in Christ. This conviction, as I suppose, is much of what makes me a Christian.

A Piece of Holy Ground

Soon after my conversion I became a member of the church where it had occurred. I regularly attended not only church but the high-school youth group, and eventually became a leader in it. Within two years I began to feel that God was calling me to the Christian ministry.

Now I must mention the single most important place in my spiritual development. Like Moses at Horeb, I found a piece of holy ground. Forest Home Christian Conference Center is in the mountains above Redlands in Southern California. Although I had been there many times previously, both as a camper and a counselor, the most important times were the three summers that I spent on the staff as assistant director of the junior-high camp, which was then called Camp Rancho. These were the summers of my nineteenth, twentieth and twenty-first years.

Let me relate some of the formative experiences that I had at Forest Home. The first was a brief and off-the-cuff speech I heard from a recent college graduate. He was from India, a Brahmin—that is, a member of Indian society's highest caste. He had been converted to Christ while in this country, had graduated from college here and was about to return home. He said that when he wrote his parents that he had become a Christian, they were shocked and horrified. They tried everything to get him to return to his senses, including arguments, threats and all kinds of devious string-pulling. When they realized that he was serious, they disowned him. His family was wealthy; he had been in line to inherit his father's business. He also loved his parents and his siblings, whom he would possibly never see again. He had to choose between Christ and all that. He chose Christ, and he was about to return to India, without a home or family, without a job, his future insecure. I remember being deeply impressed with the price that this young man had to pay. Naturally I asked myself: Was my commitment that robust? If my faith ever became that costly, could I pay the price?

At Forest Home I began to realize that I had gifts in the area of ministry. One week during my first summer on the staff Don Botsford and my boss, Richard Nazarian, urged me to prepare some talks—sort of a daily Bible hour—for a group of some fifty junior highers and their leaders who were to come to Forest Home for a week of choir camp. It was only with the greatest difficulty that I was persuaded. I couldn't think of anything worthwhile that I could possibly have to say to them. Moreover, I was quite nervous about speaking before crowds. From painful experience, I knew that my voice might elevate in pitch, my breath might shorten, and my face might redden. But I prayed about the opportunity and decided to go ahead. Although my messages were doubtless crude and my delivery unpracticed, I was not nervous, and was shocked to discover that people would actually listen when I spoke.

Also memorable was a barbecue for the staff of Forest Home on the beach at Lake Mears one balmy and starry evening. After we ate, with all of us sitting on the sand admiring the Milky Way, a visitor was asked to say a few words. He was a middle-aged man with a rich baritone singing voice, and he sang a song called "So Send I You." It was based on that verse where Jesus said to the disciples after the resurrection: "As the Father has sent me, I am sending you" (Jn 20:21). Between the verses of the song he skillfully wove a brief devotional message around the theme that we Christians are sent to continue the work of Christ in the world. It was a magical and powerful moment. In my mind's ear, so to speak, I can still hear him singing that song. That evening I had an acute sense that Jesus was sending me into the world to declare his good news and to glorify God, just as the Father had sent him. I suppose that part of the reason I am who I am today, part of the reason I agreed to write this essay, is that I still have that same sense.

But the best experience at Forest Home was that I fell in love. This was my last summer there, the summer before my senior year in college. During the previous school year I had had a date with Charis Soults. She was a classmate of mine, a beautiful and multitalented person. She invited me to one of those girl-ask-boy functions that were a feature of college life in the early sixties. It was several weeks before I reciprocated and asked her out, but when I did I was struck by how many interests we had in common (Baroque music, European cathedrals, the history of art) and how enjoyable our conversations were. By the end of the school year we were virtually at the boyfriend and girlfriend stage. She knew that I intended to return to Forest Home for the summer, and so (with no objections from me, of course) she applied there and was also hired. We fell in love that summer. I had to make sure that I did my job well and that the time I spent with her (usually from nine till eleven each night) did not interfere with it. (I had been discreetly and kindly warned by Chuck Wilson, who was my boss that summer.)

I remember particularly a long walk one night. When we stopped and sat on a large rock—a rock I believe I can still find—the full moon shone on her face through the leaves of a nearby tree. She was alluring, enchanting, captivating. Although I didn't actually propose until months later, it was then that I began to think that this was the woman for me. I had always dreamed, since about age thirteen, of falling in love with a beautiful and wonderful woman, but it had never happened until now. I later wrote this clumsy haiku:

> The moon on her face
> cast beguiling shadows—dreams
> of love taking form.

Charis and I were married after we graduated from college in 1962. We are still married today. We have raised two sons. She is my best friend, and we have been faithful to each other. We love each other more than we did in 1962.

Academic Awakenings

Let's backtrack a bit. Obviously, if I was going to be a Presbyterian minister, I had to go to college. But my mediocre academic performance in high school virtually dictated that I start off at a community college. I did, at Valley College in Van Nuys, California. There I began to awaken academically, taking classes that were challenging, and discovering the joy of thinking and learning. One professor of political science stands out in my memory, although fortunately I've forgotten his name. Apparently a believer at one time in his life, he was now an aggressive atheist. He loved to debunk the biblical miracles. On the virgin birth: "I hope by now you people are all old enough to know where babies come from." On the resurrection: "I hope you people have all learned by now that dead people stay dead." End of discussion. I recognized that his arguments amounted to nothing but bluster, and they did not bother me. But I did keep quiet in class about my beliefs; I feared he would flunk me if I challenged him.

After two years, I transferred to Whitworth College, a small Presbyterian liberal arts college in Spokane, Washington. This was an adventure, because I had never been there, knew only one person at the college and frankly knew little about it. I was a bit frightened, but also excited: since virtually no one knew me, I had a chance to start all over again, past mistakes forgotten, new impressions to make. And although I felt guilty about leaving them, it was a relief to be thirteen hundred miles away from the tensions of my California family.

Whitworth was exactly the right place for me, and I will always owe it a debt of gratitude. I went there a boy and left a man. I received excellent academic training there, but the things that happened to me outside the classroom were more important: participating in intercollegiate sports, serving as a student body officer, making lifetime friends, and (as noted) meeting Charis.

Of course I made mistakes at Whitworth too. One of them, which in retrospect is more humorous than serious, sticks out. We were playing a home soccer game against the University of Washington. Late in the game I made a long, tiring run with the ball, took a shot that should have gone in, and fell down. The shot missed, and in my frustration I slammed my fist into the ground and let out a relatively minor but nevertheless shocking and loud expletive. Everybody was startled— well, everybody except the University of Washington players. They didn't seem to mind or even notice. But there was a kind of deathly silence from my teammates and our fans. I was a student body officer at a Christian college; I was captain of the team; everybody knew I was a preministerial student. A minor slip, you might think, but nevertheless, what an example to set! I was embarrassed, and also a bit hurt by the fact that there was a certain distance between me and some of my Christian friends for a while. My teammate, roommate and fellow preministerial student Henk Wapstra, who knew my many faults better than anybody at Whitworth, actually took a couple of days to forgive me.

Academically I had wide interests, so I was never too sure what my major should be. I liked the sciences, I liked literature, I liked history. During my junior year, with no sense of purpose whatsoever, I enrolled in an introduction to philosophy class taught by Professor Lawrence Yates. An energetic lecturer with a dry sense of humor and mind full of probing questions, Yates is mainly responsible (along with his colleague Howard Redmond) for my being a philosopher today. My first reaction to the class was "Wow—do you get academic credit for doing this? This is me. This is the way I think. This is my intellectual home." Within a month, I decided that what I wanted to be in life was a philosophy professor. But I was not giving up my sense of call to the Christian ministry. I would still go to seminary. I would still be ordained. I might even serve for a time as a pastor. But eventually I would get a Ph.D. and would minister by being a philosophy professor.

I had discovered my vocation.

Anti-Catholicism has always been alien to me. I had seen with my own eyes the deep Christian commitment of some of the Catholics that I knew in Nebraska, as well as elsewhere. And so when the opportunity arose, I helped start a series of ecumenical exchanges between ten or twelve Whitworth preministerial students and an equal number of students at Mount St. Michael's, a Jesuit seminary that was then located in Spokane. At first it was slightly embarrassing to discover that the Jesuits as a group were much more mature and intellectual than we were, but those exchanges were highlights of my years at Whitworth. I made several long-time friends, especially Don Johnson, S.J. A few years later I read the Old Testament lesson at his service of ordination to the priesthood in Sacramento. But much to our mutual horror, archconservative James Francis Cardinal McIntyre of Los Angeles forbade Don from participating in or even attending my service of ordination in 1965 in North Hollywood. (I still have the incredibly baroque and triumphalist letter that the cardinal's secretary wrote to my presbytery superior.) Sadly, to the best of my knowledge, none of my Jesuit friends is still in the society. Those were innocent days, and few of us could anticipate what the late 1960s and early 1970s would do to American society, let alone to the Society of Jesus.

Seminary and Ministry

On August 24, 1962, two months after our graduation from Whitworth, Charis and I were married. The original plan was for me to go directly to Princeton Theological Seminary. But my mother and stepfather had finally divorced; I wanted to be available to help my siblings if I could, and this entailed living in the Los Angeles area for a year. (This was where the family had settled, years before, when my stepfather retired from the army.) So I enrolled in Fuller Theological Seminary, with the status of special student, so that I could take classes at the core of Fuller's curriculum.

The person who made the biggest impression on me was a man named Edward John Carnell. A native New Englander, he was tall, articulate, well read and austere. He always spoke in complete sentences and with impeccable grammar. Every day he wore a dark suit, tie and vest to class—as he once jokingly said about his attire, he was making "a last stand for culture in Southern California." He would accept no compromises. He demanded excellence of himself, and he expected it of us. One day I remember him chiding the class for a batch of papers, some of which were poorly written. He asked, "Why be satisfied with giving less than your best? Why be satisfied with sloppiness? Why not strive for excellence the next time you write a letter to your parents or even the next time you clean your apartment?"

Excellence in everything—it was a new idea to me.

The following summer Charis and I moved to Princeton, with her teaching school in Lawrenceville, and me studying. It was an exciting theological adventure to compare what I was taught at conservative Fuller with what I was taught at liberal and ecumenical Princeton. I had been one of the more liberal of the students at Fuller and turned out to be one of the more conservative at Princeton. It was John Hick's last year on the faculty of the seminary, so I took virtually every class he offered. James Barr is one of the sharpest people I have ever met, and I greatly enjoyed his lectures too, although he and I had some heavy disagreements in class. It must have made an impression on him (quite negative, I'm sure), because years later when he gave a lecture in Claremont and I introduced myself, he said, "Oh, yes, I remember you."

Once Billy Graham was invited to speak to the seminary. As a product of evangelism myself, I have always valued Billy Graham and his ministry. I think I was one of the few in the student body who supported him. In answer to a question, Billy mentioned a recent trip to Switzerland where he had spoken with two of the greatest theologians of our century, Karl Barth and Emil Brunner. Brunner had said to him, "I've read some of your books and sermons and your theology is all right, but I cringe whenever you ask people to make a decision to accept Christ." But Barth had said to him, "I'd like to correct your theology at certain points, but I admire the way you ask people to accept Christ. Man must decide!"

After seminary I served for one year (this was by design) as an assistant pastor in Burbank, California. Then I enrolled in the Claremont Graduate School for doctoral work in philosophy. During the four years of my graduate studies I worked part-time at the Claremont Presbyterian Church, a large church that is not by any means in the evangelical wing of the denomination. Nevertheless, those were four wonderful years. I noticed that the longer I stayed, the more relationships deepened, especially with the kids in my youth groups, and the more effective my ministry became. The pulpit in the sanctuary has a kind of motto carved in the wood on the inside; only the person who stands in the pulpit can see it. It is a terse but powerful quotation from John 12:21—"SIR, WE WOULD SEE JESUS." I hope that in my four years there I helped some people to see Jesus.

Providence and Tenure

I received the Ph.D. degree from Claremont Graduate School in May 1970. My first job was a one-year position as visiting assistant professor at (the then called) Claremont Men's College. Next I held a similar position at the University of California at Riverside. At the end of that year, I had a fateful decision to make. The philosophers at Riverside were making noises about my being a strong candidate for a tenure-track position that had just been authorized in their department, but CMC had invited me back for a three-year position. After a great deal of prayer, I decided to return to CMC.

The story of how I got tenure at Claremont McKenna College (as it later became) is one of the most exciting things that has ever happened to me and is to me a decisive proof of the existence of God. I was hired in 1972 as a replacement for three members of the philosophy department who were going on sabbatical leave in successive years. It was a non-tenure-track position. This academic jargon means that it was contractually understood that when the three years ended I would not be rehired. At the end of three years, however, my contract was given a one-year extension. But that had to be the end. American colleges and universities abide by the rules of an organization called the American

Association of University Professors—a sort of labor union for college teachers. And the AAUP says that people employed by one institution for seven years are considered tenured—that is, they can stay at their position until retirement if they wish.

The president of the college was in something of a quandary. He had always been rather avuncular toward me. He recognized my popularity and knew that everyone connected with the college would be happy if I were somehow allowed to stay. But he was also reluctant, in effect, to increase the size of the philosophy department by keeping me. In a day of financial crunch for private colleges, no president considered a prudent financial manager, as this one definitely was, can approve an extra, technically unneeded position. Many people were praying that I would get to stay, including my wife and me and the Christian students at the college, but it did not look promising.

It all came down to a climactic meeting on December 23, 1975, when the president met with the dean of the faculty and with the members of my department and announced that I would not be rehired. It was about 5:00 p.m. when I got word from my tired, depressed colleagues who had just returned from the meeting. Immediately I felt an impulse to walk over to the president's office at Bauer Hall. I had nothing planned, but I do have something of a stubborn streak, and I wasn't quite ready to bow to the inevitable. The president and the dean were still there, unwinding from what had been a long, difficult and wrenching meeting. They were surprised to see me. I said I hadn't come to make them feel guilty but that I wanted to hear the decision from their own lips. At the end of about thirty minutes I got up to leave. They both said how terribly sorry they were about the whole thing, and they apologized profusely that the bad news had come two days before Christmas.

Somehow I felt at peace about it. On one level it was frightening to contemplate the prospect of unemployment, especially with a wife and two boys, aged five and three, but I knew I was in God's hands. We were able to have a good Christmas. The next thing that happened that I knew about was a telephone call from the president's secretary the day school resumed in January. She said I should come and see the president. When I did, he said, "Steve, I've changed my mind. I've decided the thing to do is to treat your case as if you had been on a tenure track the whole time. Your name will go to the APT committee, and we'll let them decide whether or not you get tenure." (The APT committee is the committee on appointments, promotion and tenure; it consists of all the full professors of the college, and it decides all tenure cases.)

When I left this meeting with the president, I felt certain that I had won. I knew I hadn't an enemy in the college, and I felt sure the committee would vote me tenure. But I didn't then know the whole story. It came out only later and in bits and pieces. The president himself has never told me the story, and I think he never will. But he has told others who have relayed it to me. It seems that the president had a difficult time going to sleep on December 23. He was deeply troubled about me, about whether he had done the right thing. He finally went to sleep, only to wake up in the middle of the night convinced I should be given a chance to stay.

The end of the story is that God was with me all the way through. The APT committee voted me tenure unanimously, and I am still at CMC today. When I heard it I felt like laughing. It was the most profound joy I've ever felt, and that joy changed my life. Virtually every day since then I've thanked God for his goodness to us in those days. I attribute what happened to one thing and to one thing only—answered prayer. Whenever I think of how God proved that there are loopholes in what humanly seems inevitable, I feel a bit of the "unutterable and exalted joy" mentioned in 1 Peter 1:8. Or, as the psalmist says, "For the Lord is good; his steadfast love endures forever, and his faithfulness to all generations" (Ps 100:5 NRSV).[2]

My Vocation as Philosopher

So, in 1976, I officially became a tenured professor at Claremont McKenna College, and in 1983 a full professor. The school is a prestigious liberal arts college, part of the Claremont Colleges consortium. In some ways it was a surprise to end up here. I had always assumed that secular colleges and universities would not hire me, and that I would spend my career somewhere at a Christian college or theological seminary. The challenge that I have always accepted for myself is to do the best job that I can possibly do as a teacher and scholar. If the aim is to achieve excellence, I have probably rarely done that; if it is consistently to aim for excellence, I believe I can say that I have done that.

It has been an enormous benefit for my career to teach at Claremont. You do get a lot of acceptance around the country when you announce that you teach at Claremont—acceptance that is usually quite unrelated to your own actual abilities. But that is not what I mean. The point is that Claremont is a top-notch place in my field of the philosophy of religion (Jack Hutchison, John Cobb, John Hick and D. Z. Phillips have all been colleagues of mine). Almost every notable person in theology or the philosophy of religion passes through Claremont eventually, and it has been wonderful for me to have talked and argued with many of them.

A Christian at a secular institution is in a delicate position. You can't compromise your values or convictions, and it is a sin to "hide your light under a bushel." But you can't proselytize or preach in class either. My views do of course come out in class, and whether I like it or not I am known in Claremont as a "Christian professor." Academics who honestly have a hard time believing and even say so in class do not bother me. All philosophy professors, including those who are Christians, have a responsibility to make students face the deepest issues and strongest criticisms of religion. And it is usually a good thing that the typically vague and childish faith of religious freshmen is challenged. That is part of the educational process. Thinking through the logic of a position is what we do in philosophy. But I have nothing but contempt for those college professors who see it as their aim—an aim to be pursued with inquisitorial zeal—to turn eighteen-year-old believers into religious skeptics.

My reasons for believing in God, and indeed for being a Christian, have little to do with philosophy. They have to do, first, with certain experiences that I have had—experiences that I find myself interpreting in terms of the guidance or grace or forgiveness of God. Second, they have to do with my being part of a community—the Christian church—that accepts the existence of God and the lordship of Christ as two of its most basic and crucial tenets.

My vocation as a philosopher is certainly relevant to Christian faith, however. Almost everything I've written, in some sense or other, tries to show that Christian faith is rationally defensible. This is an important aspect of my vocation as both a teacher and a scholar. Here, doubtless, I am being negatively influenced by that professor I studied under years ago at Valley College. I've tried to argue that it is sensible to believe in the existence of God—that is, that naturalism is not the only rational worldview; that the Christian concept of God is coherent; that the problem of evil does not make theism irrational; that religious faith is not the same thing as gullibility or credulity; and that crucial Christian doctrines such as the Trinity, Incarnation, bodily resurrection and biblical authority are defensible. On a more popular level, especially in class and in talks outside of class, I've tried to challenge various contemporary philosophical assumptions like: Don't believe in anything that you can't see or touch or prove; or, Any behavior is okay as long as you feel good about it and nobody is hurt; or, It doesn't matter what you believe as long as you're sincere; or, There is no such thing as absolute truth, it's all a question of what is "true for you."

Evangelism

Once in the summer of 1985 our family spent a day at Santa Monica Beach. Our sons Adam and Nathan (then ages fourteen and twelve) were enthusiastic surfers. So after dropping them off at a good surfing spot, Charis and I drove to the pier. We ate lunch there and decided to walk along the sidewalk next to the beach. As we did so, we discovered, much to our astonishment, some street evangelism in progress. Here was a nice-looking, articulate young man speaking into a portable public-address system. Equally surprising, it turned out as we drew closer that I knew him. An InterVarsity Christian Fellowship staffworker, Cliffe Knechtle apparently specializes in this sort of thing. I knew him because he and I had been speakers at a spiritual emphasis week at Occidental College a year or so earlier.

We stayed and listened to Cliffe for about forty-five minutes. What I found most intriguing was the audience he spoke to. It was in constant flux, probably averaging between ten and fifteen people. Some were typical young beachgoers, some were older and scruffier, a few were hardened and cynical-looking. There were also a few supporters, including Cliffe's wife, with whom Charis struck up a conversation. Cliffe's style was to try to elicit comments and questions from the audience, and he was quick and clever in answering them. There was a curvaceous woman of twenty-five or so who had obviously been beaten up a few days before. She slowly rolled by a few times on a skateboard, black eyes and all, not wanting to appear overly interested, but she did stop and listen for a time. One woman in a volleyball game a few meters away shouted, "I've got a college degree and a good lifestyle—why do I need Jesus?"

But another fellow caught my attention too. He was a small, intelligent black man in his twenties wearing street clothes and carrying a book bag; he asked questions and made comments almost the whole time we were there. Nothing Cliffe said seemed to satisfy him. His most pointed and poignant question was at heart the same one asked by the volleyball player. "What good can Jesus do me?" he asked. I suppose this is the question all nonbelievers ask themselves when confronted by Jesus and the claims Christians make about him—what good can Jesus do me?

Despite being a strong believer in evangelism, I have never been a particularly effective evangelist. Why is it that some people believe and others do not? Why do some people respond positively to Christian talk about Jesus, while others are not interested? Such questions intrigue me. At the Claremont Colleges I have always been a kind of unofficial faculty adviser to the student Christian groups on campus, and usually once a year or so am asked to speak at one of their functions. I will never forget something that an InterVarsity Christian Fellowship staffworker once said to me. We were chatting in my office, and I allowed as how I sometimes felt guilty that I wasn't a better evangelist. She said, "You'll never know how much the very presence of you and the other Christian faculty here is heartening to the Christian students. They need to know that there are academic Christians, that Christian faith is academically viable."

Reformed and Evangelical

From time to time I encounter people—students, clergy, even scholars—who were raised in fundamentalism, have rebelled against it, and consider themselves in some sense damaged by it. That is far from my experience; indeed, I come at things the other way around, which may possibly account for my willingness to wear the label *evangelical*. I grew up in a broad and pluralistic denomination and am quite used to dealing with Christians with whom I would strenuously disagree on important issues. As an older teenager I came to believe (after being exposed to it) that liberal Christianity was confused and vacuous, had little of substance to preach other than ethical or political precepts that could stand well enough on their own apart from any theology at all, and that there must, therefore, be more to Christianity than what I was being exposed to. And so began a spiritual quest that ended with my adopting a theological position that is essentially Reformed and evangelical.

Today I am still a Presbyterian, a minister in the very denomination that is the historical descendant of the denomination of the church in North Hollywood in which I was converted years ago. I am an evangelical Presbyterian, and that occasionally raises tensions and frustrations in a denomination where many pastors and officials define their own theological positions over against evangelicalism. Still, the beauty of my denomination's polity as well as its rich historical and theological roots overcome all else and keep me where I am.

Let me illustrate. In recent years a source of embarrassment and anger to me and other Christians is the spectacle of pastors of certain megachurches falling into sexual immorality or financial irregularity. Aside from some nationally known figures, we have had two or three such cases in Southern California in the past year or two. Typically, these are men with egos and power needs (as well as incomes) as huge as the sanctuaries in which they preach. The saddest part of the spectacle is of course their fall. But to me the most irritating part is the ease with which they proclaim that God has forgiven them and the speed with which they emerge back in ministry again, either at the same location or another one nearby.

For all its faults, the Presbyterian Church (U.S.A.) is an ecclesiastical body in which such scenarios do not occur. If I—a minister in that denomination—were to engage in sexual or financial improprieties, I would be disciplined by my presbytery and would not be allowed to return to ministry unless and until the presbytery deemed it appropriate. The members of the presbytery would make this judgment on the basis of such considerations as whether there had been genuine repentance on my part; whether my life in the relevant respects had changed for the better; whether there was sufficient healing of the anger and pain that my actions had caused others, and so forth. The crucial difference has to do with power. Pastors of megachurches are often accountable to no one but themselves or to figurehead boards that they themselves control. I love the Presbyterian system precisely because ministers like me are accountable for our behavior to people whom we do not control.

Soccer Coach

As well as teaching philosophy, I have been the men's soccer coach here for twenty-four years. I have had a lot of success, but that is not what most moves me about coaching. The aspect of it that I dislike is the "rah-rah" part—dealing with fans, publicity and the media. What I like best is the intellectual and practical challenge of figuring how best to capitalize on the strengths of one's team and neutralize the strengths of the other team; and dealing with people, solving the various human problems one faces over the course of a season. A coach is involved in situations where people deeply care about achieving a result and are willing to expend great effort to achieve it. In my years of coaching I've seen all sorts of human conditions and situations: camaraderie and hatred, heroic achievement and crushing failure, laughter and tears, victory and defeat. (You do learn about defeat when your team has a two-goal lead at halftime in a national championship game and you end up losing!)

In this role I've tried to do two things: first, to be the best possible coach that I can be; and second, to live as a Christian in these extreme situations. I want to show that the Christian good news speaks meaningfully to the deepest levels of human experience. I am all too conscious that I've sometimes failed as a coach, as a person and as a Christian. But the level of involvement that I've had in peoples' lives in the years that I've coached, as well as the long-term friends that I've made—these are two of the most precious gifts that have ever been given me.

Renouncing Empty Promises

In the summer of 1990 I spent a few days on my family's ranch in

Nebraska. I was there, together with about sixty relatives, to celebrate the one-hundredth anniversary of the founding of the ranch. The family is almost entirely Roman Catholic, and on Sunday morning we had an outdoor Mass—conducted by the local priest—on the lawn in front of the main house. There was also a baptism. The three-week-old daughter of one of my distant relatives was christened.

Throughout the Mass I was happy to note that many of the phrases in the liturgy are ones Presbyterians would recognize. Also, the Word of God was read, the good news of Christ was preached, and the people were genuinely worshiping God. It was a pleasant experience.

However, a particular phrase in the Catholic baptismal liturgy, one that we Reformed Christians do not have in our baptismal services, caught my attention. That phrase has been much on my mind ever since. The parents of the little girl were asked to vow that they would renounce the empty promises of the devil. What a powerful phrase— *the empty promises of the devil.* Christians don't talk much about the devil these days, but we should. Far too many people are listening to those empty promises.

Especially in academia, the devil makes promises like "If you lie about yourself and your accomplishments, people will think more highly of you." Or "If you drink, or smoke marijuana, or take cocaine, you'll have more pleasure, fun, enjoyment and relaxation in your life, and less worry, stress and sense of inadequacy." Or "If you have a brief sexual fling, you'll put a little fun and excitement into your life." Or "If you refuse to acknowledge the existence of God, or the authority of God over your life, you'll be free, autonomous and happy."

These are empty promises because they all lead to destruction. I have seen people who believe them. How do Christians in academia find the strength to avoid them? Primarily by regular worship, prayer and study of Scripture, especially in company with other Christians.

In the last ten years I have become a great believer in devotional exercises and spiritual growth.[3] There are several influences in my devotional life. The first is the time I spend alone in prayer and reading the Bible every day. Often this is the most exciting part of the day for me. Hearing God's voice in Scripture and in meditation is a great joy; the Spirit will speak, I believe, to those who are open. Psalms is my favorite book in the Bible; I find it moving, comforting and challenging. The second is the time that my wife and I spend in prayer together. This is not as frequent as it should be, and is usually in response to some need that arises. But we have seen countless answers to prayer during our life together, some of them bordering on the miraculous. The third is the small group of which Charis and I are part. There are four couples, and we meet twice monthly for a meal, Bible study and prayer. Despite our busy lives, with daily fatigue a reality for each of us, this is always a meeting to which everyone looks forward. Finally, there is the faculty Christian group at the Claremont Colleges. It meets weekly for study, prayer and breakfast. This group was founded by two of us about fifteen years ago after a meeting with John Alexander, who was then president of InterVarsity Christian Fellowship. He challenged us that such a group should exist in Claremont.

People sometimes express admiration for me, but I have never had an easy time accepting praise, especially when it concerns moral or spiritual things. Whenever that happens I find myself internally responding, "If you only knew how wrong you are." I am far too conscious of my own depravity, pride and self-centeredness to accept what is being said. I know how easily I make snap judgments and say cruel things to people.

The truth is that I am not a great man but an ordinary person who is trying with the Lord's help to make it through life without stumbling. The only interesting difference between me and most other people is that I once accepted a baton that was passed to me and accordingly try to glorify God in my life. Lots of important things have happened to me—getting married, being ordained, receiving the Ph.D. degree, raising two children to adulthood, writing books, coaching teams to championships, winning awards, becoming a grandparent. But the most important thing that has ever happened in my life, the axis around which everything else revolves, occurred one night long ago when I accepted a baton that was passed to me.

Accepting the Baton

In 1976 I was invited to preach in a Presbyterian church in Grand Haven, Michigan. That church was founded in 1836, and in one room it has prominently displayed along a wall a set of photographs of all its pastors, past and present. (I was delighted to discover the picture of a man I know, the Reverend Josiah Roth, the father of my long-time colleague and dear friend Professor John Roth.) My main impression, as I walked along curiously looking at the faces, was that the nineteenth-century pastors looked stern, severe, grim and even (if I may say so with no offense intended) slightly mean. Some of them looked as if they were the kind of men (and of course they were all men in those days) whom you would not want to cross. I chuckled, because it occurred to me that some of them might have a tough time getting a call to a church if they were alive today. Today's pastors are supposed to be affable, accepting and compassionate. Expectations must have been different then.

But then I had a better thought and was flooded with a sense of awe. Looking at those faces from a hundred years ago, it dawned on me that I was part of their group. The point is not that I had preached at the Grand Haven church, as they had. It is not even that I am a Presbyterian minister, as they were. What overwhelmed me was a sense of solidarity for a larger reason—I am a member of their same community. They too had accepted the baton. They too had found their true home in Jesus Christ. Their work as Christians in the world was the same as my work. Their calling was the same as my calling. I am a follower of Jesus in an alien world, and so were they.[4]

In Matters of Religion

NICHOLAS RESCHER

Nicholas Rescher is professor of philosophy and the history and philosophy of science at the University of Pittsburgh. He is a prolific author, and his philosophical interests know no bounds. His writings include Pascal's Wager, The Riddle of Existence, Human Interests, Ethical Idealism, Rationality *and* Moral Absolutes. *He is also editor of two important journals,* American Philosophical Quarterly *and* History of Philosophy Quarterly. *Rescher has served as president of the American Philosophical Association, Eastern Division, and is a member of the Board of Directors of the International Federation of Philosophical Societies, an organ of UNESCO.*

*I*t is a task of no little difficulty for someone of a fundamentally private and reticent nature to write about his religious beliefs, since this patently involves baring in public some part of one's inmost soul. It seems to me that few other aspects of ourselves reveal so deeply and far-reachingly the sort of people we actually are as do our thoughts and actions in matters of religion.

Then again, it is hard to say if such "confessions" are ever entirely truthful—not only in the case of others but even in one's own case. As Talleyrand observed, "La parôle a été donné a l'homme pour déguiser sa pensée."[1] When it comes to explaining the major facts and decisions of our lives, it is perhaps beyond the powers of our insight—and candor—to "tell it as it actually was." But one can try.

The Start of the Long Journey

For some, religion is as meaningless as poetry or spectator sports are for others. Some people are born into a religious community and settle into it as easily as they settle into the linguistic community that surrounds them. Others go along life's route quite innocent of religious concerns, and then are unexpectedly claimed for religiosity—or its reverse—by a sudden experience of conversion that overtakes them unplanned and unasked for, like a summer cold. Still others find their religious journey long, circuitous and complex. For better or worse, I myself belong to the last category.

The family into which I was born in 1928 in the Westphalian district of Germany belonged nominally to the Lutheran-Evangelical church then predominant in that country. But this membership obtained on a rather minimal basis. The members of my family were christened, married and buried by the church, and generally attended its services for Christmas and Easter—at the most. In my own case, there were also a few confirmation classes succeeded by the rite itself. But I really cannot say that during my "suggestible childhood" religion played a more than marginal role in the lives of my parents—or in my own. Nor did this situation change for some years after my leaving Germany for the United States at the age of nine in 1938.

My teenage period confirmed the common idea that the life of a student engaged in the play of ideas and theories tends to leave one unprepared for a serious engagement in religious concerns. But I eventually experienced military service during the Korean War in my early twenties (1952-54). While I never served at the front (and indeed never went overseas), nevertheless this experience—coming on top of my being a refugee from Nazi Germany—left me acutely aware of the contingency and uncertainties of human life. This sense of vulnerability and powerlessness served to make me more open-minded toward religion and more susceptible to its influences. Accordingly, religion did not become meaningful for me until I had to some extent matured and become settled in life—after the import of death had come home to me with the loss of my father, and the experiences of adulthood and its accompanying burdens of responsibility had matured me.

The Quaker Influence

By the mid-1950s my mother had been drawn to Quakerism and had taken up work at the Friends' International Center at the University of California at Los Angeles, where I too was living at the time. After a period of attending the Quaker meeting in Santa Monica, I was ultimately motivated to join. Three aspects of the sect had a particular appeal for me: its utterly simple yet deeply meaningful mode of worship "on the basis of silence," the absence of creedal commitments that might jar a critical philosophical mind, and its dedication to human decency and the peaceable resolution of conflicts. Moreover, the entry into active membership in a Christian community was eased for me by the warm personal qualities of some of the people who then constituted the Santa Monica Friends Meeting. The Quaker emphasis on heeding that small, still voice within that continually calls us to higher and better things appealed sympathetically to my own natural tendencies of thought. It was in "centering down" in the productive silence of the Quaker "First Day" services that I gradually came to find within myself an increasing degree of Christian commitment.

In 1957 came a move from Santa Monica to Bethlehem, Pennsylvania. Throughout the period of my residence there I attended the local Quaker meeting (Lehigh Valley Monthly Meeting). It came to mean a great deal to me, counting some fine individuals among its members. I served as one of the overseers after 1959, and thus had the chance to see at close range the inner workings of a Quaker "parish." Perhaps this glance behind the curtain took away some of the magic. But I did continue to read widely in the literature of Quakerism and obtained a reasonable familiarity with its history and theology.

After leaving Bethlehem for Pittsburgh in 1961, I once again joined the local Quaker meeting—but now with a gradually diminishing commitment. It is hard to say exactly what occasioned this. Perhaps the cause lay wholly in myself. Or perhaps it had to do with the change of the times from the quiescent 1950s to the more turbulent 1960s. (Emotionally and intellectually, I was drawn to the quietistic side of Quakerism, and the political ebullience of the then unfolding Vietnam era was not to my liking.) Be that as it may, in the course of the 1960s my Quaker connection drifted away into a not altogether contented inactivity.

The Pascalian Shift to Roman Catholicism

After some time, however, I began to attend the Roman Catholic services conducted by the Pittsburgh Oratory at the University of Pittsburgh's Heinz Chapel. And as this involvement continued, a gradual change came upon my religious outlook.

Perhaps, ideally, the conversion of an intellectual to a form of religious commitment ought itself to be an intellectual product—a matter of secured conviction in theses and principles. But it certainly was not so in my case. Here it was primarily a matter of sentiment, loyalties and feelings of allegiance and kinship. Perhaps Pascal was right. If you would be a believer, he said, just go and do the things that believers do:

> You desire to attain faith, but you do not know the way. You would like to cure yourself of unbelief, and you ask for remedies. Learn from those who were once bound and gagged like you, and who now stake all that they possess. They are men who know the road that you desire to follow, and who have been cured of a sickness of which you desire to be cured. Follow the way by which they set out, acting as if they already believed, taking holy water, having masses said, etc. All this will naturally cause you to believe. (*Pensées* sec. 233, ed. Leon Brunschvicg)

The message, in effect, runs like this: Join a religious community in practice; associate with its people, attend its ceremonies, participate in its rites and rituals and socializings. Eventually you will then join the community in belief as well. So recommends Pascal, and so it was in my own case. After all, we do not come to our other allegiances—to family, to country or to culture—by reasoning but by association, custom and acculturation. Why should the matter of religion be all that different? As I see it, the impetus to religion (like the impetus to our other human allegiances) comes largely not from reason but from affects—from the emotional rather than intellectual side of our makeup.

In any case, after I had spent several years sitting on the fence as an "unofficial Catholic"—attending Mass regularly and participating in various church activities—the provost of the University Oratory, Father William Clancy, gave me a definite albeit oblique push. Taking my wife, Dorothy, aside one day, he asked her if I viewed him as somehow unsympathetic or unfriendly, seeing that in all those years I had never discussed my relationship to Catholicism with him. When I responded to this by arranging for a discussion, he put to me the question of what exactly was holding me back from joining the church. As I reflected on this, I came to realize that the answer had, in effect, to be *nothing*. And so I talked with Father Clancy in this sense, indicating that if he was prepared to receive me into the church, then I, for my part, was prepared to go ahead. And so in March of 1981 I finally did so. Bill Clancy was not only a scholar and a gentleman, but he had a deep and sympathetic insight into the heart of academically minded people. He spoke little (at least to me), but his sympathetic concern encouraged me to think things through for myself.

On Christian Commitment

There is no doubt that two intersecting factors were operative in inducing me to make a Christian commitment: a sense of intellectual and personal solidarity with those whom I could accept as role models among believers, and a sense of estrangement from those whom I deemed naively cocksure in their rejection of belief. For while I have lived almost my whole life as an academic among academics, I have always felt alienated from the easy certainties with which they generally view the world about them—confident that "they have all the answers." It has always seemed to me that the more we learn, the fewer answers we actually have, because the more questions open up. This aspect of things, which a religious outlook does or should encompass, seems to me to be something of deep and significant truth.

I myself am not a person of easy certainties. Among my favorite biblical texts is the paradoxical "Lord, I believe; help thou mine unbelief." And there is no shortage of other passages in the Old and New Testaments alike on which those alive to the mystery of things can draw for aid and comfort—texts that betray deep doubts about our ability to *know* God. As Job proclaims, "Oh that I knew where I might find him! that I might come even to his seat! . . . Behold I go forward, but he is not there; and backward, but I cannot perceive him." In the book of Psalms, the stress is often not on what we know or believe of God, but on seeking, hoping, trusting. Merely to yearn for the Lord is, in the psalmist's view, already to be well embarked on the road of faith.

Of the many forms of human failing, the failure of imagination is one of the saddest. And one of the gravest failures of imagination is that of the person who cannot manage to project the concepts of a God worthy of ardent desire—a God whose nonbeing would be the occasion for genuine grief. Compared with this, an inability to imagine a friend worth having or a spouse worth loving is a pale shadow—though all alike betoken a regrettable impoverishment of personality of the same general sort. Sensible people would clearly prefer to number among their friends someone who was willing to invest hope and trust in himself, his fellows and his world. To refrain, in the absence of preponderating reasons to the contrary, from letting hope influence belief—even merely to the extent of that sort of tentative belief at issue in a working assumption made for practical purposes—betokens a crabbed failure of confidence that has nothing admirable about it.

Religious belief alters our valuative frame of reference, enabling us to view our own lives with a clearer and more enlightened sense of priorities. Its commitment to the larger, "spiritual" values helps us to realize the extent to which various issues that many people see as supremely important are actually trivia.[1] This sort of view, at any rate, gradually became the substance of my religious outlook.

But just what was it that led me to commit myself to Christianity in the Catholic configuration? Given that my wife was Catholic, it was perhaps partly a sense of familial solidarity—the conviction that a family should be a unit. But beside this something deeper and more ideological was also at work, something that lay deep in my emotional makeup.

As a philosopher, I had to decide upon my spiritual kindred in life. Did I want to align myself with the religion-disdaining Lucretiuses, Voltaires, Humes, Nietzsches and Bertrand Russells of the world, or with its theistically committed Platos and Plotinuses, its Anselms and Aquinases, its Leibnizes and Hegels? I was free to choose those who were to be my spiritual kinfolk, and I felt myself drawn toward those who saw humanity as subject to transcendent aspirations and obligations—and for whom forms of worship and religious styles of thought really mattered.

Some people are led to deepen their religious commitment by *thought*—by reflection on the rational fabric of theological deliberations. Others are impelled by *experience*—by a reception of some sort of sign or signal. In my own case, however, it came by way of *feeling*—through awe and wonder at the mystery of existence and, no less importantly, by a sentiment of solidarity with those whom I admired and respected as part of a community of faith transcending the boundaries of dogma and doctrine. There was no dramatic episode of conversion—no flash of light came calling me from on high. I simply and gradually found myself sliding along the unbroken slope from mere participation to committed membership.

Religious commitment, after all, has two aspects: evaluation and belief. On the one hand is the belief-oriented, creedal aspect of religion that is strongly emphasized in the cognitively oriented monotheistic religions of the West, which draw much of their theological impetus from Greek philosophy. But the valuative aspect is also a significant factor—and has never quite been altogether absent from Christianity, which recognizes the pivotal role of a commitment to hope in God as the expression of a dedication to values above and beyond the ordinary selfish, materialistic, self-advantaging range. The dedication to higher values reflected in our Christian yearning for a benevolent God whose concern is not directed at us alone, but at all our fellows (enemies included) is something that ennobles us, makes us into beings of worth—into individuals whom others can rightly regard as associates in a value-sharing community of faith based on a community of hope and aspiration and not merely as cobelievers in certain formal articles of faith.

In the final analysis, then, I have become and continue to remain a committed Catholic because this represents a position that, as I see it, is intellectually sensible, evaluatively appropriate and personally congenial. Accordingly, the answer to the question of why I am a Catholic is perhaps simply this: because that is where I feel at home. It is a matter of communion—of being in communion with people whose ideas, allegiances and values are in substantial measure congenial to my own.

In any case, it was not dogmas and doctrines that drew me to Catholicism but an inner need of a sort that is difficult to describe. It was not a need for relief from a sense of sin, nor a need for relief from the intimations of mortality. Rather, it was a need for relief from a sense of isolation—the desire to feel oneself part of a wider community of spirits who are in some degree kindred, who share with oneself a sense of values and priorities geared to the spiritual dimension of our species and to a sense of human insignificance in the awesome face of the mysteries of our existence.

Queries and Replies

Yet what of the *bêtises* committed by the church—nowadays as former-ly? There they are, plain for all to see. But then what of the foolish-nesses committed by our children—or our parents? Those who give their loyalties only to the flawless have in effect resolved to do away with any and all attachments. If we respected (or loved) only those who are perfect, there would be no scope whatever for such emotions. And anyhow, what right has an imperfect Christian to demand a perfect church?

"But then you do not agree with the whole gamut of the teaching, practices, traditions and teachings of the church." Just so—I do not agree with the entire lot. No doubt this would displease my spiritual counselor, perhaps my bishop and conceivably even the pope. But is this pivotal? Did Christ come into the world for the contentment of the hierarchy or for the salvation of souls? The point is that—like them or not—I view those practices, traditions and teachings with respect, take them seriously, and accommodate myself to them as best I can. After all, these are all issues on which easy certainties are quite unrealizable. Even where I am deeply out of sympathy I do not mock but respect and try to understand. If this is an uneasy compromise, then so be it. Here as elsewhere life itself is a matter of uneasy compromises between the realizable and the ideal. A church that does not want imperfect members wants none at all. Who is the discontented hierarch to cast the first stone?

"But has religion changed your life?" In one way the answer is clearly yes. For one thing, it has humanized me, leading me to take a stronger and more sympathetic interest in the endeavors and concerns of my fellows. For another, it has enlarged my circle of acquaintances (*friends* would perhaps be too strong a word) by one very important member, namely God. Sometimes we converse. Very imperfectly, no doubt, like people communicating across the static and cross-conversations on a Third World telephone system. But still we converse—with me sometimes addressing him in prayer and and he sometimes communicating with me via that medium called conscience. "How would God feel about you doing that?" is a question I occasionally ask myself—not perhaps as often as I should, but still sometimes. While it's largely how I *feel* about things that attracted me to faith in God, the effect of this faith is largely its influence upon how I *think* about things. (For better or worse, I am not one of those whose religiosity impels them to go forth and change the world.)

It is clear to me from my own experience that philosophers—or at least some of them—need Christianity. But does Christianity need philosophers? It seems to me that the answer here is also affirmative. We humans are members of *Homo sapiens.* The need to comprehend and understand is inborn in our nature—ignorance and incomprehension are painful to us: we need knowledge for the mind as much as we need food for the body. And this is particularly true in matters that—like religion—bear in the fundamentals of our lives. The clarity and cogency that philosophy brings is accordingly something that has a potentially positive role to play in every impartial area of human endeavor, Christianity by no means excluded. No church can exist in easy comfort with its intellectuals and theologians, but no church can be a thriving concern among thinking people if it dispenses with their services.

Has being a Christian made a difference to my philosophizing? An affirmative response is indicated by the fact that religious belief has affected my professional work in two ways. On the one hand, it has stimulated my interest in the philosophical aspect of some religious issues. (These interests are particularly reflected in such books as *Pascal's Wager, The Riddle of Existence* and *Human Interests.*) On the other hand, it has also made me more sensitive to the valuative and ethical dimension of human life. (These sensibilities are particularly reflected in *Ethical Idealism, Rationality* and *Moral Absolutes.*) Being a religious person has amplified my philosophical interests, moving them beyond the "scientific" to embrace also the "humanistic" side of philosophical concerns.

European philosophical colleagues at secular institutions are almost invariably nonbelievers. And American philosophers, like American intellectuals in general, are quite predominantly so, and in this respect, as in many others, are out of tune with the wider society to which they belong. On the faculties of American universities, theists have generally been an embattled minority throughout my professional career. In view of this, I have always proceeded toward my own philosophical colleagues on a "to each his own," "live and let live" basis. Not until the founding of the Society for Christian Philosophers in the 1970s did something like a support group emerge among professional colleagues. (Rightly or wrongly, I have viewed the far older American Catholic Philosophical Association as an organization catering to colleagues—principally clerics—serving at specifically Catholic universities.) And so it is among these philosophical fellow Christians that I have found some spiritual kinfolk.

This leaves a very different question: "So you are a Christian. But are you a *good* Christian? In particular, do you live the sort of selfless life that a good Christian clearly *ought* to lead?" A painful question, this.

"Works" are doubtless not the core of Christianity, but they are clearly an essential component. A paramount duty of the good Christian is surely to be constructive, to make a difference, to make the world a better place in one respect than it would otherwise be. One certainly need not be a Christian to have this object, but one does not qualify as a true Christian without it. And in this regard I have a deep sense of inadequacy. As an academic, my efforts have been far more directed toward understanding the world than toward trying to improve it. In my case, this inclination seems to lie deeply rooted "in the nature of the beast," and I can only hope that a God who certainly realizes this will also be prepared to forgive it.

Becoming Michael

FREDERICK SUPPE

Frederick Suppe is professor of philosophy in the department of philosophy and a member of the committee on the history and philosophy of science at the University of Maryland at College Park, as well as professor of philosophy in the doctoral program of the School of Nursing of the University of Maryland at Baltimore. He was founding chair of the Maryland graduate program in the history and philosophy of science. He specializes in philosophy of science, epistemology and metaphysics, and in philosophical theology. He has published over seventy scholarly articles as well as the following books: Facts, Theories, and Scientific Observation; The Semantic Conception of Theories and Scientific Realism; The Structure of Scientific Theories; *and volumes 1 and 2 of* PSA 1976, Proceedings of the 1976 Biennial Meetings of the Philosophy of Science Association *(with Peter Asquith). He has taught at the University of Michigan, the University of California at Santa Barbara, the Indian Institute of Technology at Kanpur, the University of Illinois, the University of Notre Dame (where he was Distinguished Senior Scholar in the Center for Philosophy of Religion) and Princeton University (as National Science Foundation Visiting Fellow in Geology and Geophysics). Since writing this essay he has had to abandon avocational climbing because of arthritis in his hands, substituting a return to the flying of his youth.*

I am in a Trappist monastery in Virginia, nestled at the foot of the Blue Ridge Mountains by the edge of the Shenandoah River. I have come to find humility; I seek it in silence and Lenten penance. I have been working through the awareness exercises in Anthony deMello's *Sadhana: Way to God; Christian Exercises in Eastern Form.*[1] Back home our parish has been having Lenten prayer workshops built around videos of deMello's exercises, and I have built my retreat around them. They also were recommended by Francis Vanderwall[2]—one of the best writers on spiritual direction I've encountered.[3] It is my third day of the retreat, I've been fasting for sixty-three hours, and I have just returned from the monks' chanted Midday Prayer. I resume my spiritual exercises reading deMello's instructions: "Exercise 9: Body Prayer."

Actually, I've done some of these before joining the monks at prayer—those "exercises you could try in the privacy of your room, where you can express yourself freely with your body without the embarrassment of being seen by others."[4]

First quiet yourself through awareness of sensations in various parts of your body. . . . Sharpen your awareness by picking up even the subtlest sensations, not just the gross and evident ones. . . .

Now, very gently move your hands and fingers so that your hands come to rest on your lap, palms upward, fingers joined together. . . . The movement must be very, very slow . . . like the opening of the petals of a flower. . . . And while the movement is going on, be aware of each part of it. . . .

Become aware of the gesture itself: This is a gesture of prayer to God. . . . What meaning does this gesture have for you? Say it without words, merely identifying with the gesture.[5]

This, the basic one, I had done before Midday Prayer in the Oratory.

Now I am back in my cell, back at spiritual exercise again. I want more intimate contact with God. I continue the exercises. Before the day is over I will have experienced God, as in a quiet love affair. It will be my Song of Songs, not the great life-transforming Berlioz sort of experience of God . . . I had that thirteen months earlier. That was the beginning of a path that found me prostrate on that Trappist cell floor seeking humility. A path that would lead me to deeper, sustained and more profound encounters with God. And with the Evil One in active opposition. A journey filled with suffering and joy, with consolation and disconsolation. A journey of struggle as with God's grace I seek to integrate the scars of childhood, my personality, my sexuality, my intellect, my past and present—*my very being*—into a life of faith and devoted allegiance to God. But those struggles are stories for other times. Here is the place to tell you something of my formative years, of my struggling fitful journey to God and Christ, of how I came to crave the humility of loving surrender to God.

Opening Disquisition

Before I get to that a vexing worry must be confronted: humility, silence and obedience. The virtue of taciturnity. How is autobiographical writing compatible with these virtues? Am I not being like the Pharisees parading my "virtue" in public? To be sure, there is an element of mortification in this public confession. But isn't that like fasting loudly *(Mt 6:16-18)*? I want, I desperately seek, humility. And yet at the same time don't I want everybody to learn of it? Silence is the key to humility and obedience.

> The rule [of St. Benedict] encourages and values highly the virtue of taciturnity.
>
> This evaluation of taciturnity is based on the desire to avoid sin and practice virtue. The monk can hardly hope to avoid sin if he does not control his tongue. Neither can he realize in practice certain virtues [especially obedience and humility] unless he observes silence. . . .
>
> A second motive for the practice of silence is the necessity to observe silence in order to listen. . . . Silence is necessary so that the monk may communicate with God, may hear God speak to him in the work of God, in holy reading, in the teaching of the abbot, in private prayer.[6]

So why don't I begin here?

Why the need to go public, to proclaim my unsuccessful search for humility? Perhaps herein lies the secret of my failure: I seek it. Can one *seek* humility? Or is it a grace obtainable only by total surrender of self to God? Is the end of humility the only means to humility? Must one be humble to become humble? Or is silence the key, the path? But how to become silent? Try meditating. But thoughts intrude, wildly, without control. There are techniques. DeMello says, "Observe every thought that comes into your mind. . . . Become aware of it or of the fact you are thinking . . . make the startling discovery that while you are aware of the fact you are thinking all thinking tends to stop."[7] It works. Thinking is like introspection. C. S. Lewis says, "The enjoyment and contemplation of our inner activities are incompatible. You cannot hope and think at the same moment. . . . The surest way of spoiling a pleasure was to start examining your satisfaction. . . . All introspection is in one respect misleading. In introspection we try to look 'insides ourselves' and see what is going on. But nearly everything that was going on a moment before is stopped by the very act of turning to look at it. Unfortunately this does not mean that introspection finds nothing. On the contrary, it finds precisely what is left behind by suspension of all our normal activities; and what is left behind is mainly mental images and physical sensations. The great error is to mistake this mere sediment or trace or byproduct for the activities themselves."[8]

No human being can establish himself in silence; anyone who thinks he can, only shows that he does not know anything about silence. God alone does it. . . . It is God who must immobilize us in silence.[9]

Humility is no different. It is a state of mind—nay, a state of heart. Humility must be utterly unselfconscious. Once one looks for it, once one attempts to focus on it, it disappears—leaving only the residue of good intentions, of failed efforts.

Humility is an invisible virtue. Yet it is the most virile of the virtues because the most metaphysical: It makes us realize that we are nothing. This is the virtue that is least recognized by the world and by philosophers. . . . It goes much farther than the virtue of religion, with which it is often confused.[10]

So confession is compatible with humility if it is utterly self-effacing, if it is utterly spontaneous and undeliberate. But how can confession be an act of humility? For unless *I* take responsibility, unless *I* confess that *I* have sinned, it is not genuine confession. Confession more than anything else must be egocentric. And so it cannot be an act of humility. No, but perhaps it can be a path *to* humility. Cannot that very egocentric act of confession become the means to shed that ego? By the very act of confession can I not offer up my ego to God, as my sacrifice of atonement? The offering of myself up in contrite holocaust? Perhaps this is wherein lies the wisdom of requiring confession to a priest. For can one offer up one's ego in private? Is not the insistence "I can confess directly to God—I need no intercessory" a refusal to offer myself up in atonement? If I am unwilling to do so in another's presence, is this not a clinging to self—esteem of self, a treasuring of self, a holding on to self? The act of confession becomes inauthentic, self-conscious and proud—the antithesis of humility.

Perhaps herein lurks the resolution of paradox: public autobiographical confession, if ingenuous, possibly can be sufficiently self-effacing as to be, or approximate, an act of humility. The Pharisee's public acts were self-aggrandizing. That was the sin there. To the extent that self-reflection is self-effacing and publicly displayed with such brutal honesty as to be destructive of self-respect, then and only then is it consistent with humility. And even then only if unselfconsciously done. But the act of writing is utterly self-conscious. So humility again eludes me, though I suspect at some deeper, more profound level.

But I did promise Kelly I'd try to write an autobiographical piece for this collection. In the midst of my struggle to reconcile autobiographical writing with my search for humility I am acutely aware that the manuscript deadline fast approaches. Whether to honor that promise or not? Once again I see the impotence of philosophical argument and analysis. They are no substitute for discernment of God's will. So I abandon my intellectualizing efforts and turn instead to prayer. I ask that the Holy Spirit grant me powers of discernment: what to put in, what to leave out. I ask Jesus to be with me as friend and confidant as I try to write. I pray, "May the Spirit of the Lord be in my head, in my heart, and guide my pen." Simultaneously I cross myself, pen in hand, on the forehead, the lips and the heart—in imitation of the prayer gestures we make at Mass just before the Gospel is read. Only then do I put my pen to paper.

Formation

To begin at the beginning. I was born just before World War II, the middle of three sons, and was baptized in the Congregational Church. Memories of those early war years are happy ones. We were a close family that had good times together. I remember playing with packing crates in the backyard, my first attempts to use tools, my own brace and bit received as a present at age five. Toys for Christmas were lovingly handmade by my father and great uncle. I remember Audrey Flugel babysitting us, the Haney's L-16 La Salle car, the fear my Dad would be drafted, my first bottle of soda pop, fighting with bully David Dodds, playing Indian tossing my hammer "tomahawk" at a lug-crate target and missing and taking out the plate glass front window instead. Religious memories include wartime socials in the Presbyterian church basement where, after food, kids were entertained by silent 8mm movies of Allies shooting down Jap planes.

During the war Dad had a critical industries job that, with his age (he was 35 when it ended), kept him from being drafted. After the war we moved into our own home and Dad went back into partnership with his father in the family sewing machine and appliance business. The happy bliss of childhood was over. My paternal grandfather was a crude, obnoxious, cigar-chewing loudmouth with a strong sadistic streak. One of my most vivid childhood memories is visiting at his house, being mercilessly teased and taunted until I could take it no longer and I fled out of the door yelling, "I hate you!" and heading the three or four miles home in tears.

He treated my father the same way, only worse. Neither could really stand the other, though my father felt guilty about it. They frequently fought at the store, and when they did Dad would come home and take his frustrations out on us kids. It was extremely unhealthy for him—and for us. The slightest provocation, and we'd be punished. Never in all those years can I recall deliberately doing wrong. Whatever had been forbidden I scrupulously tried to avoid.

The NT [temperament person] is never willing to repeat an error.—David Keirsey and Marilyn Bates, Please Understand Me! Character and Temperament Types[11]

Always it seemed to be for something that nobody had ever bothered to forbid that I was punished. And in ambiguous situations he would project the worst intentions on me and punish me for them. Once I was in the front flower bed trying to make a ring of matches stuck head close to head, to see if I could make them ignite one another domino style. In the dirt flower bed there was no danger of a real fire. Just then Dad came home, upset from a particularly bad fight with his father. I was accused of *trying* to burn the house down and beaten severely. There was no such intent—but that wasn't relevant. I was always punished by being beaten, harshly, while he screamed, "You'll get this till you stop crying!" I felt intensely violated by him.

> *Physical punishment is deeply violating to the NT [temperament person] . . . he reacts to abuse of the body with what seems to be an exaggerated response, somehow seeing this abuse as a violation of his nature. Dignity usually is important to NT children, and they often are described as "prideful." Somehow, others often find this offensive and seem to take the NT's pride as a personal affront, which often presents a challenge to those around the NT to bring the NT off his high horse. . . . Parenting the NT means hands off.[12]*

Whippings continued until adolescence when, finally, I rebelled as he tried to abuse me physically and I wrestled him to the ground, pinned him straddling his chest, and pummeled his face. Never again did he try to punish me physically.

Psychological abuse was just as effective, though. By then he already had gotten into the habit of trying to provoke disobedience as an excuse to punish. He'd push, taunt—just like his father did—until you couldn't take it anymore. Then, when you'd rebel, he'd take away privileges "for showing lack of respect." In these moods he made impossible, inconsistent demands and brutally punished noncompliance. My older brother tried to obey them all. That was a factor in his own increasing instability and the mental breakdowns and institutionalizations during his adulthood. I tried a different tack: When treated irrationally and unfairly I fought back—and got a lot of punishment for my integrity. It seemed like my father especially liked to go after me, presumably because I could be counted on to break, to rebel, to show lack of respect if he kept the attack up long enough. But he had to be careful. Twice he so provoked me that I tried to kill him. He grew scared of me and threatened to send me to military school. But still he kept it up. My younger brother was scared the least. He saw that Dad played by *rules*—bizarre ones—that licensed sadistic behavior. He quickly learned to allow Dad no emotional hold over him, learned passive resistance. When accused he never fought back. He just grinned as Dad grew more and more angry. John wasn't violating any rules that gave Dad license to punish, and Dad just grew more and more frustrated.

The abuse was physical and psychological, not sexual. Alcohol was not a factor. Increasingly Dad had become like two persons: one a sadistic person, like his father; the other was a generous, kindly, caring father. The problem was, you rarely knew which father you were going to be dealing with.

There was one situation where Dad could be counted on to be the kind person—when it involved his true love, the mountains. When I was little, sleeping out, the stars scared me; nightmares trapped in mummy bags. But when I got older, and life with Dad often was un- happy and vicious, I *could* count on him being his good self in the out- doors. For it was there he was happiest, and thus the scouting days with him as scoutmaster were happy ones. Perhaps this has something to do with my return to the mountains when I'm in generally unhappy circumstances. (And now, when I'm pretty happy, I have a strong need to live in the mountains remote from population.) I have very fond memories of being in the mountains with Dad—on family vacations, on scout troop trips, and on trips with just the two of us. I have tender recollections of his getting what we mistakenly thought was appendi- citis back on Bubb's Creek in the Sierras, and carrying his and my pack out as I nursed him back to civilization and worried about his survival.

The good times sometimes were as wonderful as the bad times were hideous, and it's made reconciling the two personas of my father ex- tremely difficult.

> *Love in our world is suffering love. Some do not suffer much, though, for they do not love much. . . . If I hadn't loved him, there would not be this agony. . . . In commanding us to love, God invites us to suffer.*[13]

I can't reconcile things except through Christianity: eventually I discov- ered I didn't have to sort out or resolve my conflicting feelings about him to pray for his soul. Gradually I learned to honor my father by praying daily for his soul and trying not to think too much about him otherwise. Only very recently have I become able, through action of the Holy Spirit, to honor him by saying, "I love you. I love you despite all the despicable things you did to us." Of course, intellectually I know he was mentally ill. The fact was that he was so like his father; and family stories record that earlier generations were worse.[14] I harbor sporadic fears that I resemble him more than I would like (I look most like him of the three boys; and once, later in life, I found myself behaving, in exasperation with a whiny, spoiled little five-year-old my mother was caring for, uncomfortably like my father—taunting then punishing when the child could take no more and told me to shut up). These have been among my reasons for the conscious decision not to raise children. Some family lines ought not to be perpetuated, and I fear mine, at least through me, is one.

Church loomed increasingly important in my formation process. We attended the Presbyterian church—one that used an adaptation of the schismatic American Catholic Church vernacular Mass (including Credo, Sanctus and Agnus Dei but with sermon usually replacing the Eucharistic Prayer) as liturgy. This, I'm sure, had a lot to do with preparing me for my later love of the Mass. Early in my adolescence we got a new youth minister, Joe Easter. Joe increasingly became my surrogate father. He gave me the predictably stable male adult influence I needed. I could talk to him. He realized I was very bright and told me so. (I'd never really known that. Nobody said much positive to me. I didn't learn to read until third grade—and then over one weekend I went from remedial group to reading at the eighth- or ninth-grade level. I wouldn't accept things on authority, and often quarreled with teachers over facts and explanations. Frequently I was right. I thus was a troublemaker. Only as I got to junior and senior high did some teachers come to appreciate how gifted I was and encourage me.) But Joe Easter was the first to tell me just how bright I was.

He had me teach junior-high Sunday school. Although I was only in the eleventh grade, I wasn't satisfied with the standard curricular stuff and drew up my own teaching materials, duplicating them on an old hectograph (a gelatin precursor of Ditto). I thus began my first efforts at hermeneutics under his guidance, and got pretty good at it. I preached in church on youth Sundays—once on my maternal grandmother's death. One summer I went to church camp. It culminated with a dedication campfire where each camper threw a fagot into the fire and made a public vow. I admired Joe Easter a lot, and I prayed for the call. I'm not sure I got it then, or whether I worked myself up in intense desire. In any case, I threw my stick into the fire and vowed to become a minister. My parents were strongly opposed when they found out.

During my high school days Dad was on the citizen's advisory board for the local Salvation Army. For some reason or other we kids were volunteered to help evangelize on street corners on Friday evenings. Also, I became de facto scoutmaster for the Salvation Army troop (being in high school I was too young; some "phantom" person was listed as the "official" leader). The troop met at the Salvation Army building and so I was around there a lot. I sometimes attended services, including my first funeral (complete with brass band and a horseshoe floral wreath with "Good Luck Bessie" printed on the streamer). I was somewhat attracted to the discipline of the Army. I recall reading the officers' manual and being entranced by the rules commanding a rather stark, simple, severe lifestyle. It was my first exposure to Christian asceticism. I am much more at home with this side of Christianity than I am with the Pollyanna "Happyland" strain.

> I hope you'll accept from me a little volume I've always admired. I believe it touches on some of the fine points we've discussed this morning. "God is My Hobby." By Dr. Homer Vincent Claude Pierson, Jr. In this little book, I think you'll find, Dr. Pierson tells us very clearly how when he was twenty-one years of age he started putting aside a little time each day—two minutes in the morning and two minutes at night, if I remember correctly—and at the end of the first year, just by these little informal visits with God, he increased his annual income seventy-four percent.—Zooey in J. D. Salinger, Franny and Zooey[15]

I instinctively gravitate to the asceticism in Christianity. It is a real struggle for me to fathom its message of love. I have trouble seeing what the point of religion, of Christianity, is if it's not hard and demanding. While I briefly had fantasized about being a Salvation Army officer—trying on the discipline "for size"—I don't think I really entertained the idea seriously. I was to be a Presbyterian minister.

Meanwhile my older brother had become a Baptist. He was much into gospel music, as was Great-Uncle Harold who directed Charles E. Fuller's "Old Fashioned Revival Hour" choir. We went to lots of gospel sings and services, including the black Echoes of Eden and the Abyssinian Baptist Church. My high school social activities thus centered around church, Explorer and Boy Scouts, and mountains. And I was athletically involved—on the track team and managing the "B" basketball team as well as a recreational league team.

My paternal grandmother was sort of Christian Science, and had only an eighth-grade education. I saw lots of her because she lived nearby, had a TV, and bribed us with candy, gum and ice cream. We visited after church every Sunday. As we grew older she had less and less to offer me[16] and we grew distant. My maternal side was far more interesting, though they lived sixty miles away and we saw less of them. Grandma Cross was a former concert violinist, a "Boston Lady" who had grown up with Dwight Moody's children at one of his Christian academies where her mother was professor of organ. Grandpa Cross was one of the smartest people I've ever met—a licensed civil engineer and retired official of the Southern California Edison Company. He was very mechanical as well as intellectual, always inventing things: he designed and built his own lathe, milling machine and so forth, and had invented the heat pump for Thermador. I took after him, and in many respects he has been my role model in adult life. No adult influenced me more in my formative years. I fortunately was able to live with him half of my first year of college.

My mother took after them, having earned a masters degree and being an accomplished musician. Her thesis developed a precursor of Labanotation for recording dance movements, and was published in journal article form. She provided an intellectual atmosphere and influence at home that, augmented by the occasional good junior- or senior-high teacher, overcame the usual effects of growing up in a blue-collar, assembly-line town where around 5 percent of high-school graduates went on to any further schooling. Mom was the primary intellectual influence. She was responsible for two of her three boys going on to get Ph.D.s and for their drive to become leading scholars in their respective academic fields. (My younger brother is chairman of the Geological and Geophysical Sciences Department at Princeton and has an endowed chair there.) Dad was outclassed intellectually, but was contentious enough to hide his ignorance by challenging the claims we'd make. This usually happened at dinner, and we'd be sent to the encyclopedia for facts and evidence. Dinners were educational affairs, a training house in argument, rhetoric and scholarship. We learned to defend our views and claims. It was the chief, most important educational influence on all three of us. It made an often unhappy and intolerable home life manageable.

Nevertheless, things were not well between me and my father, and I left home as soon as I graduated from high school. Except for periodic use of a car (and later some assistance my first year of graduate school in exchange for remodeling their store), I was financially independent. I got a job as an instrumentation technician for General Electric Flight Test at Edwards Air Force Base and worked the nine months till I entered college. At Edwards I attended base chapel and was in a young adults group.

These quite possibly were the happiest days of my life. I was very good at my work, and was well liked and well regarded by my mostly older fellow-workers. (I always have felt more comfortable with people older than myself than with my peers.) It was a curious accumulation of high-tech types and desert rats—often in the same personage. There was the highest concentration of eccentrics and characters I've ever seen, and I held them in high respect for their individuality, competence and nonconformity. Life was replete with mad escapades: circling by small plane over the drive-in at low altitude to see if the movie was any good and, if it was, landing and racing by car the twenty miles to catch the last show. Celebrating the Fourth of July with half-sticks of dynamite, rescue smoke guns, 45 shells and highway flares. Underage drinking with test pilots at bars during "First Flight" parties. Driving all night to the High Sierras and hiking in with Beedle, Bill and Shorty, and having them sit comfortably to watch as I climbed Mt. Conness from a glacial approach, then immediately rejoining them to hike back out and drive back to the desert the same day—all just to prove to them that I really had climbed that peak several weeks earlier. Those days also provided me with scientific experiences that fueled my later work as a philosopher of science.[17]

Then I went to college at the University of California at Riverside—originally an experimental "honors" campus for the university system. There I discovered and fell in love with philosophy. I recall no hostility toward Christianity in any of my classes there. A spectacular course in history and thought of Western civilization gave me a solid exposure to many of the classics of Western spirituality such as the *Rule* of St.

Benedict. My medieval philosophy course with Philip Wheelwright gave me a strong grounding in St. Augustine and St. Thomas, as well as Stoic and neo-Platonist developments that strongly influenced Christian thought.[18]

Meanwhile a church fight erupted back at the Presbyterian church, and Joe Easter had been made a scapegoat and forced out. I was disillusioned. Equally influential—I'd fallen in love with academia and *knew* I wanted to be a professor. Only later did it occur to me that this could be combined with the ministry. My desire to become a minister diminished. I remember sitting in Joe's car at UCR when he came to visit me on campus and telling him I wasn't going to be a minister. In my disillusionment my belief in God dwindled. Later, through friends, I became enchanted with High Church Episcopalianism (which we snobbishly called "Anglicanism" to distance it from the usual Low-Church varieties) and almost joined; but increasingly I came to find the basis of my attraction spiritually insubstantial, being primarily an aesthetic response to the ritual. So ultimately I did not join. Eventually I left Christianity, agnostic rather than atheist, and went to graduate school in philosophy.

The climate was somewhat hostile toward religion in the Michigan philosophy department, especially among graduate students. Only George Mavrodes was an overt believer, and he was mocked for it behind his back; why, he'd even gone to Baptist seminary! Alston was in his period of lapse, and Frankena's belief was so low-profile as to be easily missed. Geach and Anscombe visited for a semester, but their Catholicism was viewed as just another of their many eccentricities. My agnosticism was not challenged.

One aspect of Christianity continued to be a part of my life: music. In high school I had discovered the very fine boys' choir at the downtown Episcopal cathedral, and attended many wonderful liturgies and concerts there, including an exceptional performance of the *Messiah* with boy sopranos, countertenors, tenors, basses, organ and harpsichord using the original Handel setting instead of the more standard Mozart orchestration. In college I was in the university choir for several years and sang a wide spectrum of the choral repertoire, including the Mozart *Requiem*. In graduate school I continued to take advantage of the many classical music offerings at Michigan. Masses, oratorios and Te Deums were among my favorite music. My love for organ music expanded to include extended exposure to the French romantics such as César Franck and Widor; memorable organ performances include ones by Anton Heiller and Pierre Cochereau.

The academic setting was stimulating and intellectually congenial. Yet there was a feeling of never quite belonging socially, of always being on the outside looking in. I was somewhat retarded socially, and I had few instincts on how to relate conversationally. It was a struggle of learning how to *imitate* social interaction, but never having the feel for it that made social intercourse fluid—be it dating or being one of the guys. It is characteristic of my personality type (INTJ) that one "seems to stand *beside* instead of *in* the stream of life, seeming to watch bemusedly as the river flows by—a little distanced, a little detached, a little uninvolved."[19] You feel an outsider, observing but not experiencing. One "experiences" communal life as profoundly inauthentic. What others do by instinct I attempted to acquire as a skill. And always it seemed an *ersatz* version, a clumsy, inauthentic performance lacking in true feeling or appreciation. When unsure of how to interact I either would withdraw or else grandstand, inappropriately dominating conversation—desperate attempts to escape the terror of a peer encounter. (Angst has not subsided with age. Today I avoid large peer events like the plague. In smaller peer group situations I struggle against instincts to withdraw, or to dominate, or to destroy the group if I can neither withdraw nor dominate. I am happier and content when there is a status differential where either I or someone else is expected to dominate.)

How does being outside looking in relate to C. S. Lewis's "Joy"—that experience "of an unsatisfied desire which is itself more desirable than any other satisfaction"—neither happiness nor pleasure. Apart from wanting it again, "it might equally well be called a particular kind of unhappiness or grief."[20] Have I experienced Joy with other people? I don't know. Have I been happy in my social dealings? Can one be happy on the outside, looking in? I think not—I don't think the desire of alienation is Joy. At least I suspect not. When am I happiest? When I seek God? Was it Joy when God called me back at Notre Dame by plunging me into the depths of profound, aching alienation? Was that being surprised by Joy? What about that calling at church camp during high school?

I do know that I am not on the outside looking in when I *do* philosophy. But within academia, within the philosophy profession, I often feel on the outside looking in. Much of what academic philosophy rewards, that for which it confers "superstar" status, seems to me intellectual game-playing, "navel-contemplatory twaddle"[21] having little to do with what I take to be the real problems of philosophy, with the examined life. (Von Neumann caught this when he defined philosophy as "the systematic misuse of words designed precisely for that purpose.") The problems that exercise me—or else how I think they should be approached—often seem unfashionable. I have no more instinct for the philosophically fashionable minuet than I have in other social enterprises. I constantly doubt whether my work is appreciated or well regarded, and I feel intensely insecure about my status in the profession. I genuinely am surprised when people I've not met know who I am and recognize me by sight at meetings, or to discover that people actually have read my works. I still don't know how to read others' signals, I don't have the instinctive understandings needed for effective social intercourse—not even in the professional setting. I thus am desperately insecure as to my status and place.

It has been that way since puberty. As a youth I sought to belong. But I felt apart, felt different. Such aloofness I fueled by an extremely poor physical self-image that made me feel profoundly less than a man. I coped by alternately shying away from competitiveness in the social arena and by efforts of hypermasculinity. A vignette captures it: Dare I think of going to the Senior Prom? No. That would require asking a girl out, and run the risk of being turned down, rejected. And it would be no wonder. Who'd want me? And if she did want me, what did that say about her desirability? (Here another memory intrudes: I have been going steady with a girl; and to prove my masculinity I am physically aggressive. We make out all the time—even in the back seat of the youth minister's car. My hands under her bra and in her pants are a regular occurrence. But since she lets me, even welcomes these intrusions, she increasingly becomes a slut in my eyes. She wants me . . .

so she is unworthy.) Back to the prom. I don't just not go. I take off school and go fishing with Dad. It's a rugged masculine trip up the East Fork of the San Gabriel River, inaccessible most of the year due to high water or closed due to fire danger. The San Gabriels are among the most rugged mountains I know. And we ford our way upstream till we come to a waterfall—impassible except when the water is somewhat low, and then only with the aid of a fixed rusty cable. We ascend the waterfall, hand over hand up the cable through the flow, packs on our backs. Above the falls fishing is spectacular. Few people get back there; we are alone. We catch our limits. And I get a good hypermasculine story to tell, to cover up my inability to risk the rejection of being refused by a prom invitee. But it's not really a genuinely masculine act of hooky—Dad has arranged this all with the principal, his Kiwanis buddy.

The prom episode is my life in miniature. Much of my life will involve courting the hypermasculine to excuse or mask a feeling of unmasculine inadequacy: flying airplanes—fueled by fantasies of screaming down the railroad tracks 18 inches off the ground hopping the semaphore signals. A plane crash I walked away from, the crumpled plane totaled, upside down. Mountain climbing, mostly solo in my younger years. Being 500 feet up a face in a chimney that starts to collapse; my only chance is to climb up faster than it collapses till I get to an escape ledge—then standing on the precipice shuddering in relief still to be alive. (That was age twenty. Later, in my forties I go back in my lonesomeness to climb the mountain by an easier route, go out on the escape ledge and look down. I don't believe I did it. I had to be crazy. . . . I *was* crazy.) Going native with the Masaii in East Africa. Sneaking into the Sudan, when I couldn't get a visa for legal entry, by hollowed-out log at flood time, getting shipwrecked and taking refuge in an Anuak village. Doping up the village chief with paregoric to make him think we were curing his tertiary syphilis—thereby buying his protection, refuge and safety in the jungle. Climbing the 45-degree ice cap of the fifth highest peak in North America and freezing my feet; ripping off the black dead skin from my toes, tossing the pieces out the window, and gulping sulfa drugs as my brother and I ride back to Mexico City in a rickety bus filled with peasants and poultry. Drinking heavily—like a man, and to cope. (Habitual, not alcoholic, drinking; when I finally decided to stop poisoning my body it was very easy to stop drinking.) Urban pioneering in downtown Washington, D.C., in the midst of the main prostitution and heroin area. Taking on the whores, pimps and pushers in open warfare. We wrestle down a hooker who is blowing her john in my basement stairwell, assaulting her, and then have *her* arrested and charged with assault. Farming. And years of affairs, orgies, sexual adventuresomeness of every sort. (As Elton John said when asked about his sexuality, "I draw the line at goats.") All efforts at hypermasculinity—all betrayed by a self-image that told me I was less than a real man. These ultimately were desperate efforts to grasp authenticity. But they were too deliberate, too contrived to be authentic. Always the outsider never feeling he belonged, always going through the motions. Experiences were like skills to be acquired; jack of all trades, master of none.

But had life remained this frantic oscillation between hypermasculine exercises and aching self-doubt, it might have proved empty but sustainably viable. Then I met someone who wanted me. I fell head over heels in love. We became lovers. In my insecurity I tried to be what I thought my lover wanted and bear full responsibility for his happiness. I evidenced most of the sociopathic marks of pseudointimacy.

> We see that these very skills we believe should promote intimacy are, indeed, used to avoid intimacy. . . . The following are some of the skills used to form pseudo-(addictive) relationships. . . .
>
> To be able consistently to lay aside your own needs for the sake of the relationship.
>
> To know how to "take care of" the other person and quickly move in to meet his or her needs.
>
> To know how to foster dependency and how to "attach" to the other in a dependent way.
>
> To know how to "compromise" personal needs, values, ethics, or morality for the relationship. . . .
>
> To have the skills (imagined) and desire to "save" the other person from the life he or she has constructed. . . .
>
> To be able to ignore aspects of the person you do not trust or like.
>
> To be able to ignore unshared values, hopes, and fears and see the other only through the eyes of illusion.
>
> To be able to accept blame and fault for anything that goes wrong in the relationship.

To be able to "hang in there" long past the point of sanity. . . .
To have the ability to accept jealousy as an indication of true love. . . .
To be able to suffer endlessly for the relationship. . . .
We have been taught that these skills lead to relationships when, in fact, they lead
one into addictive pseudo-relationships.[22]

It was an exercise in inauthenticity driven by fear of rejection. But I couldn't be totally inauthentic. There was also me, my work. So I oscillated between the two. This unhealthy relationship lasted nearly two painful decades.

Paradoxically, one good thing that happened in my disastrous, often unhealthy relationship, was my return to Christianity by converting to Catholicism in 1973.

The fire, the cross, packs of wild beasts, lacerations, renderings, wrenchings of bones,
mangling of limbs, crushing of the whole body, the horrible tortures of the devil—let all
these things come upon me, if only I may gain Jesus Christ![23]

On visits to my lover's parents, where attending Mass was obligatory, I came to know and appreciate the Mass. Eventually I fell in love with the Mass, and began attending the parish nearby our home. The priest there gave a particularly beautiful Mass and was one of the best homilists I have heard. Gradually we came to know him. Increasingly I wanted to participate fully in the Mass as a communicant—not just be an inauthentic spectator. But our sex practices were morally condemned by the church in *Humanae Vita* and other teachings, and thus were an impediment. The philosopher in me took over; I read the relevant moral theology. I came to the conclusion that a theological case could be made for the moral legitimacy of our relationship if modeled on monogamous marriage. By then the priest and I were good enough friends that I could put the following proposition to him: If I could make a strong case that my moral dissent from the church's sexual teachings was within the limits of acceptable informed theological dissent, could I be confirmed while I remained unrepentant and recalcitrant in the relationship? He discussed it with his Bishop, and the dialogue was begun on the issue—but no promises given with respect to my request. So instead of the usual catechetical instruction, we entered into a mix of instruction combined with serious moral theological dispute—which went on weekly for several years.

I became knowledgeable and adept at moral and systematic theology, mounting a case that nonprocreative sexual acts need not automatically constitute an objectively grave matter when done in a monogamous, permanent, loving relationship; that the traditional exegesis of scriptural passages seemingly condemnatory of nonprocreative practices were not (for example, the sin of Onan was not masturbation, but failure to perform a filial duty), that a relationship such as ours even could fall under the sacrament of marriage,[24] and so on. The position I articulated and defended in most respects was a close anticipation of one later put forward by a blue-ribbon committee of the Catholic Theological Society of America.[25] I made the case for my stance being within the scope of the *then* acceptable range of theological dissent. (In the later theologically more restrictive regime of Pope John Paul II and Cardinal Ratzinger, this study was to be condemned by the Vatican, as was Charles Curran's defense of masturbation not invariably being an objectively grave matter, which also figured importantly in my defense.)

Still there was no agreement to confirm me. Finally, a Vatican II reform came into play: under certain circumstances a Bishop can delegate to another priest involved in the adult conversion experience the power to confirm. The Bishop, who apparently was unwilling to set precedent by confirming me so long as I persisted in my theologically defended dissent from traditional Catholic moral teaching, granted this extraordinary permission, and I was confirmed at Mass, the Bishop absent, in February 1973—just after turning thirty-three. My confirmation name was Michael—he "who would be like God."

My lover, who remained a lapsed Catholic and seemed threatened by my participation in the full sacramental life of the church, soon began to engage in, and bring to my attention, promiscuous infidelities. I was tempted to end the relationship (though that was incompatible with an aspect of the defense I'd mounted in joining the church as dissident), but in my insecurity and fear that I was really unlovable I decided I'd rather share him than be alone. I also consulted my priest (who by then had been transferred to another parish). He advised me to leave the relationship, arguing that my lover was so immature and had such an undeveloped moral sense and conscience that no semblance of a real marriage had ever existed.[26] I resisted this advice, feeling that to act on it would have made a sham of the way I joined the church. (This was one of many opportunities to get out of the relationship of which I failed to take advantage.) So I forgave and excused the infidelities, but insisted that the relationship remain monogamous on my side.

But this was not sufficient. Pressure increasingly was put on me to join in promiscuous infidelities. With matters unresolved we moved to Washington, D.C., and in our new parish encountered a sexually active priest who had a lover and encouraged us in promiscuity.

> *But now I feel obliged to write and encourage you to fight hard for the faith delivered once for all to the saints. Certain individuals have recently wormed their way into your midst, godless types. . . . They pervert the gracious gift of our God to sexual excess. (Jude 4, NAB 1970)[27]*

Despite the fact that doing so was blatantly incompatible with the theological position on which my joining the church was predicated, I took his and another errant priest's advice as permission, and eventually gave in as a means of reducing the mounting pressure to swing, which increasingly was destroying the harmony of the relationship. I came to enjoy the orgiastic activity, and became seduced by the pleasures of the flesh sufficiently that I didn't worry about theological scruples.

> *Sin speaks to the sinner*
> *in the depth of his heart.*
> *There is no fear of God*
> *before his eyes.*
> *He so flatters himself in his mind that*
> *he knows not his guilt. (Ps 36:1-3)[28]*

After all, with my priest friends distributing communion and encouraging us in our promiscuity, I didn't have to decide between the two.

At the same time I was very busy with building up the Maryland philosophy department and with starting the history and philosophy of science program there. I was gone a lot—interviewing candidates and the like, and my lover, unhappy in an overly demanding, highly respon-

sible job, was abandoned alone nights and increasingly turned to marijuana to cope. Some bad dope, which unbeknownst to him had been
laced with PCP, resulted in a psychotic breakdown and many months
of full-time hospitalization, followed by eighteen months of day hospital. In the initial stages of hospitalization I continued to go to Mass
and cut out the promiscuous activity. But as weekend passes from the
hospital became frequent, and going to Mass was agitating and counterproductive to the cure, I didn't attend on the weekends we were
together. Attendance at Mass became more and more infrequent as
passes became regular. Eventually Mass became a thing of the past.

It was no dramatic, decisive decision to leave the Church. Rather, it
was as Father Dowling once observed: "The erosion that precedes the
major moral lapse is seldom publicly visible. Characters dissolve much
as they are built up, by a slow accumulation of seemingly unimportant
deeds."[29]

Eventually we reactivated our promiscuous lifestyle in a dizzying
sequence of one-night stands and orgies. As our relationship moved
along its counterproductive course, doing immeasurable harm to both
of us, I gradually moved from nonpracticing to nonbelieving, and eventually to positive disbelief. Toward the end I became an atheist, and
viewed the very possibility of eternal life as a bad joke.

> It might be grim and deadly, but at least it was free from the Christian God. . . . Some
> people . . . will find it hard to understand why this seemed to me such an overwhelming
> advantage. . . . I was . . . far more eager to escape pain than to achieve happiness, and
> feeling it something of an outrage that I had been created without my own permission.
> To such a craven the materialist's universe had the enormous attraction that it offered
> you limited liabilities. No strictly infinite disaster could overtake you in it. Death ended
> all. . . . The horror of the Christian universe was that it had no door marked Exit.[30]

Thus I prayed that God not exist. "The fool has said in his heart, 'There
is no God above' " (Ps 53:1).

Philosophers delude themselves into thinking their craft is one of
ratiocination. *Rationalization* is a more accurate description. For unfath-
omable reasons one stakes out one's philosophical position and *then*
seeks arguments in its defense—to rationalize the previously determined conviction. Oh, we dress it up by engaging in self-deceiving

dialectic wherein the attempt to rationalize the belief is refined, altered in usually insubstantial ways. As much as possible we try to avoid biting the bullet.

As I look back at the episode of becoming a Catholic on my terms and then the gradual compromise of that position as I slid along a path of degeneracy into atheism, I am struck by how thoroughly I was deluded by my own rationalizations. To begin with, I wanted an *easy* entree to Catholicism. I wanted to be a Catholic on *my* moral terms. I'd decided to be a smorgasbord Catholic—to pick and choose what I want of what the Church has to offer in the way of morality and doctrine.[31] But in my hubris *I* simultaneously wanted the Church's imprimatur on my choice. Then, having received a closer approximation to that approval than one could reasonably hope, I proceeded to alter the position in a process of progressively more self-deluding rationalizations. As my sexual practices became more libertine, and as my faith declined, I developed new arguments rationalizing the rejection of more and more of Catholic sexual morality and the rationalization of an increasingly more libertine lifestyle. I joined the cult of self-actualizing pleasure, arguing that promiscuity was the path to morality.

It was, after all, the age of sexual liberation. I joined in what C. S. Lewis calls

"chronological snobbery," the uncritical acceptance of the intellectual climate common to our own age and the assumption that whatever has gone out of date is on that account discredited. You must find out why it went out of date. Was it ever refuted (and if so by whom, where, and how conclusively) or did it merely die away as fashions do? If the latter, this tells us nothing about its truth or falsehood. From seeing this, one passes to the realization that our own age is also "a period," and certainly has, like all periods, its own characteristic illusions. They are likeliest to lurk in those widespread assumptions which are so ingrained in the age that no one dares to attack or feels it necessary to defend them.[32]

Open marriage was the cure—never bothering to pay much attention to what it was supposed to cure. I believed Jean Genet when he said that one could achieve sainthood through perfecting one's twisted nature in an orgy of self-actualizing perversion.[33]

If all philosophy is rationalization, wherein lies its objectivity? If ratiocination is not feasible, wherein lies the philosophical proof? Philosophical proof is like proving the metal content of coins. One puts it to the test—via philosophical counterargument. Philosophers wrangle, attack, as means to putting philosophies to the hard test. But when the ideas are the characteristic illusions of a period—as they were in the pre-AIDS, preherpes, penicillin-sustained days of sexual liberty of the 1960s and early 1970s—there is little philosophical proof undergone. "Philosophy and Sex" emerged as a field, but it was an exercise in self-indulgent liberation. Only repressive ideas were put to the proof. The libertine was left unchallenged. And so my emerging "sexual morality" was left unchallenged, which is to say embraced but unproved—except in the crucible of my own relationship. Curiously, though, it did keep the relationship alive, it prolonged the unavoidable eventual termination. Only after we abandoned sexual promiscuity and limited our gratification—sexual and otherwise—to each other did it eventually suffocate in monogamous contempt for each other.

I enjoyed the sexual freedom I had rationalized. In a sense it *was* liberating. Promiscuity provided a means of intimacy without the full baggage of a relationship, and I learned to place limited demands on intimate involvements. ("This isn't love, it's just for tonight.") And it seemed to be evidence of desirability. A one-night stand counters poor self-image, saying, "You're desirable." One conveniently ignores the fact that one's partner usually was picked up at closing time in a bar— "trash call"—a mutual act of inebriated desperation, where one held on to one's remaining shreds of self-esteem by going home with somebody, anybody, rather than risk the rejection of going home alone.

After some years the promiscuity grew stale. And an allergy to penicillin discovered in anaphylactic shock while being treated for a dose of the clap changed the odds. This, together with the specter of herpes (AIDS was not yet an issue), made me face up to the desperation of the whole routine, the ritualized impersonal sex—where a quickie in a corner was better than going home with somebody *because* it could be completely impersonal. ("Wham, bam, thank you ma'am.") I stopped the sexual adventuresomeness and became monogamous. Increasingly both of us stayed home—and destroyed each other. Clutched, clawed, in claustrophobic intimacy that became less and less physical, more and more mutually self-destructive.

> "The NT [person] . . . can become involved with . . . [persons] who might be totally unsuitable as life companions."[34]

Eventually we left the city, the gentrification jungle of restoration Washington, and moved out to a farm in the country, where we were trying to keep the relationship alive, commercially farm, and live a life of self-reliant self-sufficiency in accordance with the simple life philosophies.[35] (Or at least I was. Exactly what my lover was doing with art collection, fur coat, household of fine antiques, and 135 pieces of stemware I'm not sure.) It was, for me, the last chance I was willing to give the relationship.

However, the relationship continued to deteriorate as everything associated with me became a focus of hostile spousal reaction. The aftermath of visits from my family became dreadful exercises in recriminating rehashings of events; the price exacted for visits, or even long-distance intimacies with my family, became too high. So gradually I distanced and alienated myself from them. Fewer visits, fewer calls.

I long ago had ceased drinking as a means of coping. The university office was 131 miles away, and my normal two-night stays there lengthened to five or six per week. I'd come home for the long weekends, stay until I could stand it no longer, and then flee back to campus. Summer vacation was coming up, and I knew a summer of living together and farming wasn't viable. I realize I have to get away, in prolonged separation, if I am to get through the summer.

So I plan a long, cheap vacation (farming left us very tight financially): supersaver to California, hitch a ride to the Sierras, go backpacking for twenty-one days alone—175 miles, 40 of them cross-country high above the timberline. I luxuriate in my aloneness, resenting it when, most days, I encounter people. I trek alone; climb solo (my first serious climbing in over twenty years) up the Minarets by crampons and ice axe, back to Michael Minaret and the small glacial lake there, visiting Pete Starr's tomb about the anniversary of his solo death by fall on Michael Minaret. I climb another Minaret solo, but turn back 50 feet from the summit when things get too exposed in gusting 50 mph winds to take the unroped risk of a 1000-foot fall to the glacier below. Finally I'm tired of being in the wilderness, tired of trying to be alone. I've had my catharsis.

I come out of the wilderness, return to the farm in Virginia, and am welcomed home with the message that the relationship is over, liquidation of the livestock and other joint assets is in progress to cover resettlement costs. I do not resist this. For the first time I do not try to hold on to the relationship. I give in with relief. We draw up formal separation papers, documents for dissolving the farm business and other joint holdings, and prepare to part. The actual breaking up is the only amicable, cooperative thing we've done in months. I stay on the farm, alone. Just me, the dogs, the barn cats, two peacocks—and a Percheron mare I am to try to sell, which I do. So many years together . . . Increasingly I look on them as a total loss. I worked hard the first year not to come out of it hating my ex—and I succeed. Later I will come to a more balanced assessment.

The spring before the breakup I had developed numbness in my fingers and toes. By the time I returned from my solo trek in the Sierras it had become chronic. So in the midst of winding down the relationship I finally seek medical attention for this condition—and for a referral for some elective plastic surgery. The numbness takes priority over the surgery as my physician fears Amyotrophic Lateral Sclerosis (my father had died from ALS and there is a slight tendency for it to run in families) and I quickly am sent to neurological specialists. They preclude ALS, but the prime candidates become muscular dystrophy, AIDS and others in a litany of progressive, degenerative, nonreversible diseases. Adult-onset diabetes is the faint ray of hope. One can at least live with that! I endure endless lab tests to preclude heavy metal poisoning and other esoteric possibilities, hideous sessions of nerve conductivity studies (where electroshocks are sent down individual nerve fibers and travel time recorded) and probes stuck deep into muscle mass while computers graph responses as I twitch my impaled muscles. Finally all known aetiologies are precluded and a nonspecific diagnosis is obtained: small fiber neuropathy with attendant loss of myopathic functioning. That is, my peripheral small nerve fibers are misfiring, resulting in degeneration (necrosis?) of muscle tissues. No prognosis. "Wait six months to see if it's stable and come back." I'm unwilling to go the way my Dad did. Suicide becomes an eventual possibility. I get a copy of the Hemlock Society handbook for "do it yourself euthanasia"[36] but deliberately don't read it. I resolve not to read it until things get bad. Don't want to be morbid about all this.

I resolve to do positive things: I change my courses for the next semester so they can be easily covered if I don't live out the semester. Since I no longer was farming, I'd exercise to build up my muscles; strengthen those fibers that weren't dead to compensate for those that were. How? Hike—every week, for miles in the nearby mountains. Back to the wilderness for rejuvenating strength. I take the dogs with me.

What was it about the mountains that drew him? . . . To go to the mountains was to face God.[37]

Not so, not yet. A more elaborate plan evolves as I recall the exposed fall potential that turned me back on that Minaret: start serious rock/ ice climbing again. Not just for the exercise. But also to lay a basis for an eventual suicide being ruled an accident. (There was $200,000 of life insurance at stake.) Establish a history of high-risk sports. Then if an "accident" (either genuine, due to degeneration of nerves and muscle leading to unreliable performance, or deliberate) occurred . . .

With no prognosis there is no obvious impediment to having the elective plastic surgery. I obtain clearance and schedule surgery for over Thanksgiving break. My ex's final departure is behind schedule due to delays in closing on a new house and occurs the day I undergo surgery. In preparation I prepare an "If I die" letter for my department chairman, giving detailed instructions about completing my classes, finals and so forth, in case the admittedly low risk of not surviving should happen (the general anesthesia was the principal risk). I don't believe in God, but I'm prepared to risk dying, and I go into surgery remarkably calm. And why not? It's an alternative to suicide and I don't have much to live for anyway.

I survive. The plastic surgery is a success. My self-image improves dramatically. Furthermore, by use of Mill's methods I determine that phenylalanine (the most common artificial sweetener) is the cause of my neurological problems. I double-check this, making the numbness come and go at will, cut it out of my diet, and things remit. I don't go back to the neurologists.

Thoughts of eventual suicide are put aside, but the reawakened interest in climbing remains. No longer fueled by fear of crippling disease or earlier insecurities, climbing becomes a real passion. I begin to climb sixty-five to seventy days a year. My arms and shoulders take on a definition and hardness they never had in the most athletic days of my youth. Soon I am climbing at a much higher standard than I did in my youth. Climbing becomes just joyous celebration, fun, a delight—a frivolously entertaining form of exercise. I climb everywhere—the High Sierras, Yosemite, Tuolumne, Joshua Tree, Big Rocks, Tahquitz and Suicide Rocks in California; Seneca Rocks, West Virginia; Cannon Cliff, Cathedral Ledge, Whitehorse Ledge and other locations in New Hampshire; Stone Mountain, North Carolina; City of Rocks, Idaho; the Tetons, Freemont Canyon, Dome Rock and Devil's Tower, Wyoming; Devil's Lake in Wisconsin; the Needles and Mt. Rushmore of South Dakota; the Shawangunks in New York; Jackson Falls, Illinois; obscure bluffs in Rhode Island. I do my first big wall, do Lost Arrow Spire with its scary Tyrolean traverse finish 3000 feet above Yosemite, do classic extreme-difficulty frozen-waterfall ice climbs in the east. Constantly challenging myself. What might I be trying to prove to myself now?

Reconciliation

When one dissolves an encompassing relationship of many years, one exits with the awareness that one has absolutely no idea what one's new life will be. The only surety is that whatever hesitant plans are made in dreaded anticipation are totally unreliable. Thus as I exited our relationship I had no idea that I would resume climbing with serious intensity, that I would enter into one of the most productive periods in my scholarly career, that I would rebuild family ties and become the closest I had been since fleeing home at eighteen, that I would reconcile with the Church with encompassing intensity, that I would attempt to combine faith and my philosophy in a productive synthesis. These became the central ingredients of my postrelationship life—a life that found me the happiest I had been in almost thirty years. In many ways it is a lifestyle rather parallel to those most happy earlier days in the desert: living by myself where I spend much of my time alone, but with interesting people nearby with whom I am somewhat close; religion a part of my life; lots of physical activity including climbing; doing challenging work I like. As I had no desires for another relationship, this sort of life looked to me especially sustainable.

The renewal of family ties and the philosophical renaissance are not particularly surprising. My reconversion and return to the Church are more so. Indeed, my reconciliation with the Church was quite involuntary and took me by surprise. Yet when I related the reconversion episode, a colleague who himself was in the process of becoming a Christian said he had seen it coming. And indeed it had been. The fall of the breakup with the specter of death hanging over me, my longtime friend Ernan McMullin, a philosopher of science and a priest, visited for a series of talks at Maryland. I wanted to talk to him about what was going on morally in the Catholic Church. I was concerned about the climate of growing theological repression that surrounded the Curran case at nearby Catholic University. (I'd discussed this earlier with Father William Wallace, who knew the Catholic University situation at first hand.) I had kept up enough with Catholic moral theology to know that the lines of theological argument I had used earlier to join the church as a dissident no longer were within the limits of acceptable theological dissent, that the specifics—including Curran's position on masturbation not inevitably being an objectively grave matter since it was not inevitably an act of alienation between man and God, hence not inevitably a mortal sin—of that prior defense had been explicitly condemned by the Vatican.

I did not desire another sexual relationship. Having quit drinking many years before, and quit smoking five years before, masturbation not only had become my sole sexual outlet, it was a main technique of stress reduction. (I now understand the coping strategies of the entwined couples at Pompeii petrified in the ashes spewed from Mt. Vesuvius.) In the aftermath of my separation I was under the worst stress of my life. I saw no prospect of abandoning the masturbation practice;

but also I saw no viable theological avenue to its legitimization left within Catholicism. Not even some tricky principle-of-double-effect argument seemed availing. Masturbation in fact was the chief impediment to my reconciliation with the church, but at the time I wasn't aware of the fact. My overt concerns were more intellectualized as I tried to talk abstractly about it with Ernan. But reconciliation was the real hidden and unacknowledged agenda.

The discussion was not terribly satisfactory as I intellectualized the issue, and it really was outside Ernan's particular expertise or interest as scholar-priest. That there was an underlying pastoral concern did not come through, and no progress was made on removing the impediment. One thing did transpire, though—an invitation to come to Notre Dame the following February to give a talk and a colloquium coupled with some archival work on the Amish at Goshen College in the historical collections and the archives of the Mennonite Church. (This work pertained to a course on the simple life and Jeffersonian agrarian philosophies I had been giving at Maryland—an outgrowth of my own exercises in simple, agrarian life. My attraction to the ascetic here had taken a secular manifestation. Indeed, I was interested intellectually in the extent to which such a life could be divorced from its Christian origins—to whether a secular rationale could be substituted.)

I went to Notre Dame. I lunched with Ernan and Michael Buckley, S.J., a theologian who was then Executive Director of the Committee on Doctrine for the National Conference of Catholic Bishops. A week or so before, Pope John Paul II had given a speech declaring *all* questions of traditional Catholic moral teaching on sexual matters outside the bounds of legitimate theological debate. Again, without consciously realizing that the real agenda was its threat to my reconciliation, I asked what was going on. I thought it was a theological question I was asking—something about changing claims on the status of Encyclicals— but Michael's response was political. "Let's see, that speech was written by Mngr. Cafarra . . . I wonder what he's up to?" After doing my archival work at Goshen, I returned to Notre Dame Saturday evening. Sunday I went to Mass at Sacred Heart Church on campus to see what was reputed to be a particularly elegant, aesthetic Mass with fine music in one of the most impressive large churches in America, and to watch

Ernan concelebrate it. I told myself it was the aesthetic experience I sought, for I long had loved the choral and organ religious works and the poetry and ceremony of a well-celebrated Mass. I was very much taken by the Mass that day, very moved and caught up in it. It was an unbelievable high. The Gospel reading was the parable of the prodigal son. I felt I belonged. Then, as *everybody*—except me, it seemed—went up to take communion, I experienced the most profound feeling of alienation and emptiness I ever have experienced in my life. I felt absolutely abandoned. I experienced what hell permanently must be like. I was profoundly disturbed.

God was calling me back to the church!

> *Late have I loved you. . . . In my unlovingness, I plunged into the lovely things you created. You were with me but I was not with you. . . . You touched me, and I burned for your peace.*—St. Augustine[38]

I wrestled with it. I wondered if it was just the aesthetics of the Mass. Was it a genuine call? That night I attended an exquisite performance of the Duruflé *Requiem* in Sacred Heart Church; a 6 a.m. simple Mass the next day; other Masses. Finally I entered the confessional. It was the most terrifying thing I'd ever done. More terrifying than facing the possibility of a slow, degenerative, hideous death had been. I knelt. Trembling I said, "Forgive me Father for I have sinned. It has been well over a decade since I last went to confession." How to confess so many years of debauchery and sin in a confessional line before Mass?

> *"But you have sinned with many lovers, and yet you would return to me!" says the Lord.* (Jer 3:1)

I simply said, "My principal sin has been total alienation from God. All my other sins are attendant upon that." A blunt, general confession.

The priest asked a few questions. I indicated the general nature of my disastrous relationship and its role in that alienation, and that the relationship had been terminated. Granting absolution and setting penance, the priest wisely remarked that there was much more going on here than could be dealt with adequately in the brief time available to us. The most crucial thing was to rebuild my extremely fragile refound faith. My penance: find a priest who I could talk to at length on how to rebuild that faith. I walked out—to find Mass just beginning. It was the fifth Mass I'd been to in forty-eight hours. I took Communion.

Then I contacted Ernan, as he knew the background to my situation fairly well, and asked him to be the priest with whom to satisfy my penance. Ernan cleared his loaded calendar to give me the entire next morning, and we met in my room at the Morris Inn on campus. I related what had happened. He responded, "I've always been a firm believer in Divine Providence." It was exactly what I needed to hear at that moment. Ernan's concern was in part that there most likely would be limited spiritual resources in my rural Protestant community (with one Catholic mission parish for 512 square miles).[39] He advised me to involve myself in weekday Mass while on campus in the city, where there would be richer resources. He also advised me to become involved in the life of a parish. Then he said, "You're like me, Fred. You can't separate your personal and professional interests. You've got to bring them together some way." He suggested that I read in the sacramental theology literature and also on the historic Jesus for a start. The latter topic caught me by surprise. I'd reconciled with the Church and God. Only with his suggestion did it hit me that Jesus was involved too. I bought out the bookstore in these areas, and Ernan gave me a copy of E. P. Sanders's magnificent *Jesus and Judaism*[40] as a starter.

Soon I began to work on *a posteriori* religious knowledge and its relationship to scientific knowledge from the perspective of my own quasi-realistic account of science.[41] As an outgrowth of the reading Ernan had set for me in sacramental theology I drafted a paper on the metaphysics and epistemology of transubstantiation, which I later presented at Notre Dame and to the Society of Christian Philosophers. Later I would spend a sabbatical year studying patristics, St. Thomas, and spiritual and systematic theology while Senior Scholar in the Notre Dame Center for Philosophy of Religion. Gradually my reading and thinking expanded to include the spiritual and systematic theology literatures. I would reactivate the long untaught "Topics in Philosophical Theology" course at Maryland. My first topic: Christian concepts of spiritual perfection and their ancient precursors. I had taken Ernan's advice to combine my religious and my professional life with a vengeance.

But I had worked equally hard on rebuilding my faith. Quickly I became a daily communicant—whether in the city or out on the farm. I became active in the life of my local parish, made friends, and to my surprise found extremely rich spiritual resources there. I prayed regularly, prayed from the *Liturgy of the Hours*, regularly kept Ernan appraised of my progress, and solicited his advice. Six weeks after my reconciliation I wrote Ernan the first of several long progress reports.

> My faith is becoming rich, fecund, and the dominant force in my life. And it is a faith in a 2 1/2 personage Godhead (I still don't relate to the Holy Spirit as a personage—though it is very real to me as a force emanating from God . . .). The last couple of days there has come into me an inner joy—hard to describe, hard to contain—I can't recall ever having before. It came during morning Mass yesterday and it hasn't left. I'm so blessed happy! It had elements of being a kind of personal Pentecost—though I'm not speaking in tongues.

That inner joy has become a recurrent event. Sometimes I leave Mass feeling as if I am walking a foot off the ground. I went on to report that "Although it now is to the point I am enjoying being a Christian a lot, it's been a lot of hard work—very hard work—getting to this point, and I continue to work very hard at becoming increasingly more Christlike and at one with God." Ernan was a good spiritual advisor, crucially helpful in rebuilding my faith. My efforts at spiritual progress were noticed in my parish, and some months later I was invited to become a lay eucharistic minister. A strong faith integrated into my daily routine rapidly was emerging.

My colleague Allen Stairs and I talked about my reconversion experience, and we began meeting weekly for a Christian discussion/dinner together. Allen was exploring his way toward eventually becoming confirmed as an Episcopalian. We reinforced each other's efforts. We discussed Christianity around the office as well, and others began to join in the debate. A remarkable transformation occurred at the department as a result. Colleagues previously hostile to religion began to bite their tongues. Some graduate students came to me to discuss issues of faith. One said, "Since I respect you very much as a philosopher, I have to take your belief seriously. Tell me about your faith." Religious content began to show up as examples in classes—not just Allen's and my own. Later I would direct a senior honors thesis on Sts. Thomas Aquinas's and John of the Cross's treatments of faith and reason and introduce Christian theology into the University's curriculum.

The Resurrection Continues
Gradually my faith strengthened. To follow Christ is to be truly transformed.

> We were indeed buried with him through baptism into death, so that, just as Christ was raised from the dead by the glory of the Father, we too might live in newness of life. . . . We know that the old self was crucified with him. (Rom 6:4, 6)

But to follow Christ is not to undergo a single act of conversion or reconversion. The crucifixion of ourselves is an ongoing process. The only end to a conversion story is the timeless finale of the City of God where one will bask eternally in the Beatific Vision. Where to bring my tale to an end when there is no natural stopping point to my story? Perhaps it will suffice to note the struggles that have come with deepening faith.

Relationship to my father. How as a Christian do I relate to my father who abused me yet loved me? Earlier I noted that I had dealt with this by praying for his soul at Mass. God did not long indulge me such easy resolution. I had arranged an eight-day retreat over Thanksgiving 1990, to work on abandonment of self-will to God. There it proved to be God's will that I confront the scars of abuse and my relationship to my father in what proved to be a remarkably intense retreat. Through the presence of the Holy Spirit, under the aid of extraordinary spiritual direction, I became able to view the abuse suffered at my father's hands as a gift *of* God[42] for which I should and could be grateful. Then through extremely vivid imaging exercises I neutralized the memories of his abuse and my attempting to kill him, and reduced the memories of good times with him to realistic proportions—thereby emotionally putting the abuse behind me and reducing my father to occupying a modest positive place in my psyche. The next step was to go to his grave two days after Christmas. There I talked to him, telling him how much he had screwed up my life and my older brother's. I told him that his behavior had been despicable. All this was put matter-of-factly and without discernible anger. But I also told him, genuinely and honestly, that I forgave him, that I'd come to see his abuse as a gift of God. And that I prayed daily for his soul. I tried to say, "I love you," but couldn't make the words come out. I prayed to God that forgiving him would be enough. God said no, and some months later through the aid of the Holy Spirit I finally came to say, with conviction, "I love you, Dad. Despite all you did to me."

Asceticism. Nevertheless, many scars of abuse remain. I fled home at eighteen to get away from the abuse. When you are abused you are made to feel guilty about it, that you *deserve* to be abused. I needed to be abused, and I found a lover who could take my father's place as abuser. Indeed, I sometimes wonder whether I made him into an abuser to fill my needs. Finally the relationship ended after extracting great costs from both of us. Could I, after thirty-two aggregate years of abuse, now make a life free of abuse? I am drawn to the dark side of Christianity, to penitential practices and Christian asceticism. Are these surrogates for abuse? Am I attempting to make God and the church my next abusers? If not, why do I have so much trouble identifying with the love message of the Gospels?

My sexuality. My return to the church did nothing to resolve my theological problems over masturbation. It is clear to me that had such intellectual resolution been the sole path to my reconciliation, it never would have happened. Philosophy is a terrible way *to* faith. God called me, and preempted the philosophical/theological issues. I obeyed. I had no choice. But, as I rebuilt my faith, what to do? I vacillated. Sometimes I tried not to masturbate. Sometimes I tried to argue that since I wasn't convinced it was sinful it was OK. But I also was acutely aware that when I first converted to Catholicism I did so on *my* terms, and the result was a weak faith that didn't last. Philosophy increasingly loomed in my mind as a threat to faith if I allowed faith to be subordinate to it. Finally I said, "This time I buy the whole thing, without reservation or hesitation." Part of the attraction of Catholicism is that it is a hard, demanding morality. I didn't know if the church's teaching on masturbation was morally binding on me or not. But I decided to preempt the issue. "I'll take a vow of chastity—and that will settle the issue." I did.

I subordinated my philosophy to my faith.

This worked for several years as my faith strengthened. But then God again refused to let me take the easy way out. I am a sexual being, created in God's image. And it proves inauthentic and unhealthy repression merely to deny that aspect of my being. Restudying the Church's teachings on human sexuality convinces me of the soundness of my earlier critiques of her supporting argumentation. But the libertine sexual morality I earlier championed now strikes me as no better. Again philosophy proves impotent. I turn away from philosophical analysis and speculation to prayer as I struggle to learn how to integrate my sexuality into the Christ-following life, as I seek a healthy Christian perspective on my sexuality. My problem is not one of unwillingness to follow God's will. It is one of discerning what that will is.

Gradually I have come to repudiate the homophobia I flirted with earlier in my reconciliation with the Church. Unchristian lack of charity toward homosexuals and homosexuality constitutes an unacceptable accommodation of my sexuality within the gospel message. Increasingly I fear that this essay will be misappropriated as a vehicle of oppression by "Christian" homophobes bent on perverting Christ's message of love into a campaign of hate.

Can I confront and struggle with these deeply existential and spiritual issues surrounding my sexuality without jeopardizing or losing my faith? Will the Church allow me to?

Philosophy and faith. Repeatedly since reconciliation I had subordinated my philosophy to my faith. Yet Ernan has advised me to integrate the two. Bas van Fraassen, also a convert to Catholicism, and I have had several searching talks about this issue. We agree that philosophy, especially philosophical theology, *is* hazardous to faith. (Atheism may be even more an occupational hazard for theologians than philosophers.) But Ernan *is* correct: as a matter of psychological fact, *I* cannot separate philosophy from what is important to me in life. I have no choice but to integrate the two. The issue becomes, How to do so without jeopardizing my faith?

My early efforts involved praying to St. Thomas, who so effectively combined the two, for intercession.

Just as bread is nourishment for the body and virtue for the soul, so is spiritual prayer nourishment for the intellect.—Ponticus[43]

They also involved subordinating the philosophy to my faith. I have begun work on the metaphysics and epistemology of Catholic dogma. Fortunately, for Catholics there is a "truth of the matter" here to be accommodated. If I want to do the metaphysics of transubstantiation, six *de fide* principles must be accommodated and three *sententia certa* ones are not lightly to be rejected. These become design constraints on my philosophical work. The issue becomes, Can I do a metaphysical and epistemological analysis fully consistent with these design constraints? If so, I succeed. If not, the failure is mine—I wasn't clever enough to pull off the design problem. Such failure is a comment on me and my performance, not a threat to the dogma or the faith. My priorities here seem in order, and thus the threat to my faith minimal. In the moral arena there is no such firmly established body of dogma (indeed there is great controversy as to how binding even Encyclicals are); perhaps sometime later my faith will be powerful enough to enable me to work in the moral theology arena without spiritual threat. But that is a long way off. I'm still rebuilding my faith.

There remains a far deeper, more profound threat from philosophy that I have completely failed to resolve. As a philosopher I am a system-builder who, like Kant, wants to tackle the big issues—full-blown metaphysical and epistemological systems. To take on such projects, to persevere in them, to publish one's results as I am doing for *a posteriori* and scientific knowledge in *Facts, Theories, and Scientific Observation*—these seemingly require one giant ego to fuel the whole process. Despite all my self-doubts typical of an INTJ personality, my ego has proved adequate to the task so far. But such egomania is quite at odds with the sort of Christian I want to be. One of my greatest failings as a Christian is insufficient humility.

Is humility psychologically compatible with philosophical productivity—productivity that so far has been fueled by one obnoxiously outsized yet highly insecure ego? Part of the personality profile of the INTJ bordering on the INTP is

a recalcitrance . . . —even from an early age—to accept without question in the domain of ideas even a widely accepted authority. . . . This recalcitrance to established authority tends to make [them] . . . seem unusually individualistic and even arrogant.

[They] often report . . . that they are haunted by a sense of always being on the verge of failure. . . . Constant self-doubt is the[ir] lot. . . .

Once caught up in a thought process, that thought process seems to have a will of its own, . . . and they persevere until the issue is comprehended in all its complexity. They can be intellectual snobs and may show impatience with others less endowed intellectually. This quality . . . generates hostility and defensive behaviors on the part of others, who may describe the INTP as arrogant.[44]

It fits. Might this demon be my muse?

Twenty-two years ago I tried to quit smoking and developed a total writing block. I had to choose between not smoking and tenure. I chose tenure. Ten years ago I again quit smoking—one of the harder things I've ever done. Key to my success was a willingness to pay the price of never writing again. I was spared that price. Thomas Philippe writes, "It is very sweet to surrender to God, but also very difficult. It requires total renunciation of our intellect and reason."[45] Will the price of humility be ceasing to be a philosopher?

I try to convince myself it need not inevitably be so. St. Thomas Aquinas was by all accounts a humble man of great faith, intellect and philosophical productivity. On the advice of a confessor I have prayed many days to him that he will intercede on my behalf to utilize my intellect and philosophical talents to serve God, and to do so in a way that deepens my faith and teaches me humility. I pray that St. Thomas will intercede to let me learn that what is good in my philosophy is *God's* doing, that *I* can claim only what is inferior, confused and wrong. My prayers are beginning to be answered. I am convinced that *Facts, Theories, and Scientific Observation* is a far better book than *I* am capable of producing. Writing it thus has been extremely humbling. What is good in it clearly is *not* my work. I discussed this during confession with my Capuchin priest back home, Father Martin—a wise and holy confessor. He told me to say that—to thank God—in the preface. I do.

The idea that one might pray to St. Thomas—for whom no real

173

miracle ever has been attributed save that of the herrings—initially was mind-boggling when it was assigned to me as penance. But crazy as it all seems, it does seem to help, and I became increasingly comfortable at St. Thomas joining St. Michael the Archangel and St. Bernard of Menton as my patron saints. (Michael is my confirmation name, and St. Bernard of Menton is the patron saint of mountaineers.) I pray that I too can make some contribution *qua* philosopher to that advancement. But, to be honest, I'd settle for just deep faith and the virtue of humility.

You should put away the old self of your former way of life . . . and put on the new self, created in God's way in righteousness and holiness of truth. . . . and do not leave room for the devil. (Eph 4:22, 24, 27)

The unresolved question is whether, without a wholesale and perhaps unrealistic change of personality, I can imitate St. Thomas in combining philosophical profundity with true humility and deep faith. Perhaps it would suffice to publish my philosophico-theological contributions in Carthusian anonymity. Yet, "if any man wishes to come after me, he must deny himself" (Lk 9:23; Mt 16:24; Mk 8:34). Is anything less than total obliteration of ego and shedding of personality enough?

Philosophy thus remains a constant, profound threat to faith and humility for me, and I struggle on with the unresolved conflict.

Trusting God. The issue here in part concerns Christian perfection. Is anything less than total devotion to God[46] a form of rejecting God? Can one follow God by merely avoiding sin, or ought one strive to root out all imperfections in relentless cultivation of the theological and cardinal virtues? St. Dorotheus says, "This is the way we are. It doesn't matter how many virtues a man may have, even if they are beyond number and limit. If he has turned away from the path of self-accusation, he will never find peace."[47]

But to attempt to do more than God commands us—is that not the hubristic sin of thinking that one can *earn* one's salvation? Is it not to trivialize Jesus' agonizing hideous death on the cross in atonement for our sins? For if one can be justified by good works and cultivating the virtues then Jesus' death was gratuitously unnecessary.

Yet in no way can a man redeem himself
or pay his own ransom to God;
Too high the price to redeem one's life;
he would never have enough. (Ps 49:7-8)

I am attracted to the darker side of Catholicism. Lent is my favorite liturgical season. Penances, mortifications and denials give me comfort, a sense of security rooted in devotion to God.

Our conduct should be modeled on that of Christ dying on the cross.[48]

The fifty days of Easter are difficult. This period of joyous celebration leaves me fearful and insecure. If I'm not fasting and denying, if I give in to celebrating, I will grow soft—and I'll fall away from God once again. And if I do, I'll lose the resurrection gift; I'll be damned. So I get agitated long before Pentecost and want to reintroduce penances and mortifications. Clearly my trust of God is too little. My God is too small.

I know that I can be saved only through the grace of God. I know that I cannot merit everlasting life by my own efforts. So what is the point of good works, penances, mortifications, the attempts at Christian perfection beyond the mere avoidance of sin? It is, I think, something like this: grace is like an efficient cause. Grace can cause me not only to believe but also to do what is good. That is why no merit accrues to me for the good in me or produced by me. That is God's gratuitous gift. But grace, the action of the Holy Spirit, can be causally efficacious only against certain causal prerequisites, certain background conditions. These are under my control, and I can allow or withhold them. When I withhold them, the action of grace is inhibited, blocked. That is why responsibility for the evil I do accrues to me. Indeed, such responsibility accrues to *any* imperfections in what I do. For God's grace is sufficient to perfect me in all that I do—if only *I* would let it.

Original sin is the capacity, transmitted from Eden on through the procreative process, that humans possess to resist or to block the actions of grace. Spiritual discipline consists in strategies and efforts for minimizing the effects of original sin by reducing the extent to which one blocks or inhibits grace. Denials, mortifications and penances are not only reparations for sins. When voluntarily undertaken they are steps toward cultivating the virtues—toward becoming the sort of person who is more disposed to allow the Holy Spirit and the graces of God to be efficacious in oneself. At a crude level, this involves the avoidance of sin.

Our dear Lord does not blame us for the same things that others do.[49]

But the avoidance of all sin leaves one far short of Christian perfection. To stop there is to undervalue the prospects of the Beatific Vision.

Again I try to intellectualize a spiritual problem. *My problem* is that I am scared that if I don't indulge in spiritual exercises, in good works, in various acts of faith, I will once again reject God. I do not delude myself here. I fully have within me the capacity to turn my back on God and to walk away once again. In my disconsolation over that realization, through dark nights in which I have become so desperate that I have had to pray to God for extra grace merely to be able to be open to the sufficient grace already granted me, I came to realize that I lack in myself even the resources to accept God. My very faith, my very acceptance of God, is not in my power. It is a gratuitous gift of God, and I struggle to make that realization more than episodic in my life. Because of all the abuse, the suffering, I don't really trust love. I don't believe in love. But God is love. My resort to practices to earn God's love, my difficulties trusting God and my difficulties relating to the love message of the Gospels all are of a piece. I must learn to trust God if I am to learn to love.

Closing Disquisition

Meanwhile I continue seeking to follow God and Christ—but with fits, starts, doubts, backsliding and much self-incrimination. My feeble efforts are humbling. My sinful past alone should be humbling. Yet there is hope. I realize that those who tempted me as I turned away from God are not responsible for my evil. While I would not have rejected God in one big step, I willingly made a series of capitulations to evil that cumulatively rejected God. I bear the full burden of responsibility at every step. But that is not enough. I must forgive those who tempted me. I must be grateful for those hurts from my father and others that propelled me toward God. Just as God forgives the Enemy I must forgive my enemies. But who is my greatest enemy? Myself. So I must forgive myself. To forgive myself is to accept myself. Is this not the ultimate act of humility?

> Humility goes deeper than repentance. It allows us to be detached even from our faults and to avoid the sterile regrets that imply resentment toward or discontent with ourselves.[50]

If I know myself well enough to forgive myself, do I not thereby have sufficient incentive to keep silent? For isn't to forgive to forget? And isn't forgetfulness just the inner silence I seek? To forget, to silence these earlier hurts and gain inner tranquility, must I now excise the egoistic demon muse? Will the price be philosophical silence? Perhaps not, for

> If when . . . [the Holy Spirit] comes he finds you humble, silent and trembling at the words of God, he will rest upon you and reveal what God the Father has hidden from the wise and prudent of this world. You will then begin to understand the things Holy Wisdom could have told his disciples on earth.[51]

Jesus says, "Whosoever wishes to come after me must deny himself." Do I risk following him into the deep silence of obedient humility?

I am coming to see that my self-doubts, my insecurities, are a gift from God. *They* are the seeds of humility. They are my hope for humility. My error has been to try to overcome them, to build self-esteem. The self-doubts are true. I must give in to them, accept them for the truths that they are and that they reveal.

Becoming *Michael*

Shortly before his death I spent a couple of days with my friend and former colleague Alan Donagan. Later his wife, Barbara, would write me,

> You know the importance of his Christian faith to him. I know how glad he was to see and talk to you in February. He told me that you had had a long, interesting, and satisfying talk, and that he felt that your return to the church had brought you happiness and peace.

During the Last Supper discourses, Jesus says to his disciples, "Peace I leave with you; my peace I give to you. Not as the world gives do I give it to you. Do not let your hearts be troubled or afraid" (Jn 14:27). A peace that would lead them to suffering, imprisonment, martyrdom. "It is a fearful thing to fall into the hands of the living God. Remember the days past when, after you had been enlightened, you endured a great contest of suffering. . . . You need endurance to do the will of God and receive what he has promised" (Heb 10:31-32, 36).

Yes, Alan. In my faith, in my struggles to live it, I am at peace. That peculiar peace that comes from Christ. That peace, with all its unresolved tension, that the prodigal son felt when he finally came home to a loving, forgiving Father. The peace that comes from becoming he "who would be like God." The peace of finally becoming Michael.[52]

The Vocation
of a Natural Theologian

RICHARD SWINBURNE

Richard Swinburne succeeded Basil Mitchell as the Nolloth Professor of the Christian Religion at Oxford University. Prior to this appointment, he held positions at the universities of Oxford, Leeds, Hull, Maryland and Keele. Swinburne is universally acknowledged as the premier rational defender of Christianity of our time. His important works in defense of Christianity include The Existence of God, The Coherence of Theism, Faith and Reason, The Evolution of the Soul *and* Revelation.

*A*s far back as my memory stretches, I recall having thought in Christian terms; and from early years I recall having prayed. Since neither of my parents was Christian, any human contribution to this process must be attributed to my early schooling. By the time I had passed through a British "public school," completed my military service, and come up as an undergraduate to Oxford University in 1954, being a Christian was, I claimed to myself, the most important thing in my life. I also loved argument and found myself with a natural theoretical interest in big questions. The latter led to my reading philosophy, politics and economics (with the weight on philosophy) for my B.A. degree. My home, my school, my military service (spent learning to speak Russian, supposedly the language of the enemy in a future war) and above all my university were all highly intellectual places, where I was exposed to all the achievements and current attitudes of the modern academic world. These attitudes were, it seemed to me, basically anti-Christian. The ethics of sophisticated intellectuals were very different from the ethics of traditional Christians.

The Conflict Between Materialism and Christianity

A materialist worldview, very different from the traditional Christian worldview, was supposed to be what science favored; and the "scandal of particularity," God becoming incarnate in Christ in human history, was indeed regarded as a "scandal," that is, absurd, by contemporary intellectuals. There was a great belief in progress, and progress seemed to mean leaving Christianity behind. But my instincts favored traditional Christianity; and the fact of this conflict between traditional Christianity and the modern intellectual worldview did not in itself disturb me too much. There's plenty in the New Testament to suggest that it might well be expected that Christianity should be a minority allegiance. Besides, as I said, I enjoyed argument—and the more people and the more clever people there were to argue against, as far as I was concerned, the better. (If you think that this attitude of mine was less than perfectly Christian, you could well be right!)

But what *did* disturb me very much is that the church didn't seem to take this conflict seriously. Preachers preached pious sermons that simply failed to connect with modern science, ethics and philosophy; they expounded biblical texts and preached attitudes. And the answer to such questions—Why should one believe the Bible? Does it not presuppose an out-of-date science? Are not moral truths mere matters of opinion? Why should one suppose that there is a God at all?—was that religion was a matter of "faith." But the preachers had nothing to say about why one should take a leap of faith, and why one should take it in this direction rather than that (that is, in favor of this religion rather than of that rival worldview). The church's lazy indifference to modern knowledge appalled me; and I saw that, even if as many as 20 percent of the population of the United Kingdom still went to church in 1954, things wouldn't go on like that unless Christianity could fit in better with the intellectual worldview.

In due course I came to realize that behind this "lazy indifference," as I saw it, lay a theological attitude. There were theological "justifications" of why reason had no part to play in establishing the foundations of the Christian theological system. The most influential modern systematic theologians were German, of whom the best known was Karl Barth. They derived their philosophy from the Continental tradition in philosophy of the past two hundred years. This includes such very diverse figures as Hegel, Nietzsche, Heidegger and Sartre. But it seemed to me—and has seemed to most Anglo-American philosophers—that what characterizes them all is a certain sloppiness of argument, a tendency to draw big, vague, general pictures of the universe, without spelling them out very precisely or justifying them very thoroughly, a kind of philosophy geared toward literature rather than toward science. And the philosopher who above all influenced the theologians was Søren Kierkegaard, who thought that the choice between worldviews was a highly nonrational matter.

Now I did not wish to deny that the practice of religion is chosen; it does indeed involve giving your life generously for a supremely worthy purpose. But it needs to be shown that the purpose is indeed worthy—that the Christian way of living on earth is a good way; and that involves showing that the Christian theological system, which explains *why* it is a good way, has some reasonable chance of being true. There is no point in confessing your sins to God or worshiping him if he almost certainly doesn't exist. And if the modern work throws up some reasonable arguments that suggest that he almost certainly doesn't exist, they need to be treated seriously and shown to be unsound. To ignore them is insulting to God, who has given us our reason and allowed us to use it to such good effect in theoretical and practical science. But, alas, the systematic theology fashionable in the 1950s had no resources for dealing with such matters.

The Legacy of Logical Positivism

While appalled by the church's attitude toward modern knowledge, I had been acquiring some of the latter in the form of philosophy as taught at Oxford in the late 1950s. The broad stream of careful and rational argument about big metaphysical issues that has characterized European philosophy since the Greeks had reached an odd stage. In the

Anglo-American world at large the skepticism of Hume has given rise to logical positivism: the view that the only real things are sense impressions and (possibly) material objects of a size visible to the naked eye, and that our knowledge is limited to past, present and future alterations of sense impressions and material objects. And not merely our knowledge is limited; talk about anything else is meaningless. This view was codified in the verification principle, which says that the only propositions that are meaningful are ones that can (in some sense!) be verified by observation. And hence, said the verificationists, all claims about the nature of space and time, about which moral views are true, and of course about God, are not false but meaningless.

In Oxford this logical positivist background had led many philosophers to hold that the only job left for philosophy was to teach people what words mean in ordinary use, and so to help them avoid using words to state meaningless philosophical theses. If you understood what "cause" meant, that is, how it was applied in ordinary situations, you couldn't be tempted to say such a meaningless thing as "God caused the world"! The high priest of Oxford "ordinary language" philosophy was J. L. Austin. I attended many of his lectures and classes and count myself fortunate to have done so. I learned something about the subtleties of ordinary language, and the need to start from words used in their ordinary senses, even if thereafter one introduces new technical terms by means of the former. Metaphysical language must take off from and be explained in terms of ordinary language. "Ordinary language" philosophy however had no sympathy for anything that went beyond ordinary language. But it taught one clarity of statement and thoroughness of argument. I valued Oxford philosophy greatly for its cultivation of those virtues. But there seemed to me no good reason for believing the dogmas that lay behind the practice. In particular there seemed no good reason for believing the verification principle, but even if one did assume it, so long as you do not interpret "verified" as "conclusively verified" but as "confirmed or supported by evidence or argument," then why shouldn't great metaphysical theories, including Christian theism, be verifiable and so meaningful?

So I disliked Oxford philosophy for its dogmas, but I liked it for its tools of clarity and rigor; and it seemed to me that someone could use its tools to make Christian theology again intellectually respectable. And I came to believe it to be my Christian vocation to make a contribution to this process. I was going to become a priest, but I became a professional philosopher instead. I went on to do graduate work in philosophy—I took the two-year Oxford B.Phil. in philosophy (the normal course at Oxford at that time for intending professional philosophers) and then a one-year diploma in theology.

Yet it seemed to me that the centerpiece of the modern worldview was not Oxford or any other brand of professional philosophy, but modern theoretical science—the physics of relativity theory and quantum theory, the biology of evolution, the genetics of DNA—which many people thought counted against the traditional Christian worldview. And here I felt very ignorant, as I had studied little science at school. I needed to study these great developments thoroughly. I was fortunate to be awarded three years of research fellowship (at Oxford and then at Leeds, in the years 1960-63) after my philosophical and theological studies; and I devoted them to learning much modern science and much history of science—how we had got to where we are. And I studied "philosophy of science," then a very ill-cultivated branch of philosophy in England, which is a study of the meaning and justification of scientific theories—and especially of the criteria that scientists use to judge one theory as well evidenced and another as ruled out by data, and of whether those criteria are ultimate or whether they can themselves be justified by some general principle of rationality or logic.

Justification of Scientific Theories

My study of science showed me one thing very quickly and very obviously. The great theories and predictions of modern science concerned matters far beyond observation: atoms and electrons and now quarks, far too small to be observed in any literal sense; and galaxies and quasars and the "big bang," far too distant in space or time to be observed in any literal sense. If we insist that to be meaningful a theory has to be "verifiable" in the sense of conclusively verifiable by observation, modern science would be rendered meaningless. Yet since it quite obviously isn't meaningless—as everyone in any way touched by the modern worldview would have to admit—theories could be meaningful without, in that sense, being verifiable. I saw, and in due course Oxford philosophy itself came to see, that the verificationist dogma was fatally flawed. What makes scientific theories *meaningful* is not their verifiability but the fact that they describe their entities ("atoms") and their properties ("velocity," "spin") with words used somewhat similarly to words used for describing ordinary mundane things. Atoms are somewhat like billiard balls, only very much smaller; they are also somewhat like waves, only not waves in media like water—words have to be used somewhat analogically in order to describe what atoms are like. Any attempt to describe them won't be totally adequate but can give us quite a good idea of what atoms are like. And scientific theories (or hypotheses) were *justified* insofar as (1) they lead us to expect the phenomena we observe around us, (2) the phenomena would otherwise be unexpected, and (3) they are simple theories.

The criterion of simplicity is crucial. If the only evidence in favor of a scientific theory was its success in leading us to expect what we observe, then we would never have any justification for any prediction about the future. Let me illustrate this by a simple example. Suppose that you are a scientist studying the relation of two variables (x and y); you have made six observations so far and you find, say, that x and y are related as follows:

$$\frac{x\ 1\ 2\ 3\ 4\ 5\ 6}{y\ 1\ 2\ 3\ 4\ 5\ 6}$$

You seek a general formula connecting x and y that will allow you to predict a future value of y for a new value of x. An infinite number of formulas are possible, all equally successful in leading you to expect what you have observed so far but diverging in their future predictions. For example, all formulas of the form $y = x + z\,(x-1)\,(x-2)\,(x-3)\,(x-4)\,(x-5)\,(x-6)$, where z is some constant, are like this. But of course you think that one of them ($y = x$) is better justified than the others; and this is because it is simpler. The simpler theory is that most likely to be true.

Scientists use this same pattern of argument to argue to the existence of unobservable entities as causes of the phenomena that they observe. For example, at the beginning of the nineteenth century scientists observed many varied phenomena of chemical interaction, such as that substances combine in fixed ratios by weight to form new substances (for example, hydrogen and oxygen always form water in a ratio by weight of 1:8). They then claimed that these phenomena would be expected if there existed a hundred or so different kinds of atoms, particles far too small to be seen, which combined and recombined in certain simple ways. In their turn physicists postulated electrons, protons, neutrons and other particles in order to account for the behavior of the atoms; and now they postulate quarks in order to explain the behavior of protons, neutrons and most other particles. What we postulate must enable us to predict (at least with some probability) what we observe when other theories do not; but the criterion of simplicity remains crucial for choice among the infinite number of theories that do so predict.

The simplicity of a theory is not just a matter of mathematically simple formulas connecting given variables (as in my example), but of few laws, each connecting few variables; the theory postulating few entities, few kinds of entity, few properties, few kinds of property. We could always postulate many new entities with complicated properties to explain anything that we found. But our theory will be supported by the evidence only if it postulates few entities, which lead us to expect the diverse phenomena that form the evidence. It is sometimes said that we can test between theories equally successful in predicting observations so far by a new test—in my example observe the value of y for $x = 7$—and that will rule out most of those theories. But it will still leave us with an infinite number of theories (incompatible with each other in their further predictions). It is sometimes said that "background knowledge," our general knowledge of how the world works in neighboring fields of inquiry, will help us to choose between competing theories without recourse to simplicity; we choose the theory that "fits best" with that background knowledge. But "fits best" turns out to mean "fits most simply." And anyway when we are considering big theories, such as the general theory of relativity, they purport to explain so much (such as about all of mechanics, optics and electromagnetism) that there is not much left by way of theories of neighboring fields with which they can fit. Simplicity remains the ultimate criterion of choice between such rival theories. According to an old Latin saying, *simplex sigillum veri*—"The simple is the sign of the true." To be rendered probable by evidence, a theory must be simple.

The Justification of Religious Belief

But once I had seen what makes scientific theories meaningful and justified, I saw that any metaphysical theory, such as the Christian theological system, is just a superscientific theory. Scientific theories each seek to explain a certain limited class of data: Kepler's laws sought to explain the motions of the planets; natural selection seeks to explain the fossil record and various present features of animals and plants. But some scientific theories are on a higher level than others and seek to explain the operation of the lower-level theories and the existence in the first place of the objects with which they deal. Newton's laws explained why Kepler's laws operated; chemistry has sought to explain why primitive animals and plants existed in the first place. A metaphysical theory is a highest-level-of-all theory. It seeks to explain why there is a universe at all, why it has the most general laws of nature that it does (especially such laws as lead to the evolution of animals and humans), as well as any particular phenomena that lower-level laws are unable to explain. Such a theory is meaningful if it can be stated in ordinary words, stretched a bit in meaning perhaps. And it is justified if it is a simple theory and leads you to expect the observable phenomena when you would not otherwise expect them. Once I had seen this, my program was there—to use the criteria of modern natural science, analyzed with the careful rigor of modern philosophy, to show the meaningfulness and justification of Christian theology.

At this time I discovered that someone else had attempted to use the best science and philosophy of his day rigorously to establish Christian theology. I read part one of the *Summa Theologiae* of Thomas Aquinas. He too started from where the secular world was in his day—the thirteenth century—and used the best secular philosophy available, that of Aristotle, instead of the initially more Christian-looking philosophy of Plato; and he sought to show that reflection on the observable world, as described by Aristotelian science, led inescapably to its creator God. The *Summa* doesn't start from faith or religious experience or the Bible;

it starts from the observable world. After an introductory question, its first main question is *Utrum Deus Sit*, whether there is a God; and it provides five "ways" or arguments from the most evident general phenomena of experience: that things change, that things cause other things, and so on—to show that there is. I do not think that those five ways work too well in detail; and it is interesting that often where the argument goes wrong it is not because Aquinas had relied unjustifiably on Christian theology but because he had relied too much on Aristotelian science. While I realized that the details were not always satisfactory, it seemed to me that the approach of the *Summa* was 100 percent right. I came to see that the irrationalist spirit of modern theology was a modern phenomenon, a head-in-the-sand defensive mechanism. In general, I believe, it is the spirit of St. Thomas rather than the spirit of Kierkegaard that has been the more prevalent over two millennia of Christian theology. But each generation must justify the Christian system by using the best secular knowledge of its own day; and that is why true disciples of St. Thomas cannot rely on the *Summa*—they have to carry out Thomas's program, using the knowledge of their own day.

Before I could put my program into practice I needed to develop thoroughly this understanding of science to which I was coming, and I needed to establish my credentials in this area in order that those who respect such work might listen to what I had to say when I began to write about religion. So when I obtained my first teaching post at the University of Hull in 1963, I devoted most of the next ten years to writing on the philosophy of science. Respect for the pronouncements of science is such a major component of the modern intellectual outlook that investigating the nature, limits and justification of such pronouncements is a vitally worthwhile task on its own, quite apart from any consequences it might have for religion; it is also a fascinating task. I wrote two substantial books in this area: *Space and Time* (1968) and *An Introduction to Confirmation Theory* (1973). The former worked up from an analysis of our talk about distance and temporal interval to such big questions as whether there is only one space and time, why space has three dimensions and time only one, and why causes precede their effects. It had a lot to say about the interpretation of relativity theory; and was in that way a case study of the meaning and justification of a famous scientific theory. The book on confirmation theory was crucial for my later thinking. Confirmation theory is the axiomatization in terms of the mathematical calculus of probability of what makes what probable, or confirms it (that is, increases its probability). I sought to show that the criteria by which scientists judge the worth of theories, which I described above, can be captured by that calculus, and especially by a famous theorem of that calculus, Bayes's theorem.

Apart from a short book, *The Concept of Miracle*, and a few articles, I had published nothing on the philosophy of religion before 1972. I was then ready to change gears. In that year I became professor of philosophy at the University of Keele and began to write a trilogy on the philosophy of theism, the claim that there is a God. The first book of that trilogy, *The Coherence of Theism*, was concerned with what it means to say that there is a God; the second book, *The Existence of God*, was concerned with whether there is a God, and it argued that it is significantly more probable than not that there is; and the third book, *Faith and Reason*, was concerned with the relevance of arguments about the existence of God to the practice of religion.

Scientific Versus Personal Explanation
The basic idea of *The Existence of God* is that the various traditional arguments for theism—from the existence of the world (the cosmological argument), from its conformity to scientific laws (a version of the teleological argument), and so on—are best construed not as deductive arguments but as inductive arguments to the existence of God. A valid deductive argument is one in which the premises (the starting points) infallibly guarantee the truth of the conclusion; a correct inductive argument is one in which the premises confirm the conclusion (that is, make it more probable than it would otherwise be). Science argues from various limited observable phenomena to their unobservable physical causes, and in so doing it argues inductively. My claim was that theism is the best justified of metaphysical theories. The existence of God is a very simple hypothesis that leads us to expect various very general and more specific phenomena that otherwise we would not expect; and for that reason it is rendered probable by the phenomena. Or rather, as with any big scientific theory, each group of phenomena

adds to the probability of the theory—together they make it significantly more probable than not.[1]

When explaining phenomena we have available two different kinds of explanation. One is *scientific explanation*, whereby we explain a phenomenon E in terms of some prior state of affairs F (the cause) in accordance with some regularity or natural law L that describes the behavior of objects involved in F and E. We explain why a stone took two seconds to fall from a tower to the ground (E) by its having been liberated from rest at the top of the tower 64 feet from the ground (F) and by the regularity derivable from Galileo's law of fall that all bodies fall toward the surface of the earth with an acceleration of 32 ft/sec^2 (L); E follows from F and L. And, as I noted earlier, science can also explain the operation of a regularity or law in some narrow area in terms of the operation of a wider law. Thus it can explain why Galileo's law of fall holds for small objects near the surface of the earth. Galileo's law follows from Newton's laws, given that the earth is a body of a certain mass far from other massive bodies and the objects on its surface are close to it and small in mass in comparison.

The other way that we use all the time and see as a proper way of explaining phenomena is what I call *personal explanation*. We often explain some phenomenon E as brought about by a person P in order to achieve some purpose or goal G. The present motion of my hand is explained as brought about by me for the purpose of picking up a glass. The motion of my legs earlier toward a room is explained by my purpose of going there to give a lecture. In these cases I bring about a state of my body that then itself causes some state of affairs outside my body. But it is I (P) who bring about the bodily state (E) conducive to producing that further state (G) rather than some other.

The kind of explanation involved here is a different way of explaining things from the scientific. Scientific explanation involves laws of nature and previous states of affairs. Personal explanation involves persons and purposes. In each case the grounds for believing the explanation to be correct are, as stated earlier, the fact that to explain the cited phenomenon and many other similar phenomena we need few entities (for example, one person rather than many), few kinds of entities with few, easily describable properties, behaving in mathematically simple kinds of ways (such as a person having certain capacities and purposes that do not change erratically) that give rise to many phenomena. In seeking the best explanation of phenomena we may seek explanations of either kind, and if we cannot find a scientific one that satisfies the criteria, we should look for a personal one.

We should seek explanations of all things; but we have seen that we have reason for supposing that we have found one only if the purported explanation is simple and leads us to expect what we find when that is otherwise not to be expected. The history of science shows that we judge that the complex, miscellaneous, coincidental and diverse needs explaining, and that it is to be explained in terms of something simpler. The motions of the planets (subject to Kepler's laws), the mechanical interactions of bodies on earth, the behavior of pendula, the motions of tides, the behavior of comets and so forth formed a pretty miscellaneous set of phenomena. Newton's law of motion constituted a simple theory that led us to expect these phenomena, and so was judged a true explanation of them. The existence of thousands of different chemical substances combining in different ratios to make other substances was complex. The hypothesis that there were only a hundred or so chemical elements of which the thousands of substances were made was a simple hypothesis that led us to expect the complex phenomena. When we reach the simplest possible starting point for explanation that leads us to expect the phenomena that we find, there alone we should stop and believe that we have found the ultimate brute fact on which all other things depend.

The Cosmological Argument

The cosmological argument argues from the existence of a complex physical universe (or something as general as that) to God who keeps it in being. The premise is the existence of our universe for so long as it has existed (whether a finite time or, if it has no beginning, an infinite time). The universe is a complex thing with lots and lots of separate chunks. Each of these chunks has a different finite and not very natural volume, shape, mass and so forth—consider the vast diversity of galaxies, stars and planets, and pebbles on the seashore. Matter is inert and has no powers that it can choose to exert; it does what it has to do. There is a limited amount of it in any region, and it has a limited amount of energy and velocity. There is a complexity, particularity and finitude about the universe that looks for explanation in terms of something simpler.

The existence of the universe is something evidently inexplicable by science. For, as we saw, a scientific explanation as such explains the occurrence of one state of affairs in terms of a previous state of affairs and some law of nature that makes states like the former bring about states like the latter. It may explain the planets being in their present positions by a previous state of the system (the sun and planets being where they were last year) and the operation of Kepler's laws, which postulate that states like the latter are followed a year later by states like the former. And so it may explain the existence of the universe this year in terms of the existence of the universe last year and the laws of cosmology. But either there was a first state of the universe or there has always been a universe. In the former case, science cannot explain why there was the first state; and in the latter case it still cannot explain why any matter exists (or, more correctly, matter-energy) for the laws of nature to get a grip on, as it were. By its very nature science cannot explain *why* there are any states of affairs at all.

But a God can provide an explanation. The hypothesis of theism is that the universe exists because there is a God who keeps it in being and that laws of nature operate because there is a God who brings it about that they do. He brings it about that the laws of nature operate by sustaining in every object in the universe its liability to behave in accord with those laws (including the law of the conservation of matter, that at each moment what was there before continues to exist). The universe exists because at each moment of finite or infinite time, he keeps in being objects with this liability. The hypothesis of theism is like a hypothesis that a person brings about certain things for some purpose. God acts directly on the universe, as we act directly on our brains, guiding them to move our limbs (but the universe of course is not his body).

As we have seen, personal explanation and scientific explanation are the two ways we have of explaining the occurrence of phenomena. Since there cannot be a scientific explanation of the existence of the universe, either there is a personal explanation or there is no explanation at all. The hypothesis that there is a God is the hypothesis of the existence of the simplest kind of person that there could be. A person is a being with *power* to bring about effects, *knowledge* of how to do so and *freedom* to choose which effects to bring about. God is by definition an omnipotent (that is, infinitely powerful), omniscient (that is, all-knowing) and perfectly free person: he is a person of infinite power, knowledge and freedom; a person to whose power, knowledge and freedom there are no limits except those of logic. The hypothesis that there exists a being with infinite degrees of the qualities essential to a being of that kind is the postulation of a very simple being. The hypothesis that there is one such God is a much simpler hypothesis than the hypothesis that there is a god who has such and such limited power, or the hypothesis that there are several gods with limited powers. It is simpler in just the same way that the hypothesis that some particle has zero mass or infinite velocity is simpler than the hypothesis that it has 0.32147 of some unit of mass or a velocity of 221,000 km/sec. A finite limitation cries out for an explanation of why there is just that particular limit, in a way the limitlessness does not. God provides the simplest stopping-point for explanation.

That there should exist anything at all, let alone a universe as complex and as orderly as ours, is exceedingly strange. But if there is a God, it is not vastly unlikely that he should create such a universe. A universe such as ours is a thing of beauty, a theater in which humans and other creatures can grow and work out their destiny, a point that I shall develop further below. So the argument from the universe to God is an argument from a complex phenomenon to a simple entity, which leads us to expect (thought does not guarantee) the existence of the former far more than it would be expected otherwise. Therefore, I suggest, it provides some evidence for its conclusion.

The Argument from Design
The teleological argument, or argument from design, has various forms. One form is the argument from temporal order. This has as its premises the operation of the most general laws of nature, that is, the orderliness of nature in conforming to very general laws. What exactly

these laws are, science may not yet have discovered—perhaps they are the field equations of Einstein's general theory of relativity, or perhaps there are some yet more fundamental laws. Now, as we have seen, science can explain the operation of some narrow regularity or law in terms of a wider or more general law. But what science by its very nature cannot explain is why there are the most general laws of nature that there are; for *ex hypothesi,* no wider law can explain their operation.

The conformity of objects throughout endless time and space to simple laws cries out for explanation. For let us consider to what this amounts. Laws are not things, independent of material objects. To say that all objects conform to laws is simply to say that they all behave in exactly the same way. To say, for example, that the planets obey Kepler's laws is just to say that each planet at each moment of time has the property of moving in the ways that Kepler's laws state. There is, therefore, this vast coincidence in the behavioral properties of objects at all times and in all places. If all the coins of some region have the same markings, or all the papers in a room are written in the same handwriting, we seek an explanation in terms of a common source of these coincidences. We should seek a similar explanation for that vast coincidence which we describe as the conformity of objects to laws of nature—such as the fact that all electrons are produced, attract and repel other particles, and combine with them in exactly the same way at each point of endless time and space.

That there is a universe and that there are laws of nature are phenomena so general and pervasive that we tend to ignore them. But there might so easily not have been a universe at all, ever. Or the universe might so easily have been a chaotic mess. That there is an *orderly* universe is something very striking, yet beyond the capacity of science ever to explain. Science's inability to explain these things is not a temporary phenomenon, caused by the backwardness of twentieth-century science. Rather, because of what a *scientific* explanation is, these things will ever be beyond its capacity to explain. For scientific explanations by their very nature terminate with some ultimate natural law and ultimate physical arrangement of physical things, and the question with which I am concerned is why there are natural laws and physical things at all.

There is available again the simple explanation of the temporal orderliness of the universe, that God makes protons and electrons move
in an orderly way, just as we might make our bodies move in the
regular patterns of a dance. He has *ex hypothesi* the power to do this. But
why should he choose to do so? The orderliness of the universe makes
it a beautiful universe, but, even more importantly, it makes it a universe that humans can learn to control and change. For only if there
are simple laws of nature can humans predict what will follow from
what—and unless they can do that, they can never change anything.
Only if they know that by sowing certain seeds, weeding and watering
them, they will get corn, can they develop an agriculture. And humans
can acquire that knowledge only if there are easily graspable regular-
ities of behavior in nature. It is good that there are human beings,
embodied minicreators who share in God's activity of forming and
developing the universe through their free choice. But if there are to
be such, there must be laws of nature. There is, therefore, some reasonable expectation that God will bring them about; but otherwise that
the universe should exhibit such very striking order is hardly to be
expected.

The form of "argument from design" that has been most common in
the history of thought and was very widely prevalent in the eighteenth
and early nineteenth centuries is the argument from spatial order. The
intricate organization of animals and plants that enabled them to catch
the food for which their digestive apparatus was suited and to escape
from predators suggested that they were like very complicated ma-
chines and hence that they must have been put together by a master
machine-maker, who built into them at the same time the power to
reproduce. The frequent use of this argument in religious apologetic
came to an abrupt halt in 1859, when Darwin produced his explanation
of why there were complexly organized animals and plants, in terms
of the laws of evolution operating on much simpler organisms. There
seemed no need to bring God into the picture.

That reaction was, however, premature. For the demand for explanation can be taken back a further stage. Why are there laws of evolution that have the consequence that over many millennia simple organisms gradually give rise to complex organisms? No doubt because

these laws follow from the basic laws of physics. But then why do the basic laws of physics have such a form as to give rise to laws of evolution? And why were there primitive organisms in the first place? A plausible story can be told of how the primeval "soup" of matter-energy at the time of the "big bang" (a moment some 15,000 million years ago at which, scientists now tell us, the universe, or at least the present stage of the universe, began) gave rise over many millennia, in accordance with physical laws, to those primitive organisms. But then why was there matter suitable for such evolutionary development in the first place?

With respect to the laws and with respect to the primeval matter, we have again the same choice: saying that these things cannot be further explained or postulating a further explanation. Note that the issue here is not why there are laws at all (the premise of the argument from temporal order) or why there is matter-energy at all (the premise of the cosmological argument), but why the laws and the matter-energy have this peculiar character of being already wound up to produce plants, animals and humans. Since the most general laws of nature have this special character, there can be no scientific explanation of why they are as they are. And although there might be a scientific explanation of why the matter at the time of the big bang had the special character it did, in terms of its character at some earlier time, clearly if there was a first state of the universe, it must have been of a certain kind; or if the universe has lasted forever, its matter must have had certain general features if at any time there was to be a state of the universe suited to produce plants, animals and humans. Scientific explanation comes to a stop. The question remains whether we should accept these particular features of the laws and matter of the universe as ultimate brute facts or whether we should move beyond them to a personal explanation in terms of the agency of God.

What the choice turns on is how likely it is that the laws and initial conditions should by chance have just this character. Recent scientific work has drawn attention to the fact that the universe is fine-tuned.[2] The matter-energy at the time of the big bang has to have a certain density and a certain velocity of recession; increase or decrease in these respects by one part in a million would have had the effect that the

universe was not life-evolving. For example, if the big bang had caused
the quanta of matter-energy to recede from each other a little more
quickly, no galaxies, stars or planets, and no environment suitable for
life would have been formed. If the recession had been marginally slow-
er, the universe would have collapsed in on itself before life could be
formed. Similarly, the constants in the laws of nature needed to lie
within very narrow limits if life was to be formed. It is, therefore, most
unlikely that laws and initial conditions should have by chance a life-
producing character. God is able to give matter and laws this character.
If we can show that he would have reason to do so, then that gives
support to the hypothesis that he has done so. There is available again
the reason (in addition to the reason of its beauty) that was a reason
why God would choose to bring about an orderly universe at all—the
worthwhileness of the sentient embodied beings that the evolutionary
process would bring about, and above all of humans who can themselves make informed choices as to what sort of a world there should
be.

A similar pattern of argument from various other phenomena such
as the existence of conscious beings, the providential ordering of things
in certain respects, the occurrence of certain apparently miraculous
events in history and the religious experiences of many millions is, I
claimed in *The Existence of God*, available to establish theism (when all the
arguments are taken together) as overall significantly more probable
than not.

In Defense of Christian Doctrine

My trilogy was finished in 1981. It concerned merely bare theism—the
meaning, justification and relevance of the claim that there is a God.
But Christianity claims a lot more than that. Along with many other
religions, Christianity involves a view of human beings that distinguishes them sharply from ordinary material objects. And here I knew
that entrenched very deeply in the modern wordview was a materialist
doctrine—that a human was nothing but a very complicated material
object, a highly sophisticated robot. That doctrine seemed to me, on
grounds quite independent of theology, to be totally mistaken. I devoted the next five years to developing a case for substance dualism—that

there are two parts to a person, body and soul; the soul is the essential part, and its continuing constitutes the continuity of the person. Christian theology vitally needs this view—for if there is to be life after death, the essential part of the person must be something other than the body, which can be reduced to ashes or even simple chunks of energy. My defense of substance dualism and of connected doctrines about the nature of humanity (such as possession of free will) was published in final form in *The Evolution of the Soul* in 1986.

My treatment of this issue was a prolegomenon to the treatment of specifically Christian doctrines. I have now settled down to work on a tetralogy on the philosophical issues involved in Christian doctrines. (I say "philosophical" issues because Christianity is a historical religion, and some of its doctrines require historical evidence to support them. A philosopher does not feel competent to treat that; but one can show where we need historical evidence and how much relevance it has to an overall case, for which other grounds can also be provided; and that I have sought to do. Thus we need historical evidence to show that Jesus was crucified and rose from the dead; but it needs philosophical argument to show that this has cosmic significance.) My treatment of specifically Christian matters coincided with my move back to Oxford to a chair entitled "The Nolloth Professorship of the philosophy of the Christian religion."

The first volume of this planned tetralogy, *Responsibility and Atonement*, was published in 1989. When we do good or harm to each other, various members of a set of moral notions have application—we are guilty or meritorious; we need to repent and apologize and make reparation; others need to forgive us or, as the case may be, express gratitude or reward us; or they may punish us. Part one of *Responsibility and Atonement* was devoted to analyzing these notions and seeing when they apply— to the dealings of humans with each other. Part two then applies the results of part one to analyzing the meaning and justification of those Christian doctrines that utilize these notions to describe the relations of God and humanity—such as doctrines of sin and original sin, the atonement, eternal punishment and our eternal reward.

In all my works on the philosophy of religion my approach has been to start from where secular humanity stands, develop a philosophy of that area of thought, and then show how that philosophy leads to a Christian understanding of things in some respect. In *Responsibility and Atonement* I started from the human's limited moral understanding of obligation and supererogatory goodness, and argued thence to a conclusion about our moral status in relation to God. In the earlier trilogy I began with the inductive standards implicit in science. In my next book, *Revelation*, published in 1992, I start from ordinary sentences having meaning and develop thence a philosophy of meaning, before I move on to theological matters. There is no other way to proceed in the philosophy of religion if its results are to be made rationally acceptable to those who are initially nonreligious. Hence the philosopher of religion needs to be more than an amateur in other areas of philosophy; and I have written, at least at article length, on most other such areas. All philosophy concerns exciting and important issues; and, hard work though it is, I have enjoyed discussing the issues with colleagues, learning from their work, and, I hope, advancing things a bit further in all the areas of philosophy in which I have worked.

My book on revelation concerns the Christian claims to announce truths revealed by God. That work investigates what would be evidence that the creeds and the Bible are revealed. The prior philosophical questions concern how meaning can be conveyed by analogy and metaphor within the false scientific and historical presuppositions of an ancient culture; I treat these in part one of that work before applying my results to the Christian claim. I plan two more books of my tetralogy—one on the doctrine of God, treating the specifically Christian doctrines of the Trinity and the Incarnation; and one on providence and evil—dealing with the problem of evil more fully, in the light of specifically Christian doctrine, than I was able to do in *The Existence of God.*

When that last book is finished, I do not see myself as having anything further to say at book length on the philosophy of religion. I shall have said what I have to say. But I hope to continue to publicize and defend what I have already said, in various ways; as well perhaps as writing books on certain philosophical theses—for example, about simplicity and necessity—underlying some of my writing on the philosophy of religion but falling centrally within other branches of philosophy.

How much influence all this writing will ultimately have, I have, of course, no idea. But I believe I have already had a small influence in edging Christianity a bit further into the forum of intellectual respectability; and in my more collected moments, I am immensely grateful for the privilege of having been allowed to do so—grateful to God; grateful to my atheistic philosophy friends for their tolerance and openmindedness toward an odd colleague; and grateful to the public which, unknowingly and indirectly, has paid my salary for philosophizing for all these years. Nor, of course, have I been alone in trying to do what I have done. A considerable number of philosophers in the Anglo-American empiricist tradition, mainly in the United States, have been working in their various ways to relocate Christianity in its proper place at the middle of a rational, scientifically sensitive worldview. I am immensely grateful for their work and their personal friendship.

Final Reflections

I am very conscious that my intellectual development has been largely a matter of systematizing and justifying what I believed in a very vague way forty years ago. Although my views on lesser matters have changed, my worldview has not. I am well aware that I do not like changing habits or attitudes, and that there is an explanation of my intellectual development that has some initial plausibility—that I am simply too "pig-headed" to allow myself to change my mind under the pressure of experience and the force of the arguments of my philosophical opponents, to which I have been exposed during my philosophical career. All that I can plead in my defense is that holding a true view about very big metaphysical issues matters to me enormously, and I do honestly believe that if I judged that experience or argument led to a position contrary to that of my youth, I would not have concealed that fact from myself. I have no wish to worship a God who does not exist, and in consequence I have sometimes found myself beginning to pray, "O God, if you do not exist, help me to see that fact"!

Do I ever doubt the central claims of the Christian faith? If the question means, am I less than absolutely confident that those claims are true, the answer is yes. I am absolutely confident about very little, not even the existence of an external world and "other minds." But I judge that there is a significant balance of evidence in favor of both of these positions and in favor of Christian theism. If the question means, do I devote time to examining objections to Christianity, the answer is obviously also yes. It's my job. I think that everyone, Christian or non-Christian, ought to spend some time, in however amateur a way, examining the pros and cons of one's creed; and not just once in one's youth, but at intervals throughout one's life.

Over many years whenever some objection has occurred to me, I have written it down as something in due course to be explored fully. And exploring such objections fully has, I believe, led me to see facets of truth that I would not otherwise have glimpsed. Thus, anyone with any moral sensitivity must consider the fact of pain and suffering to constitute a prima facie objection to the existence of an all-powerful and all-good God. But taking the objection seriously, instead of concealing it from oneself, involves exploring just what sort of a world we think an all-powerful and all-good God ought to have made. Starting to spell out that alternative in detail led me[3] to realize that if God made a world without suffering, it would be a world in which humans had little responsibility for each other and for other creatures. Seeing that that alternative is not obviously better than the present world led me to see something about goodness—that there is more to it than tingles of pleasure—and about God—that his goodness is shown in the freedom and responsibility he gives to his creatures.

I have found generally that what this simple example shows holds for more complicated and difficult examples. Doubt (in the second sense) is good for belief. And learning more about what God is like and in particular what his goodness amounts to is good for prayer. Preachers never tire of telling us that knowing about God is one thing and knowing God is another; but although these are distinct, it would be very odd if you could know God at all well without knowing quite a lot about him (whether or not you have the philosophical expertise to put that clearly into writing). After all, we know an ordinary friend better when we know something about that person's history and character.

Despite this point, I must admit that much of my prayer and worship is pretty "dry." Nevertheless, worshiping our Creator is the first human duty—to fail to acknowledge publicly and privately the goodness of God is a very deep failing of total insensitivity to ultimacy and ingratitude to our supreme benefactor. And I am in general pleased to worship, Sunday by Sunday, in the way in which God has provided, in the Eucharist. And thereby by using not merely the "bare bones" of the ceremony recorded in the Gospels, but the prayers and fuller ceremonies that Christians have used for hundreds of years, one unites oneself in worship not merely with Jesus Christ, the celebrant of the first Eucharist, but with all Christians who have joined in the Eucharist since then. Ancient prayers, ceremonies and confessions of faith save us from the poverty of expression and narrowness of vision of "spontaneous" prayer.

Jesus Christ founded a church, and to be a Christian involves belonging to that church. But the church is divided, and so one has to belong to the church by belonging to a part of the church, that part which seems to one best to reflect the organization and doctrine that Christ willed his church to have. I was baptized at the age of fifteen in the Church of England, that is, as an Anglican (in American terms, an Episcopalian), and I have remained an Anglican ever since. But I have never felt altogether comfortable as an Anglican. No one ought to be content with belonging to a sect, preserving its independence from the rest of the church that Christ founded. We ought all to work for the unity of Christ's church, which is meant, I believe, to be the unity of an organization that would find its natural center in a primacy—of honor—in a reformed papacy. But there is also another reason why I am uncomfortable as an Anglican; and that is that the Church of England does not seem to treat with sufficient seriousness either the totality of commitment demanded of Christians or the importance of teaching true doctrine. If I lived in Russia or Greece, I would probably feel more at home in the Orthodox Church. But, living in England, I remain an Anglican, and I value the Church of England for its sacramental worship, its respect for scholarship, its tolerance and its humility.

My involvement in the church has been confined to involvement in its primary activity of worship (and in other prayer and sacraments) as an ordinary member of the congregation. Though I have in a minimal way joined in the social functions that are necessary for the corporate fellowship of the church, I have not belonged to church committees, edited church newspapers or sung in church choirs. I constantly repeat to myself as my excuse St. Paul's words that "there are diversities of ministrations"; and mine, insofar as I understand it, is to write, lecture and teach in a secular context.

I am an impatient person, and I have never enjoyed the present as much as I ought to have done. As with most people, the less pleasant aspects of life have diverted attention from the more pleasant ones. My family life has not been an ideal one; and it is understandably easy to let that divert one from the success and comfort of life in other respects. But I have always looked forward. I look forward now to completing all those academic projects; and, please God, I look forward also to what God will do with me when this life is over. But fear and trembling are the only proper attitudes with which a Christian may appear before his Creator. And I pray that God may give me the time and the grace to prepare for that day.

A Philosopher's Religious Faith

MORTIMER J. ADLER

Mortimer Adler is director of the Institute for Philosophical Research, chairman of the board of editors of the Encyclopaedia Britannica, *and honorary trustee of the Aspen Institute. His distinguished seventy-year career includes professorships at Columbia University and the University of Chicago; he has also lectured at St. John's College and the University of North Carolina at Chapel Hill. Adler's work as an educational reformer led to the development and publication of* The Paideia Proposal. *The most recent of his fifty books include* A Second Look in the Rearview Mirror, The Great Ideas: A Lexicon of Western Thought, Desires, Right and Wrong: The Ethics of Enough, Haves Without Have-Nots: Essays for the 21st Century on Democracy and Socialism, Truth in Religion, Intellect: Mind Over Matter, *and* How to Think About God.

My interest in theology antedated by many years my interest in religion. In my view of the matter, I had no religious upbringing. My parents may have thought otherwise.

In my preadolescent years, I was taken by my mother and my maternal grandmother to religious services in a Reform synagogue on Saturday mornings, but without any effect on my mind or soul. The inoculation did not take, or the patient was too intransigent. The dose may have been too slight.

Jewish Upbringing

My father was born in Bavaria and came to the United States in his late teens. He was brought up in an Orthodox Jewish household, and the ritualistic habits of his youth persisted. My mother and my grandmother, who lived with us, catered to his dietary scruples, and he, in turn, tolerated the rest of the family's transgressions of or deviations from them. If I thought about his orthodoxy at all, I regarded it as an anomaly, a vestige of the old country that he could not shake off, but totally out of place and meaningless in the world in which we were living.

My father's orthodoxy did not prevent us as a family from celebrating Christmas as well as Hanukkah, and Easter as well as Passover. The difference between secular and religious holidays did not mean anything to me, though I am sure that I enjoyed what went on at Christmas and Easter better than I did at Hanukkah and Passover. Of course, we observed the Jewish holy days on Rosh Hashanah and Yom Kippur, but only my father fasted on the latter day. For me, they were two days that I did not go to school.

I went to high school when I was twelve and a half years old, and I was at that stage of my schooling when the time came for me to go through the Jewish rite of passage known as bar mitzvah. I remember quarreling with the rabbi about the speech that I was to give to the congregation on that occasion, but the points in contention were philosophical, not religious. I do not recall the rabbi's ever asking me whether I believed in God. I simply had to memorize enough Hebrew to appear to read, while reciting, a passage from the Old Testament. It was an act of filial, not religious, piety on my part. I was simply an obedient boy, complying with my parents' wishes. My parents may have taken it more seriously than my joining a fraternity or my becoming a Boy Scout, but it had no more spiritual content for me than that.

In my adolescent years, and especially when I was in college, I gave up my ambition to become a journalist, cherishing the hope of becoming a philosopher instead. I ceased to have anything to do with the Jewish religion. My mother no longer expected me to go to synagogue with her on Saturday mornings. My father never mentioned my irreligiosity. For all intents and purposes, I was a pagan—and a somewhat rebellious one at that.

It was through my study of philosophy, not through religious obser-
vances and rituals, that I became interested in God—as an object of
thought, not as an object of love and worship. It was the God of Aristotle and of Spinoza, not the God of Judaism and of Christianity.
When I graduated from college at twenty and started to conduct great
books seminars with Mark Van Doren, I first came into contact with
the Treatise on God in the *Summa Theologica* of Thomas Aquinas.

The intellectual austerity, integrity, precision and brilliance of that
book, incomparably different from all the philosophical books that I had
read up to that time, and much more exciting to me, put the study of
theology highest among all of my philosophical interests.

What for Aquinas were his articles of Christian faith, I was willing
to take as postulates or assumptions that called upon him or anyone
else to engage in philosophical thought for the sake of discovering their
implications or consequences. What for Aquinas was philosophy serving as the handmaiden of theology in the process of faith seeking
understanding was for me just a philosophical exercise, as exacting in
its demands on the intellect and as rigorous as higher mathematics.

Natural and Philosophical Theology

In the next twenty or thirty years, I read all the treatises in part one
of the *Summa Theologica* and many of the later parts, dealing with moral
theology, but not all of the *Summa.* I also read St. Augustine's *Confessions*
again and again, as well as his *City of God,* his *Enchiridion* and his essay
on *Christian Doctrine.* I became acquainted with the thought of St. Anselm, as well as with the doctrines of the great Jewish theologian Maimonides (whom Aquinas referred to as *the* rabbi) and with Aquinas's
criticisms of the errors of Averroës (the Arabic philosopher whom
Aquinas referred to as *the* commentator for his contributions to the
study of Aristotelian philosophy).

Since at this time I had no religious faith, my preoccupation with
theology was entirely philosophical, and I did not yet fully understand
the relation of the three domains of theology: sacred, natural and philosophical.

All, or almost all, of the theologians in the Middle Ages (whether of
Jewish, Christian or Islamic religious faith) were sacred or dogmatic

theologians. Their religious faith, or the dogmas of their religions, provided them with the unquestionable principles of their theology. I learned from Aquinas that their faith was a gift from God. They had faith by the grace of God, not by a voluntary act on their part, an exercise of what William James called "the will to believe."

On the other hand, the three branches of theoretical philosophy according to Aristotle were physics, mathematics and metaphysics; and in Book Lambda of his *Metaphysics* we find Aristotle's theology—his teaching about God, the prime mover or first cause of an eternal (or, more precisely, an everlasting) cosmos or universe.

This is not sacred or dogmatic theology, but purely philosophical theology. From the point of view of the medieval Jewish and Christian disciples of Aristotle, he was a pagan theologian. That did not prevent them from borrowing arguments from him when they tried to prove the existence of God, even though Aristotle's conception of God differed so radically from the God in whom they believed that, while acknowledging his pagan attempts, they should have pointed out his serious errors.

There is a third domain in which theological thinking occurs. In addition to sacred or dogmatic and philosophical or pagan theology, there is something usually miscalled "natural theology," which is apologetics. A medieval example of Christian apologetics is found in a work by Thomas Aquinas entitled *Summa Contra Gentiles*, addressed to the Jews and Moors in Spain. It is written as if it were philosophical theology, but that it is not, because it was written by a Christian and not by a pagan. There are theses and arguments in the doctrine it attempts to teach that no pagan, but only a person of Christian faith, could have affirmed and developed.

The first principles of Christian apologetics are principles of reason, not dogmas of religion. However, as the history of such natural theology reveals, it is for the most part the work of individuals who are not pagans, but persons of religious faith, by virtue of which they assert about God and about humankind's relation to God propositions that cannot be on purely rational grounds.

Such Christian apologetics, which is neither dogmatically sacred theology nor philosophically pagan theology, became in modern times, beginning with the *Meditations* of Descartes, the work of philosophers who were also Christians or of Christian divines who also tried to be philosophers. A prime example of such work is the late-eighteenth-century treatise by an Anglican priest, William Paley, entitled *A View of the Evidence of Christianity* and a later work entitled *Natural Theology*.

These works were required reading for entrance to Cambridge University until the end of the nineteenth century. The Gifford Lectures in the twentieth century at the University of Edinburgh produced books in natural theology by scientists and philosophers who were also Christians. In my judgment, few if any of these books, and many more like them, are sound as works in philosophical theology, because they are not written by pagans.

I did not fully understand the philosophical deficiencies of what in modern times was called "natural theology" until fairly late in my life, when I finally wrote the book I had been preparing to write for many years: *How to Think About God* (1980). The subtitle of that book was *A Guide for the 20th-Century Pagan*, and on its title page, the word *pagan* was defined as "one who does not worship the God of Christians, Jews, or Muslims; irreligious persons." Furthermore, chapter three informed the book's readers that the book was not only written for pagans but also written by a pagan.

As what follows will show, it is much easier to be a philosopher without religion than to be a philosopher after acquiring religious faith. It is much easier to have blind faith, but that is not an option open to a philosopher. If one has religious faith, one then has the obligation to think about the dogmas of that religion.

I suspect that most of the individuals who have religious faith are content with blind faith. They feel no obligation to understand what they believe. They may even wish not to have their beliefs disturbed by thought. But if the God in whom they believe created them with intellectual and rational powers, that imposes upon them the duty to try to understand the creed of their religion. Not to do so is to verge on superstition.

A Pagan Thomist
Stories that I have told elsewhere anticipate what remains to be told

here. I have reported how I came to join the American Catholic Philosophical Association in 1932 and the steps that led me to deliver my address "God and the Professors" at the opening session of the First Conference on Science, Philosophy and Religion, sponsored by Rabbi Louis Finkelstein of the Jewish Theological Seminary of America in New York City.[1]

Without becoming a Roman Catholic, I had become a Thomist in philosophy as a result of my intensive study of the *Summa Theologica* of Thomas Aquinas. For the give and take of philosophical discussion, I found fellow Thomists in the American Catholic Philosophical Association a more receptive audience for the books and essays that I was then disposed to write than were my colleagues at the University of Chicago, or the professors of philosophy at other secular universities.

The Dominican House of Studies in Washington, D.C., published a magazine called *The Thomist*. After delivering a paper on the demonstration of democracy at the annual meeting of the American Catholic Philosophical Association in 1939, Father Walter Farrell and I coauthored a book-length series of essays entitled "The Theory of Democracy," which was published in *The Thomist* in successive issues from 1941 to 1943. *The Thomist* also published my long essay "The Problem of Species" (which elicited a storm of adverse criticism from my fellow Thomists) and the essay I contributed to a special issue of the magazine in 1943, celebrating the sixtieth birthday of my friend Jacques Maritain. That essay, entitled "The Demonstration of God's Existence," attempted to show why the five ways of proving God's existence presented by Aquinas in part one, question two, article two did not succeed. That elicited an even greater storm of protest from the Thomists.

During these years and also in the following decade, I was a frequent guest at the Dominican House of Studies in Washington, D.C., and also at the Benedictine Abbey in Collegeville, Minnesota, where I gave lectures at St. John's University, run by the Benedictine monks. I also gave lectures at the University of Notre Dame and became a close friend of Father John Cavanaugh, its president then, and later of Father Theodore Hesburgh, his successor.

I am sure that many of my Roman Catholic friends wondered why I did not become a Roman Catholic, but with the one exception of

Father Robert Slavin of the Dominican House of Studies, none of them ever broached that question explicitly in conversation with me.

There were moments in the late 1930s and throughout the 1940s when I put that question to myself. As I look back at the answers that I gave myself, I think the reasons I gave were superficial. They cloaked my disinclination to become religious. I simply did not wish to exercise a will to believe; and from what I understood about faith as a supernatural, theological virtue, which was a gift of divine grace, my will was not moved by faith.[2]

When Clare Boothe Luce, who had herself then recently converted to Roman Catholicism, made a strenuous effort to convert me, I explained to her the difference between dead and living faith—faith without hope and charity and faith that is enriched by the other two theological virtues, hope and charity. I told Clare that simply being able to understand Thomist theology was what Aquinas called dead faith. It was not enough to carry one into a Christian religious life.[3]

I should add here that my first wife, Helen, was born an Episcopalian. My Jewish father and mother were reconciled to that mixed marriage. The two sons that Helen and I adopted, Mark and Michael, were baptized and confirmed in the Episcopal Church, and I attended religious services with them at the Church of the Redeemer, in the neighborhood of the University of Chicago, also attended by T. S. Eliot when he was a visiting lecturer there. Father Francis Lickfield, the rector, and I became good friends, but, as I recall, he never tried to convert me.

My second wife, Caroline, was also born an Episcopalian, and our two sons, Douglas and Philip, were baptized and confirmed in the Episcopal Church. As a family, we became members of the parish community of St. Chrysostom's Church in Chicago, of which Father Robert Howell was the rector; and, as in the earlier case of Father Lickfield at the Church of the Redeemer, Father Howell became a friend, but he never raised any question about my becoming a baptized Christian.

There is one other coincidence that I should mention. Father Howell had a close friend in Chicago, Father William Casady, who was the rector of Grace Episcopal Church downtown in the Chicago Loop. I had complained to Caroline that many of the sermons we had heard together in the churches we attended in San Francisco and in London were not, in my judgment, sufficiently theological in their exegesis of the Gospel text appointed in the liturgy of the day. On the occasion of a party for me, to which Caroline had invited Fathers Howell and Casady, she mentioned my complaint about sermons. Father Casady responded at once by inviting me to deliver a sermon at his church. He followed that up with a letter asking me to deliver a sermon on Mother's Day, May 11, 1980.

I did so, avoiding the text that was appointed for that day in the church calendar. I tried to explain the relation between the Mosaic Decalogue and Christ's two precepts of charity, on which, Jesus said, "hang all the law and the prophets." The title of my sermon was "The Old Law and the New," and since it was delivered on Mother's Day, I gave special attention to the commandment about honoring "thy father and thy mother, that the days of thy life may be long in the land the Lord thy God giveth thee."

Since then, I have delivered about twelve sermons in Grace Episcopal Church in Chicago and in Christ Episcopal Church in Aspen, and in other Episcopal churches elsewhere. About half of these sermons were delivered before I became an Episcopalian, and half after my conversion to Christianity, not from Judaism, but from being an irreligious person.

Caroline, who has listened to all the sermons I have given, thinks that they are not good pastoral homilies. They are not exhortative at all, but entirely explicative and exegetical—philosophical disquisitions about biblical texts and points in Christian doctrine.

All the facts I have just mentioned are in the background of my conversion to Christianity in 1984. Before I try to explain that event, there are two preambles to it, both philosophical, that I must report. One is the address I gave at the opening Conference on Science, Philosophy and Religion in 1940, entitled "God and the Professors." The other is my continuous effort, from 1943 to 1978, to improve the philosophical arguments for the existence of God—revision after revision of a lecture on that subject, all of them having their seed in my dissatisfaction with Aquinas's five ways of proving God's existence.

My writing *How to Think About God* in 1979 was the culmination of all those efforts from 1943 on. It was also a crucial step in my becoming a religious Christian. When I wrote *Philosopher at Large* in 1974-75, I did not foresee the book I was to write in 1979; for in the closing sentence of chapter fourteen I wrote: "Whether or not I shall ever be able to resolve the difficulties I have encountered in all earliest attempts to construct a valid proof of God's existence, the best judgment I can reach about the matter would, in my opinion, be a fitting close . . . to my philosophical career."[4]

It turned out to be much more than that, as I will relate after I have dealt with the two preambles that I mentioned above, which preceded *How to Think About God.*

From Philosophical Theologian to Religious Believer

Though I had become a person of Christian faith when I wrote *Truth in Religion* in 1990, I tried to write that book as a work in philosophy, not as a work of Christian apologetics. If I did not wholly succeed in this endeavor, my 1940 address "God and the Professors" was a philosophical statement about religion at a time when I was not a person of Christian faith.

In that essay I stated eight propositions about philosophy in relation to science that should be affirmed—or if not affirmed, then the denials should be rationally defended. The conference should not consist of professorial papers on loosely related topics, but rather of issues joined and disputed. The propositions set forth, which I affirmed, would most probably be denied by others and thus become the focus of debate. I meant this to be the case of the eight propositions I presented with respect to religion, as well as with respect to the propositions I stated about philosophy.

My essay on the philosophy of religion in 1991 reaffirmed, in a somewhat different manner, the eight propositions enumerated forty-nine years earlier in 1940. But it went further. The subtitle of *Truth in Religion* was *The Plurality of Religions and the Unity of Truth.* The unity of truth required that any religion that claimed truth—factual, not poetical, truth—for its beliefs had to be consistent and compatible with whatever truths were known at the time, with certitude or probability, in history, science and philosophy.

Among the plurality of religions that claimed truth for their beliefs, those that were in conflict with one another in such claims could not all be true; as, for example, theistic religions that are monotheistic and those that are polytheistic, or religions that are theistic and religions that are nontheistic. Therefore, with regard to truth in religion, we are confronted with the question, Which of the recognized world religions has the best claim to being true, or which among them has a better claim than others?

In the concluding chapter of *Truth in Religion*, I enumerated the considerations that individuals should have in mind when trying to answer this question for themselves. If the religions of Far Eastern origins do not claim to be supernatural knowledge, based on divine revelation, then they are theoretical or moral philosophies masquerading as religions. Even as counterfeit religions, if they are polytheistic or nontheistic, then their philosophical doctrines come into conflict with the truths of philosophical theology, and must be rejected. That leaves the three monotheistic and revealed religions of Western origin: Judaism, Christianity and Islam. These conflict with one another in their truth claims. If one has a better claim to being true, the others may partially share in that truth. Each is compatible with the truths affirmed in philosophical theology, but all three may not be equally compatible with the established truths of empirical science and history.

I thought of four other considerations that must be taken into account in deciding which of these three religions might have a better claim to being factually true. I enumerated them as follows:

One involves the matter of proselytizing: Should not a religion that claims logical and factual truth for its orthodoxy engage in missionary efforts to convert others to its belief?

Another criterion is the differing eschatology of these three religions—their views about the ultimate destiny of the individual human being or of mankind as a whole, their views about immortality, and about life after death, about divine rewards and punishments, and about salvation.

Still another is the difference in their views concerning the immanence as well as the transcendence of the supreme being.

A fourth criterion of the greatest importance is the extent to which God's self-revelation involves mysteries—mysteries, not miracles. Mysteries are articles of religious faith that exceed our natural human powers of knowing and understanding. They may be intelligible in themselves, but they are not completely intelligible to us.[5] Since I was a believing Christian when I wrote *Truth in Religion*, I felt that my own religious faith might be ill-concealed in the enumeration of those four considerations, which certainly favored Christianity over Judaism and Islam. Was I writing as a philosopher or as a Christian apologist defending the truth claims of his own religion? With this in mind, I concluded the book with the following paragraph.

As a philosopher concerned with truth in religion, I would like to hear leading twentieth-century theologians speaking as apologists for Judaism, Christianity, and Islam engage in a disputation. The question at issue would be which of these three religions had a greater claim to truth. It being conceded that each has a claim to some measure of truth, which of the three can rightly claim more truth than the other two?[6]

In 1979, when I wrote *How to Think About God*, I was not yet a Christian. I wrote that book as a pagan for pagans. As I said earlier, the argument therein for God's existence was, for me, the satisfactory culmination of fifty years of dissatisfaction with the arguments adapted by Aquinas from Aristotle in his statement of the first three ways of proving God's existence.

In that fifty years, I had written lecture after lecture trying to do better as a pagan philosophical theologian. In that fifty years, I had finally learned how to turn St. Anselm's so-called ontological argument from being an invalid argument for God's existence into an illuminating way of coming to understand what God is like and unlike. In that period, I learned from Thomas Aquinas and from Étienne Gilson of the Sorbonne, his disciple, the crucial premise in the proof of God's existence—not to be found in the *Summa's* Treatise on God, but in later treatises in the first part of the *Summa*, especially the Treatise on Creation and the Treatise on the Divine Government. Hence I would say that my *one* argument that concludes with affirming God's existence beyond a reasonable doubt (not with certitude beyond the shadow of a doubt) is Thomistic even though it does not appear in his *Summa Theologica* in the words of the formulation that I gave it.

This is not the place to summarize the analysis and reasoning in *How to Think About God.* But I might here call attention to a number of points that I regard as original contributions on my part. One was explaining that any sound argument for God's existence as the ex nihilo cause of the existence of the cosmos must assume that the cosmos always existed and did not have a beginning, as the first verse in Genesis proclaims. That is a matter of faith, not of reason, and so on the contrary assumption, which does not beg the question, God causes ex nihilo the cosmos by preserving it in existence, or by preventing it from ceasing to be.

Another point was that God as cause of the existence of the cosmos is not to be thought of as the first efficient cause in a chain of causes (and certainly not as the prime mover) but as the *only* cause of being, acting *directly* on the cosmos as a whole that is radically contingent (or capable of not being as a whole). The superficially contingent things, which are component parts of the cosmos, never totally cease to be but merely undergo transformation when they perish, as animals do when they die.[7]

The most important points of originality appeared in the epilogue of the book. Reading the *Pensées* of Pascal, I had been impressed by his statement that the God of the philosophers was not the God of Abraham, Isaac and Jacob, or of Moses and Jesus. But Pascal merely said that and did not explain why that was so, in what respects the God of the philosophers was deficient, and how that conception of God was related to the God believed in by faithful Jews and Christians.

The sound argument for God's existence that I claimed to have formulated did not conclude with *belief in God,* but only in a philosophical affirmation of God's existence. The divinity thus affirmed to exist closely resembled the God believed in by faithful Jews and Christians in all the negative traits of a supreme being—immateriality, eternity (which means "nontemporality"), infinity, uncaused. It also includes certain positive traits, such ontological perfections as omnipotence, omnipresence and omniscience, and even such analogically understood perfections as living, knowing, willing and God's freedom in his act of creation.

But there is one perfection that the philosophical conception of God does not include and that cannot be established by purely philosophical reasoning. That is the goodness of God—not his ontological perfection, but his benevolent love of his creatures, his providential government of and care for them, his being a gracious God who is both just and merciful, who answers our prayers and forgives our sins.

I therefore concluded by saying that the soundest rational argument for God's existence could carry us only to the edge of the chasm that separated the philosophical affirmation of God's existence from the religious belief in God. What is usually called "a leap of faith" is needed to carry anyone across the chasm. But the leap of faith is usually misunderstood as being a progress from having insufficient reasons for affirming God's existence to a state of greater certitude in that affirmation. That is not the case. The leap of faith consists in going from the conclusion of a merely philosophical theology to a religious belief in a God that has revealed himself as a loving, just and merciful Creator of the cosmos, a God to be loved, worshiped and prayed to.

The God of the philosophers is not a God to be loved, worshiped or prayed to. A God who is not concerned with human destiny by being law-giving and grace-giving is the God of philosophical and irreligious deists, not the self-revealing God of religious theists.

I think I have said enough about *How to Think About God* (published in 1980) to explain how that was the penultimate step in my progress from being a philosophical theologian to being a religious believer in God. What remain to be told are the events in 1984 that attended my leap of faith.

The Leap of Faith

In March of 1984, after a trip to Mexico in February, I fell ill, probably from a virus that I had picked up there. The illness was protracted. I was in the hospital for five weeks and then in bed at home for several months or more. Though I underwent all the diagnostic tests and procedures that the physicians could think of, the illness was never adequately diagnosed; and the cure, when it finally came, involved numerous antibiotics and two blood transfusions that brought my red corpuscle count back to normal.

During this long stay in the hospital I suffered a mild depression, and often when Caroline visited me I would, unaccountably, burst into tears. Father Howell, the rector of St. Chrysostom's Church, also visited me, and once when he prayed for my recovery, I choked up and wept. The only prayer that I knew word for word was the Pater Noster. On that day and in the days after it, I found myself repeating the Lord's Prayer, again and again, and meaning every word of it. Quite suddenly, when I was awake one night, a light dawned on me, and I realized what had happened without my recognizing it clearly when first it happened.

I had been seriously praying to God. But had I not said at the end of *How to Think About God* that no one who understood the God of the philosophers as well as I thought I did would worship that God or pray to him? Only if, by the gift of grace, one made the leap of faith across the chasm to the God of religious Jews and Christians would one engage in worship and prayer, believing in a morally good, loving, just and merciful God.

Here after many years of affirming God's existence and trying to give adequate reasons for that affirmation, I found myself believing in God and praying to him. I rang for the night nurse and asked for paper and pen, and with great difficulty—for I was at that time not very mobile in bed—I managed to sit up and scrawl a letter to Father Howell. Caroline transcribed the letter for me the next day and then typed it out before sending it to Father Howell. It was dated April 1, 1984.

In the letter I told Father Howell of the conflicts and difficulties in my life and thought that had been obstacles to my becoming a Christian. I told him that when he prayed for me at my bedside, I wept and was convulsed. With no audible voice accessible to me, I was saying voicelessly to myself, "Dear God, yes, I do believe, not just in the God my reason so stoutly affirms, but the God to whom Father Howell is now praying, and on whose grace and love I now joyfully rely."

I went on by saying that "Caroline, I know, will receive this news with as much joy as you. She and I have talked about how our Christian marriage would end up. It has been a good marriage, but would not have been fulfilled without the step I am now prepared to take." I ended the letter by asking Father Howell to pay me a visit after I returned home.

He did and, on April 21, I was baptized a Christian by Father Howell in the presence of Caroline. A year later, at Father Howell's request,

I took the pulpit at St. Chrysostom's Church and gave an account of my conversion to the congregation, of which I had been a nonbelieving member for many years.

In that brief address, I reminded them that two years earlier I had given three Lenten talks about the substance of my book, *How to Think About God*, which had just been published. I reminded them especially about what I had to say concerning the leap of faith—that no one in his right senses would pray to the God affirmed in philosophical theology, but only to a God believed in and worshiped for his love and care, his grace and providence. I told the congregation of Father Howell's visit to me in the hospital and how at last I had been moved to prayer, which I recognized as an act of faith on my part, a living faith with hope and charity to complete it. I said that I still had residual difficulties—things that I still do not understand, and may never fully understand. But these, I said, do not matter. I ended by quoting Mark 9:23-24, where Jesus says to the father whose child is ill: "All things are possible to him who believes"; to which the father replies: "O Lord, I do believe, help thou my unbelief."

As I look back now upon the years of my life since then, I think I have not been as good a Christian as I promised myself I would be. To whatever degree I possessed moral virtue before I became a Christian, it was not augmented, certainly not to a heroic degree. I may probably be no worse a Christian than the many who confess their sins in church on Sunday—for having done things they ought not to have done and failing to do things they ought to have done—repent of their sins and ask for forgiveness.

If I have not been a sinless Christian, I have at least been a thoughtful one. I have pondered the mysteries that in the concluding pages of *Truth in Religion* I said were some of the things to be considered in deciding where greater truth was to be found among the three monotheistic religions of Western origin. For both Judaism and Islam the God believed in is entirely transcendent—outside the cosmos as its creator and governor. Only for Christianity is God both transcendent and immanent—at once the eternal Creator of the cosmos and the earthly redeemer of humankind, as well as its indwelling spirit, omnipresent as well as omnipotent. This is, of course, the mystery of the Trinity—the one God, of which there are three persons or aspects, the one God who is both in heaven and on earth.

When dogmatic theologians conceive of themselves as engaged in the process of faith seeking understanding, they acknowledge an insuperable limit to that process. The limit consists in the mysteries of faith, which, however intelligible they may be in themselves, will never be fully intelligible to us on earth. In the concluding section of this essay I will briefly report the thinking I have done, since I became a Christian, about the mysteries of Christian faith.

The Mysteries of Christian Faith
Inseparable from the mystery of the Trinity is the mystery of the incarnation of the second person in Jesus Christ, one person with two natures, divine and human, and the mystery of Christ's passion on the cross, his resurrection and ascent into heaven. This complex mystery requires us to try—albeit unsuccessfully—to understand heaven as a purely spiritual place, totally distinct from this vast physical cosmos, as well as in eternity and totally timeless.

The Nicene Creed contains words that refer to all the elements in the complex mystery. Its most important words are those that declare the Son to be of *one substance* with the Father, words that apply to the Holy Spirit as well. All three persons of the Trinity are "one substance," which is to say that they are existentially one. In the physical cosmos anything that is existentially one entity or substance cannot be in two places at the same time. But God is a purely spiritual being, not in physical time or space, and so it can be said of God that he is existentially both transcendent and immanent. This is, of course, unimaginable (for nothing spiritual is imaginable), but it is not unthinkable.

We must be forever cautious to remember that the word *spiritual* has *only a negative meaning* for us: *not*-physical, *not*-material, *not*-corporeal. We must forever remember that we have no positive meaning for the words *spirit* and *spiritual*. That is why Maimonides insisted that all the properties we attribute to God are negative, and why Aquinas went beyond that (adding such positive properties as living, knowing and willing) by explaining that when used of God and his creatures these words are used analogically. God lives, knows and wills, but *not* in the sense in which creatures like us live, know and will.

In short, we fail miserably in our attempt to understand God if we ever allow ourselves to employ our imagination. The realm of spirits and the spiritual is utterly beyond the power of our imagination, which is rooted in our sense experience of the physical, material and corporeal world. That is why the fundamentalist literal reading of the words in sacred Scriptures or in the Nicene Creed—many of which have sensible, physical connotations—is such a disastrous mistake. It makes a mockery of the Christian faith and its mysteries.

Thinking About Heaven

I kept thinking about the mysteries at the heart of my Christian faith. My mind kept returning to the word *heaven*, which too many Christians, I feared, imagined as a place somewhere out there or up there in physical space, from which the second person of the Trinity descended and to which he ascended after his resurrection.

I remembered, of course, St. Augustine's interpretation of the word *heaven* in the first sentence of Genesis. The word used there referred to God's creation of spiritual creatures, the angels, as the word *earth* referred to all of God's physical creatures, not to the planet earth. Several verses later in the first chapter of Genesis, the physical earth and heaven—that is, this planet and the skies above it—are mentioned as being created in the order of the six days. Augustine's interpretation of the word *heaven* in the first verse avoids a contradiction with the reference to the physical skies and seas in the later verse, which the fundamentalists, reading Genesis literally, do not observe.

The trouble with the word *heaven* is that it has both an eschatological meaning in Christian theology and a physical meaning in ancient astronomy and modern cosmology. In the centuries before Christ, Aristotle used the word in a book, the title of which in English is *Of the Heavens.*[8] In even earlier centuries, the Old Testament, unknown to Aristotle, not only in Genesis but in many of its later books referred to heaven as the abode of God.

I arranged a conference at Christ Episcopal Church in Aspen to be held in August 1991. At that conference I called attention to the fact that the Egyptian, Chaldean, Greek and Alexandrian astronomy of antiquity knew a universe no larger than the solar system and the stars that were visible to the naked eye. The Ptolemaic astronomy of the Hellenistic era had the same limited scope. That was the very small known physical world at the time of St. Augustine and at the time when the Nicene Creed was formulated. The known cosmos did not increase in size in the thirteenth century when Thomas Aquinas wrote his *Summa Theologica;* nor did it change in size when the astronomy of Galileo, Copernicus, Kepler and Newton was substituted for that of Ptolemy. The telescopes of Galileo and Tycho Brahe made little difference because the observational power of their primitive instruments was so slight.

Under these circumstances it was almost impossible to prevent most Christians from imagining heaven as if it were a physical place up there beyond the visible sun, moon and stars. So too, the words "came down from heaven" and "ascended up to heaven" were imagined as physical directions. Even the phrase "resurrection of the body" led most Christians at that time to imagine heaven as a place where the physical bodies as well as the souls of the blessed would live together in eternal life after their earthly death. Whether any Christian theologians during these centuries totally escaped making such grave errors, I do not know. Their writings are not explicitly clear on these points.

Unfortunately, as I found out at my Aspen conference in 1991, many persons of Christian faith still hang on to these ancient and medieval superstitions about heaven. They appear to be disappointed when told that they are not going to rejoin their departed loved ones in a bodily reunion in an afterlife in the world to come. This is true even of those who have been informed by twentieth-century cosmology about the millions of galaxies beyond the one constellation in which our tiny solar system exists. They have been informed about the recession of the furthest galaxies known to us; and those acquainted with Albert Einstein may even remember his statement that the universe is finite but unbounded.

For there to be factual, as distinguished from poetical, truth in Christian theology in the twentieth century, it must be consistent and compatible with what we now know about the physical universe in terms of twentieth-century cosmology. We cannot allow our imaginations to give physical meaning to such words as *up there, out there* or even *beyond* the physical cosmos. A purely spiritual realm is simply *other than* the realm of physical, material, corporeal things.

It should always have been so understood, though the error in thinking otherwise of heaven may have been more excusable when Christians in antiquity and in the Middle Ages were misled by imagining heaven as if it were a place in the physical universe.[9]

If heaven as well as hell is a purely spiritual place, then our understanding of both must turn on our relation to God, whose kingdom is in heaven. Heaven is the place where those who love God are in the presence of God and where they enjoy heavenly rest in the beatific vision or contemplation of God. Hell is the place where those who do not love God deprive themselves of God's love, and of the knowledge of God through the beatific vision. The damned in hell do not suffer bodily fires or tortures. Their punishment is a pain of loss, not of sense.

I concluded the Christ Episcopal Church conference in 1991 by asking why we should not expect progress in Christian theology in the centuries to come. If we abide by Augustine's second precept for interpreting sacred Scriptures, we should look forward to changes and improvements in Christian theology that are in accord with progress in our scientific knowledge.

I will not live long enough to see the unforeseeable changes and improvements that are bound to occur; but on one point about the future I may be excusably blind. I do not foresee future progress in our scientific knowledge that will require any advances in philosophical theology. I feel secure in my rational affirmation of God's existence and of my understanding of the chasm between that philosophical conclusion and belief in God. I thank God for the leap of faith that enabled me to cross that chasm.

A Belated Return

TERENCE PENELHUM

Terence Penelhum is professor emeritus of religious studies at the University of Calgary in Alberta, Canada, where he was formerly professor and head in the philosophy department, dean of Arts and Science and director of the Calgary Institute for the Humanities. He has been president of the Canadian Philosophical Association and an editor of the Canadian Journal of Philosophy. *He has held visiting faculty appointments at the Universities of Colorado, Michigan, Washington, British Columbia, Waterloo and California at Berkeley. He is a fellow of the Royal Society of Canada and has received the Canada Council Molson Prize and the Alberta Achievement Award. He has also been awarded honorary doctoral degrees from the Universities of Lethbridge, Lakehead, Waterloo and Calgary. His books include* Survival and Disembodied Existence, Religion and Rationality, Problems of Religious Knowledge, Hume, God and Skepticism, Butler, *and* David Hume: An Introduction to His Philosophical System.

I was born in southwest England and spent all my boyhood there. My father was a railway worker: dependable, regular, unambitious; my mother, the daughter of a country policeman who died from injuries before her birth, was a complex and unsettled personality, with ambitions that could have been satisfied easily had her husband been even moderately wealthy, but which led her instead into discontent, stress and overwork.

I was the elder of two sons. Our parents loved us inordinately, in part because, in spite of their love for one another, their own ill-suitedness made their relationship chronically uneasy, and they could agree in their determination to sacrifice themselves to us. They had the English working-class parents' tendency to be overprotective of their children when they had to face the not-very-hard knocks that came their way through the requirements of outer institutions like schools. My prize-winning classroom performances were a source of great pride to them. I am deeply grateful for the fact that they always encouraged me in career and educational plans that can only have seemed wildly overambitious to their friends. This meant I went on, at the end of my secondary school years, to the immediate and intense study of philosophy. My parents were not just fond and foolish over this. They wrote to a helpful and wise lady at the University of London about the possible imprudence of studying philosophy. She advised them not to discourage me if I seemed good enough to do it well. I was in fact able to obtain generous scholarship support throughout my undergraduate and graduate career.

Early Religious Attitudes

My family belonged to the Church of England, and as a child I was taken to church regularly and was well instructed in Sunday schools. For some time I showed a consistent childlike piety. For a period of some four or five years, however, my parents became influenced by Christian Science. This is a sect toward which I have never since been able to assume the attitude of easy derision shown it by both Christian and non-Christian philosophers. Its thought may be egregiously confused; but it has no religious monopoly on this. I can well recall the exemplary serenity of one of the lady readers whom we came to know, and who had been converted to Christian Science through the dramatic physical healing she experienced from it. I also recall very clearly one occasion during the war when we were attending a service and the air-raid sirens sounded. The service was moved to a supposedly less vulnerable part of the building (I think a corridor). Another of the readers made the comment that the move had been made to conform to government regulations, but that since we were all in the care of God's love, where could we possibly be safer? Such a direct and simple absorption of the New Testament preaching of Jesus (and there was no particle of anxiety) is something I much aspire to now, and have rarely encountered. If it was combined with muddled metaphysics, I am not so consumed by analytical fervor as to believe that this matters greatly.

This brief period introduced me to the possibility of deriving unorthodox results from biblical texts. My recollection may now be faulty; but a frequently repeated juxtaposition of readings yielded the following argument: All things were made by him, and without him was not anything made that was made; God saw everything that he had made, and behold, it was very good; *ergo,* evil and disease do not really exist. The well-known dismissal of the belief in the reality of evil as "error" follows from this conclusion, and the perhaps muddled, but certainly very real, spiritual life of the few Christian Scientists I knew rested in no small measure on this argument.

That the texts did not always lend easy support to mainline orthodoxy was something that I came to learn during my adolescence from more sophisticated popular writings, especially those published in Britain at that time by the Rationalist Press Association. These were essentially antireligious tracts, and included such works as Paine's *Age of Reason* and the popular lectures and essays of T. H. Huxley. Through these I came to be aware of the more obvious problems of biblical criticism, and to think that the theory of evolution undermined not only the historicity of the Genesis creation and Fall narratives but also the doctrines historically associated with them.

I came to drift away from the piety of my childhood years, though I still attended Church of England services fairly regularly: partly, I suspect, because it enabled me to air, even parade, my apostasy to evangelical friends who were conveniently distressed by it. Needless to say, although I attended, I did not offer myself for confirmation.

This form of adolescent rebellion coincided with the beginnings of a genuine, though initially untutored, interest in philosophy, which led me on Saturday mornings (when others were occupied outdoors) to ride the train to our county town and borrow bags of books from the library—books that I did not understand very well, but that absorbed my interest extremely. Inevitably I gravitated toward philosophers who fed my incipient unreligiousness, such as Schopenhauer. If I could not read them, I read about them. I managed to gain an uncomprehending acquaintance with enough philosophical classics to persuade my Edinburgh University director of studies, a year or two later, to admit me at once into the honors philosophy program. (Norman Kemp Smith had recently retired, and I was told that during his hegemony no one had been permitted to enter this program until the second year of university study.) The result of this early phase in my intellectual development was that I always supposed philosophy to be an activity that addressed the same human concerns that religion addresses, and I have always found it hard to summon more than a prudential interest in those areas of philosophy that are least obviously connected with those concerns, such as logic or philosophy of language. I suspect that my motivations here are not unusual, at least for the period.

To Edinburgh University

This tale has now come to the time when I left home and went to the university. In personality I was the mixture of precocity and immaturity my history would lead one to expect, with my besetting sins being those of the mean and self-protective variety, rather than those of the passionate and red-blooded sort.

I was immensely fortunate, I now think, that I began my formal study of philosophy in Edinburgh. It was in any case a wonderful place in which to be a student: one of the world's truly beautiful cities. Although the greater days of Kemp Smith and A. E. Taylor were over, it was still a place where the Scots philosophical tradition that had come down from the Enlightenment was very strong, where the discipline was central in the curriculum, and where we were expected and helped to read the great classical figures in detail.

Some of my best fellow students in the subject were deeply committed Christians who were to proceed to theological study at New College. The Scots Presbyterian tradition has always outclassed the Anglican in the philosophical capacities of its ministers, and this superiority reflects the more important place philosophy has in its national cultural life. Although I was quite inadequately grateful at the time for the privilege of being initiated into this national tradition, rather than into the self-conscious amateurism of English philosophy, I have been very grateful in the years since. The Scots revere and practice philosophy, but see the need to keep it in its proper place. I recall a friend quoting one of our teachers, Alan Fairweather, who had said that philosophy was a wonderful servant but a disastrous master. Hume of course would have agreed. It was not advice I followed very well.

My years at Edinburgh were blessed in another and profoundly important way. I met and fell in love with the fellow student who later married me and came with me across the world. She too was English and had come to Edinburgh by choice. At the time of my writing this, we have been married for forty-one years, and the undeserved and unwavering and unslavish love that she has given me has taught my ungenerous spirit something of what love is, and has been the primary manifestation of grace in my life. She has always been a steadfast Anglican, and she lived for years in the quiet hope that I would find my way back to the fold. She has always been singularly lacking in the particular vices that have most marred my own character.

Early Philosophical Views

I was fortunate, on graduation, in obtaining a scholarship, named after Alexander Campbell Fraser, which took me to Oxford. There I found myself in the midst of the new and self-consciously revolutionary philosophical environment of the early fifties. I was ill-prepared for it; not because I had not been trained adequately in philosophy, but because the ferment of new thinking, most of it still unpublished, had not then reached the more conservative Scottish environment. While I emerged from Oxford with the degree I sought, the significance of much of what I heard only became clear to me after I had moved on. I was always afterward viewed as an analytical philosopher by colleagues, and was deeply influenced by the new methods, attitudes and prejudices; yet I never felt within me more than the most partial identification with the influences that were so altering the way I thought and sounded.

One of the many forms of ambivalence with which I live is this philosophical one: while unable to think and write in any other than an analytical way (I genuinely cannot pen sentences that I do not myself feel I completely understand), and while deeply suspicious of the obscure and the technical, I have never lost the conviction that analytical philosophy, especially in the form then current in Oxford and assiduously spread abroad, is frequently sterile and frivolous and undeserving of the status it inherited in the university curriculum from the years before Wittgenstein. Although I later had good success as a teacher, I always found it hard to introduce students to philosophy using analytical writings: their value seemed, and seems, to me to be that of ironing out the furrows of puzzlement on the brows of people who had been bewildered by issues that others had identified. Such an activity, though satisfying enough, is only worth making a career of if the puzzles one attends to are deep enough.

Whatever the ambivalence, I came to see myself for a time as just another, lesser, analytical philosopher, and found it virtually impossible, with my best efforts, to discuss the subject profitably with philosophers who had not been exposed to what was then still a new virus. When I began to teach in Alberta, however, my original training was at least as important as my recent finishing, as I was forced at once into lecturing on history of philosophy to large classes of students who were, for the most part, studying this as a propaedeutic to philosophy of education. They had to have Plato; and it was useless to talk to them about Ryle without Descartes, or Wittgenstein without Hume and Kant. Although I have never worked so hard in my life as I did preparing these first classes, I have always been immensely grateful for the philosophical and pedagogical discipline that they gave to me. There is no substitute for the learning process entailed by preparing classes on complex arguments for student conscripts who are only potential specialists in the rarest of cases; one learns not to count on the common fund of assumption and prejudice that an audience of intending professionals supplies. Getting problems clear for the audiences I had entailed getting those problems clear for myself, and allowed no self-deception about when I had managed to achieve this. It was here that the analytical obsession with clarity became, again, so important.

The new cultural environment in which I began to teach in the early fifties in Alberta was one in which Christian faith was still much more common than it is now, and the much-discussed process of secularization had proceeded less far than in the larger urban centers of Europe and eastern North America. The university itself was secular and indeed anxious about the (largely imaginary) hazards of location in the "Bible belt" of the prairies; but the students and faculty contained many Christians of all denominations, and religion was still a potent political force. In this milieu, an audience on religious themes was easy to guarantee; and I acquired a certain reputation through public addresses on the supposedly new philosophical critiques of religion familiar to philosophers through the "Theology and Falsification" debates. My views on these matters were wholly derivative. I was, however, encouraged to include midlevel teaching on philosophy of religion in my repertoire, and I did have enough conscience to seek to place these fashionable debates in the context of more traditional philosophical theology. I therefore began to study Aquinas seriously for the first time and to reflect more widely on the philosophical credentials of Christianity.

My ambivalences on these questions prevented me from taking the crisply negative stance on them that philosophical fashion would have dictated, and I began to make a philosophical virtue out of seeing and describing both sides of every question. The printed result of this was a book called *Religion and Rationality,* which fell more or less stillborn from the press in 1971. This was several years later than it might well have appeared: I had, by this time, moved from Edmonton to our province's other campus in Calgary, where I had succumbed to the specious blandishments of institutional and departmental administration. When the book did appear, it was a monument of studied neutrality. Religion (by which I meant what I called moderately sophisticated biblical Protestantism) could not, I argued, be shown to be rational in the strong sense implied by traditional natural theology; that is, it is not *irrational* to deny any part of it. Nor, however, is it contrary to reason, in the sense of being conceptually incoherent or contrary to known scientific truths, to assent to it. Given the spiritual rewards some find in it, it is therefore, in this weaker sense, rational, though not metaphysically economical, to participate in it. Participation, however, is something that requires a decision that philosophy cannot make for a person. All the philosopher can do is make it clear that each side in the debate has a reasonable case, and a reasonable set of responses to offer to the criticisms of the other.

There is much in this volume I still think is correct, though it was already dated when it appeared. It was the philosophical expression of the personal position of someone who had backed away from the pure negativity of his adolescent years, but was now content to drift in comfortable and polite indecision, not choosing the austerities of open unbelief or the submission of reentry into the church, but letting life pass by while his wife saw to the religious education of his two beautiful children, and his students applauded his supposed insights but had the personal wisdom not to emulate his fence-sitting. In the inner recesses of my mind I felt I would eventually return to the fold from which I had drifted. But of course not yet.

The Study of Other Religions

Some further years went by; the writings multiplied, the indecision continued and fed my career preoccupations very conveniently. (Irreligious analytical philosophers found me undisturbing, for example. I think they still do.) As a result of some complex institutional developments, I found myself, by the end of the seventies, a member of a new instructional unit in our university. It had been decided to begin a religious studies department, which, in keeping with the needs of a public secular university, would provide academic instruction on many of the major religious traditions of the world: Western (Judaism, Christianity, Islam) and Eastern (primarily Hinduism and Buddhism). Its specialist students would be required to balance their studies between them. It was also to include a small number of instructors whose task would be to make students of these traditions aware of the philosophical and sociological dimensions of the academic study of religion, and thereby to encourage critical reflection upon them. The last ten years of my teaching career (until my retirement in 1988) was spent in this latter capacity. This was a great professional privilege, and provided me with several important demands and opportunities that most philosophers of religion do not have.

In the first instance, much as living in a country where one's first language is not spoken forces one to use another, it forced me to attend as best I could, with my limited scholarly resources, to the teachings and spiritual insights of religions other than the one I knew, and to see them as the live and open options that they are for so many. This, in turn, made me see my task as a philosophical teacher as that of making intellectual sense of those teachings and insights and enlarging my own imagination and that of my students so that their consequences, and the challenges that science and secular culture offer them, can be understood. My analytical skills became, even more, tools that had to be used to unravel and think through worldviews to which I had never attended before. I do not think I attained too much in the way of sophistication in non-Christian thought; but I do think I was able to help others know where it could be found and to recognize it when they encountered it. Most particularly, I was no longer able, or even tempted, to equate "religion" with the tradition I had known myself; and I did find it necesssary to see that tradition not only as one that had to confront the challenges of science and secular culture but as one among others faced with similar challenges. I was also blessed with some very fine and mature students, some of them well-informed refugees from the aridities of the philosophical traditions I knew so well.

It is perhaps of interest to say that the regional culture, though now greatly secularized compared with the one I entered thirty years ago, is still more significantly Christian than much of North America. Those students who enter the university from religious homes are, in my experience, rarely disturbed or antagonized by philosophical debate; what they find more difficult are the apparently skeptical implications of biblical studies.

Coming Home

For an indecisive and overprudent person, such opportunities reinforced my tendencies to drift and to indecision, by providing everproliferating grounds for them. But in spite of this, I found myself in 1978 asking our parish priest if he could present me for confirmation. I still find it hard to say what led to this—what factors in my own thinking and feeling served as the vehicles of the mercy of God. I cannot look back upon any conversion experience, and feel no kinship with, and at most a mild envy of, those who do. I can hazard some suggestions, however.

I think I had come, in the first place, to the realization that there was no reason, other than pure vanity and slothfulness, *not* to take this step. This is a most uninspiring entry to make in a spiritual autobiography, but truth demands it. For a long time I had stayed at home alone on Sunday mornings, being "too busy" with class preparation to accompany my family; but in these latter years I had been attending church with my wife with more regularity, and although my not having taken communion could not have failed to gain notice, I was clearly viewed as a full member of the congregation of our parish. My drift had been toward a renewal of the membership of my youth. My undoubtedly prudential and timid soul was also aware that time was passing, my health was less robust, and whatever was I waiting for? To take the formal step would be to come home. In such unpromising spiritual processes the mercy of God was at work.

There was another reason, not creditable either, and harder to state accurately. Our son died, suddenly and accidentally, a few days before his nineteenth birthday. His death, needless to say, was a great trauma for us and for his sister. No parent, especially a career-minded father, can experience this grief without major admixture of guilt, and I was deeply conscious of many failures of love. Praying for the repose of his soul was, and is, the only thing left to do for him. I do not say I turned back to the church because of guilt. (Not that this would have been an inadequate reason.) I say rather that these prayers for the dead were and are necessities for me, and I could not and cannot believe them to be unnecessary or unefficacious.

Our priest was cooperative in a way that (appropriately) dismayed me. He knew, because I had said, that I had all sorts of intellectual difficulties with the faith that I would go on sorting out, or failing to sort out, forever. He wisely treated them as irrelevant, and on the day when the bishop confirmed me I remember the nearest thing in my life to a distinctively and unambiguously religious experience: a strong sense, in the presence of those (the bishop, his chaplain, our priest and of course my wife) who had made this step so easy for me, that it was, indeed, unbelievably easy: that all obstacles had been imposed by myself, and that they had melted away when God's minister had quietly ignored them and not argued. (I should explain that my confirmation took place in this private setting, rather than in the publicity of a church setting, as a concession offered, as part of the openness I speak of, to what seemed my delicate health at that time.)

Christian and Philosopher

That was thirteen years ago. I have not made this step appear dramatic or turbulent, because it was not. There was a long time before I took it, and there has been a time since I took it; but I was never conscious of a clear moment of decision, or an occasion of Augustinian drama. I shall try to say something now about my life as a Christian (or someone who attempts to be one) and, in particular, given the purpose of this volume, how I see my work as a philosopher in relation to this change. I do not now teach, but I still try to think and to write, and my view of these activities still matters to me as much as ever.

I have said that I always believed philosophy to be an activity driven by the same human concerns as religion; and for me, at least, this has always been true. This does not make the life and thinking of the Christian philosopher a harmonious matter, since there is no doubt that in the case of the *Christian* religion, these concerns are met differently by the philosophical schools with which Christianity has coexisted, from the way in which the Christian must try to meet them. For the Christian believes that the message of redemption and healing that he or she has received not only is transforming but is the truth. While faith and belief are not the same, certainly one includes the other. I myself find my unquestioned identity as a philosopher mixes uneasily with my attempted identity as a Christian. This uneasiness manifests itself in my experience in several ways.

There is first, and least importantly, the fact that most academics, let alone most philosophers, are not Christian, and that the era of Dover Beach, when those who have no faith experience at least a vague regret at the fact, is long gone. Insofar as this has created an environment in which the Christian philosopher feels anxiety about professing the faith he or she has, it is deplorable, but I suspect it will pass. Those who are stridently antireligious are shaking their fists at the empty sky; and the very entrenchment of secularity makes them anachronisms. We shall now face a world in which our faith is seen as an optional oddity; but, in North America particularly, optional oddities are easily received socially, and the Christian will probably have an easier fate than the more truculent of our Marxist colleagues are about to experience. For myself, the worst I encounter when I talk about philosophy of religion is smaller audiences. I speak here of colleagues, however, not students.

But there are more serious inner clashes between the philosophical and religious strands in my psyche. They derive from the fact that I find myself an *unrepentantly* philosophical being, which puts me at a mental distance from most of my fellow Christians. Here my philosophical character has been intensified by my acquaintance with religious studies. I have become aware of the multiplicity of religious and secular worldviews, each supported by reasons, each felt and experienced, many institutionally developed and expressed, and each having resources for fending off and explaining away the claims of the other. I have found it easy, professionally, to assume the stance of each and all of them for pedagogical purposes. And I think it a mark of human enlightenment to be able to enter imaginatively into these alternative visions, since each of them is a vision that is lived by rational beings.

As a philosopher, I find that my intense awareness of the multiplicity of rational alternatives makes me feel deep alienation from fellow Christians who appear to be blessed with certainty, and with a correlative perception of the obvious falsity of such alternatives. To be frank, I do not feel their certainty to *be* a blessing: better, surely, I cannot help telling myself, to be Socrates tentative than a pig without questions.

I cannot forbear developing this a little further. Some of the Christian *philosophers* I know and admire seem at times to me to view philosophy merely as a set of defensive weapons with which to fend off arrows launched by alien attackers; to have escaped, or lived without, the wonder and puzzlement of philosophy, and to be not philosophers but armored warriors of the faith. I am not like this, and cannot bring myself to wish to be.

I must recognize, however, that in thus seeming to make a virtue out of hesitancy and ambivalence, I seem indeed to run counter to the Scriptures. The faith that is said by Jesus, again and again, to be the source of healing and to characterize the citizens of the kingdom is a faith that seems to leave no room for doubt, hesitation or ambiguity. So I have a chronic unease about my identity as a philosopher and its compatibility with my identity as a Christian, an unease that generates an obsessive concern with problems about the nature and epistemic status of faith itself.

This might lead one to expect my attitude toward doctrinal questions within the faith to be a liberal one. Here, however, I join with those many others in the church who have philosophical predilections in having an instinctive preference for theological conservatism. This preference comes from a philosopher's low pain threshold in the face of fuzziness and muddle. So although I applaud his recognition of the community of motivation between religion and philosophy, I am frequently irritated by Tillich in a way I am not by Aquinas or Barth. I should also say that in my own Anglican communion, my history of wondering whether or not I could conscientiously participate in the liturgy has made me one of those who now face liturgical change with very great reluctance. (For my sins, and there can surely be no other explanation, I find myself on a church commission charged with evaluating those very changes.)

My theological conservatism does have limits, however. Here I do not find myself attributing my attitudes to philosophy, but to my absorption of the wider scientific culture. Some theological options seem to me totally closed, and the consideration of them to invite justified ridicule from the most sympathetic enquirers. Such are beliefs in a historical Fall, or a physical ascension. I cannot bring myself to entertain such claims seriously or, therefore, to adopt any forms of biblical interpretation that would require this. We know too much to continue to encase our Christian teachings in antiquated cosmologies in the way such options require.

I am more uncertain about how the Christian should respond to the moral trends of our time: not the trends in moral behavior, but the trends in moral thinking. Clearly the New Testament cannot be the sole source of anyone's moral decisions on matters of global politics, environmental crises and sexual revolution. I have to say that the Judeo-Christian tradition deserves many of the strictures leveled against it by environmentalists, but that moral progress in this sphere is a matter of learning new things that our Christian gospel has for the most part not addressed. In matters of sexual equality, the gospel has within it principles that can be nourished and developed to meet the challenges that our day and age makes us heed.

Finally, a word about the philosophical difficulties within the faith itself. Naturally my return has changed my hopes and fears and opinions on some of these; but less than might be expected. Philosophy is full of challenges to beliefs that all, or some, people have; and the philosopher must often continue to hold a belief that he or she sees no way of justifying, and to which indeed the objections continue to mount. What is important is not that one have all such objections answered, but that one continue to seek such answers and not resort to Johnsonian dogmatism or, worse, facile skepticism. The Christian philosopher does not have to suppose that all the difficulties in the books are resolved; only that some of them can be and have been, and that the rest are not altogether intractable. I spent a good deal of professional time, for example, on questions about life after death. I have not suddenly joined those who believe, as I know some do, that there are obviously no problems about the coherence of this belief; on the contrary. But I have come to realize that my very real philosophical bewilderments, like those problems in secular epistemology that I first learned of when starting to study philosophy, can and do coexist in one and the same mind with the beliefs that they challenge. The coexistence is uncomfortable, and to the rational being an inescapable and perpetual demand for resolution; but it need not, I hope, negate the possibility of faith. Whether the latter is something I have is not for me to say. I can only hope that my desire for it is not something that the kind of philosopher I have become makes it impossible, under the mercy of God, to satisfy.

Vocatio Philosophiae

LINDA TRINKAUS ZAGZEBSKI

Linda Trinkaus Zagzebski is professor of philosophy at Loyola Marymount University. She is the author of Divine Foreknowledge and Human Free Will *(Oxford University Press, 1991) and the editor of* Rational Faith: Catholic Responses to Reformed Epistemology *(University of Notre Dame Press, 1993) and has published articles in metaphysics, philosophy of religion and epistemology. She is on the executive committees of the Society of Christian Philosophers and the American Catholic Philosophical Association and has directed three regional conferences of the SCP in Los Angeles. Zagzebski is on the editorial board of* Faith and Philosophy.

Writing autobiography, it must be admitted, is a self-indulgent activity. Just living is difficult enough. Living reflectively is even more difficult. Living reflectively out loud is yet more difficult, and what is worse, it is fraught with temptations. The autobiographer becomes the principal character in a narrative of which she is the author. But there is a tension between the roles of author and character. As author, she must pass judgment; as principal character, she is still in the process of living the life that will some day be judged. Her natural tendency is to protest, "Not yet! I have not finished." And even if the story passes scrutiny for veracity, how likely is it that it will be interesting? How many good novels have characters who could have written the novel themselves? How many fine biographies are autobiographies? To attempt the task of autobiography is probably foolish. In any case, it is risky. The fact that I have agreed to write this story at all is probably a sign that foolhardiness is part of my character.

Childhood

I was born at the beginning of the baby boom right after World War II, a second-generation native Californian. My mother came from a poor Irish Catholic family and was training to be an opera singer, an aspiration totally opposed to her family's expectations and values. She had to decide whether to try for her lifelong dream with no assurance of success and plenty of assurance of family resentment, or to play it safe. She did the latter and gave up her career aspirations the day she married. But that was not the end of her dream; she made sure I went the other way.

My father was a young lawyer in the army who had been a friend of my mother's family since she was fourteen. While visiting the family on a three-day leave in May of 1945, he took my mother and grandmother out to dinner, proposed, and married my mother two days later. My mother tells me that that was their only date, if you can call it that.

When the war ended soon afterward, my parents joined the flood of American servicemen and their brides who came back to California to start their families. New communities sprang up all over, full of young couples beginning married life in the booming postwar period. The San Fernando Valley, where my parents settled, was transformed in just a few years from bean fields and citrus groves to hastily built housing tracts. Churches could not be constructed fast enough to keep up with the population explosion, and at first my parents had to go to Mass in a tent. In no time all the new babies began reaching school age, and our parish built a school, but the demand for classrooms far outstripped the building rate, and my first-grade class was packed with sixty-five pupils. No wonder the nuns in those days had to clamp down hard on discipline! They were mostly young, inexperienced girls themselves, some still working for their college degree, knowing little of educational theory and even less of child psychology. The fact that these women could keep their sanity at all is reason enough to admire them.

The fifties were a great time to grow up. We lived in a close-knit neighborhood where many of the families had children my age and that of my younger sister. Violence and evil existed only in stories and on television. The focus of our lives was the church and the parish school, and that gave me a sense of being different, since Catholics were a distinct minority in our neighborhood. My memories of my childhood religion are vivid, mostly involving the more sensuous aspects of Catholic religious practice such as processions in the incense-filled church, where I solemnly walked as the organ played, dressed in my First Communion dress and veil and carrying a bouquet of flowers. There were also May crownings of the statue of the Virgin Mary in the schoolyard with wreaths of flowers, praying the rosary with my class, collecting holy cards, singing in the children's choir. The priest had to come to our house to give me my First Communion because I had rheumatic fever and had been confined to bed for many months, which meant I missed most of second grade. My mother taught me herself in consultation with the teacher, and not knowing how much was enough, she had me way ahead of my class when I returned to third grade the following year.

During my elementary-school years I especially enjoyed reading lives of the saints. I do not think I have ever had role models or heroes except for those saints. As I got older it saddened me that I could no longer relate to any of them the way I had when I was young. What was considered saintly in a woman did not appeal to me, while what was considered saintly in a man left out too much of my own feelings and desires. But while mourning my loss, I was aware of being exposed to many holy lives, and the experience of knowing holy people is still the most important evidence to me for the truth of Christianity. Of course, we read Bible stories and had to memorize the Baltimore Catechism, but the emphasis throughout my religious education was on spirituality and the sacraments.

I went to the same parochial school from first through eighth grade. My life was safely circumscribed in an area of a few square blocks. My family did not travel, although we did occasionally go for Sunday drives, but in spite of the very narrow range of my direct experience, I was exposed through the books in my home to a world incomparably greater than anything I had experienced for myself. My school afforded the same combination: the narrowest range of direct experience along with the widest scope for the spirit. While greatly restricting our freedom by dictating our activities for the greater part of the day, both at school and at home, due to large quantities of homework, it gave us a sense of a world that not only went far beyond ourselves but went beyond this world altogether. My teachers, both religious and lay, had a remarkable religious imagination. I remember thinking I knew just what heaven was like. Unfortunately, I cannot remember now *what* it was like.

From an early age everybody told me I was wonderful—parents, family friends, teachers, the parish priest—and I was silly enough to believe it. By the time I was old enough to realize that my belief was based on inadequate evidence, it was too late; the effect on me was permanent. In spite of every effort to have an objective view of myself, I still cannot escape the sense of being wonderful. While I recognize the irrationality of this view, I cannot prevent its affecting the way I think of God, other people and even such highly abstract philosophical questions as the connection between Being and Goodness. As philosophers, we usually like to pretend that most of our philosophical positions are arrived at exclusively through something called "reason," but I believe that even the most careful thinker is heavily influenced by qualities of temperament, and that these qualities unify the pattern of one's beliefs. Reason alone underdetermines coherence, and it does not give one's belief system a style. Religious faith helps to produce such a style, and that is probably why the minds of the great theistic philosophers of the past are interesting in a way that is rare among the more arid minds of even the best nontheists.[1] This is not to say that religion gives one a personal style; that is still up to the individual. But it gives one's beliefs a flavor, a strength and an intensity lacking in those whose beliefs are *merely* beliefs.

The message that I was wonderful had another side, as so many of life's messages do, and in this case the other side was the strong sense of sin that was cultivated in us at home and in school. In our daily religion classes we were often presented with stories of children in typical situations, and we were supposed to figure out what the child should do. It turned out to be very easy to sin. Even the slightest angry word to an obnoxious sibling or a delay in obeying our parents would offend God. But we were also taught that our sins would be cleansed through the sacrament of penance, so we developed the sensibilities of alternating remorse and joyful gratitude. The very fact that we were capable of both good and evil showed us our importance. Each of our mundane acts had cosmic significance. We marveled at the majesty of God and the wonder that our own small selves could be raised to the level of sanctification. Of course, our religious feelings were magnified far beyond the level of any feeling encouraged in childhood today, and some psychologists blame the church for giving us such a sharp sense of guilt. But I suspect that people who are not capable of very strong feelings of personal guilt are probably not capable of very strong feelings of love either.

The terror of being in sin fostered in my childhood was well expressed by John Henry Newman, a writer whom I did not know at the time:

> It is better for the sun and moon to drop from heaven, for the earth to fall, and for all the many millions on it to die of starvation in extremest agony, as far as temporal affliction goes, than that one soul, I would not say, should be lost, but should commit one venial sin, should tell one willful untruth, or should steal one poor farthing without excuse.[2]

I do not recommend contemplating these words for too long without the counterbalance of acknowledging and accepting forgiveness.

Once I reached seventh and eighth grade, I was occasionally asked to teach some of the classes in the lower grades—usually math or grammar. It seems that one or two teachers sometimes found herself at a loss about how to teach some of the basic skills, and I apparently had the ability to explain these things to younger children. I was also asked to read to the kids, give them spelling tests, and supervise their in-class writing assignments when their regular teacher had to be out of the room. Sometimes even in my own class I was asked to explain a subtle point of grammar to the class when the teacher found herself at a loss.

High School and University

After elementary school I attended Providence High School, which at that time was an all-girls' Catholic school, across the street from Walt Disney Studios. In ninth grade my lay religion teacher exposed me for the first time to the theistic arguments of Thomas Aquinas. I remember her saying to us, "Young ladies, it is now time for you to develop a more adult faith. It is not enough to just believe what you have been taught since birth. You are now old enough to know the *reasons* for your belief in God and in the Catholic faith." It is interesting to contrast my experience at fourteen with Alvin Plantinga's well-known example of the fourteen-year-old theist who believes in God because that is what she was taught. Plantinga says her belief is "properly basic" and uses this example to defend his claim that belief in God can be and often is justified even if it is not based on propositional evidence of any kind. In my education it would not be denied that it is possible for theistic belief to be justified in the way described by Plantinga, but there is no doubt that it was thought to be epistemically superior to have reasons.

We debated the cosmological argument in that class, along with the divine attributes. I usually took the devil's advocate position because no one else seemed able to do so. I discovered puzzles in God's attributes that had not occurred to my teacher and was particularly taken with the problem of divine foreknowledge and human free will. Many years later my first book was to be on this dilemma. It is interesting that while I thought the theistic arguments important, it did not bother me that it was so easy to find fault with them. In fact, that made them all the more fascinating. Imagine how boring natural theology would be if the arguments had the same strength as the proof of the Pythagorean theorem! In his autobiography Bertrand Russell relates his investigation into these questions at the same age with a very different result. My reaction was to find the arguments immensely thrilling, and my attitude toward them was curious tolerance. After all, I was aware of being young and having lots of time to figure things out in the future. I wonder if I'll feel the same way when I'm eighty.

Fortunately for me, my religion teacher was both open-minded and smart. She seemed genuinely delighted that I was able to come up with a continuous stream of rebuttals to her defenses of Christianity. Throughout my high-school years she had it in her head that I would go into philosophy. I thought that strange since in my last year of high school I all but ignored everything but math and physics. I thought she obviously did not know me very well.

The girls in my school were all sheltered young women. Only once or twice during my four years did I hear of a girl who had to leave school because she was "in trouble." Disciplinary problems usually involved coming to school wearing too much makeup or talking in class. The worst offense in the school behavior code—that than which nothing worse could be conceived—was smoking in uniform. My worst offense was chewing gum in the auditorium.

The fact that my school had no boys was a great advantage. I did not have to spend time primping in front of a mirror between classes and manipulating a seat next to my current heartthrob, thereby missing most of the class lecture. The amount of time I spent primping on Saturdays getting ready for dates was quite enough. More important, I did not have to compete with boys for the attention of teachers. There is a growing body of evidence that mixed classes tend to perpetuate gender stereotypes and that girls educated in all-girls' schools are more apt to succeed in high-status professions or business.[3] I am not able to say whether the girls at my school became more successful than their peers at coeducational schools, but I can say that we were treated as if our education was important, and a career was definitely treated as a viable option for those who wished it. Our laboratory facilities were not impressive, nor was our school library, but I fell in love with physics there and decided to become a physics major in college. I wonder if I would have felt constrained to choose a more traditional feminine pursuit if I had not attended a girls' school. In any case, I was the first student from my high school ever to be accepted at Stanford. My acceptance paved the way for others. The next year they accepted two more, and the following year, another. I don't know what happened after that.

I had a lot of status in my little school, primarily academic, although probably enhanced by the fact that my boyfriend was admired. However, I was never in the really popular girls' circles. Even then I found a greater similarity of interests with boys than with girls. I remember learning about psychological differences between males and females in my senior class on marriage and the family, which I rejected as so obviously false as not to be worth serious consideration. I later learned that in some ways I am atypical, but amazingly enough, what is unusual about me has never hurt me. In fact, it has been a decided advantage.

The supreme moral problem for my friends and me in high school was how long a kiss could last before it became a mortal sin. Naturally, we did not want to be deprived of one microsecond of our boyfriends' caresses. It never occurred to us that it was not absolutely essential to go to the very brink of mortal sin before stopping. So much for the childhood concern that even venial sin was to be avoided at all costs.

The big worry of family and school (next to the threat of boys) was the evils of secular universities. The teachers at my school spent an inordinate amount of time warning us about the terrible world "out there" and telling us how we would have to be on guard. My principal, while clearly delighted that one of the school's own had been deemed acceptable to one of the great universities in the country, cautioned me to attend a Catholic college instead. I stood my ground in telling her that I had every intention of going to Stanford. After all, I reasoned, if my father was willing to borrow to the hilt to pay for it, it must be worthwhile. Besides, I thought of it as the first great adventure of my life, and it did not disappoint me.

My speech at graduation was an appeal for young women to do the extraordinary, to dream dreams their mothers had not thought of, to try, even if they failed. Since Bob Hope was the principal speaker and spoke immediately after me (his daughter was in my class), television news cameras were present and videotaped my speech. On the news that night it was reported that I had given a "feminist" speech. I had always associated the word *feminism* with suffragettes of a previous era and so was not sure how to take this appraisal.

Now I have to admit that my feminist credentials are not very good. For one thing I do not accept the feminist line on abortion; for another, I actually *like* the metaphysics of modality, the philosophy of time, theories of meaning and reference, the logical paradoxes, and other areas of philosophy that are said to appeal more to the male mind. I know that many women have experienced mistreatment in a variety of forms and find themselves always on the outside looking in to a world made for men. When I look at problems such as sexist language and institutions that discourage women from attaining positions of power and authority, I strongly agree with the feminist line. On the other hand, my personal experience has not primarily been one of discrimination or mistreatment. I am not denying that I have been disadvantaged in some respects, but in other respects I think that being a woman has actually been an advantage. For example, people will usually remember someone who stands out in some way more readily than someone who is just like everybody else. When I gave my first paper at a conference, I was the only woman in the room. (I did not notice this at the time; it was pointed out to me later.) People remembered me more easily because I was a woman. If the same paper had been given by a man, I wonder if the reaction would have been the same.

My first year at Stanford was probably the most joyful of my life. I had had no idea there were so many talented people in the world my own age, and the fact that there were more than twice as many male as female students meant that I could go out as much as I wanted, and that turned out to be almost every night. I studied, of course, but that was a form of fun for me, and the truth is, it still is. When I think that I am actually paid for doing what I would want to do anyway, I am so full of gratitude at my good fortune that it is hard to work up much righteous indignation at the low salaries of academics. In fact, I've never gotten over my amazement that I get paid at all.

Stanford's curriculum made no firm distinction between lower- and upper-division courses, nor even between undergraduate- and graduate-level courses. A student was allowed to take any course whatsoever. This meant that there were graduate students in some of the classes I took as a freshman. My first quarter I chose as an elective a course in Chinese philosophy from the noted scholar David Nivison. Since there were so many upper-division and graduate students in the class, I decided that I had best keep my mouth shut, but it never occurred to me to drop the class. I had never heard of such fascinating stuff before, and I suppose it appealed to my romantic love for the exotic.

Right away I realized that I was not sufficiently prepared to be a physics major. I was only average in the accelerated calculus class, and while I did well in physics, I was not very good at the laboratory part of the courses. I immediately changed my mind about the major but continued to take physics courses while sampling as many other fields as I could. I thought about majoring in French, then anthropology, then history. Finally, in my junior year I decided that the only thing exciting and difficult enough to keep my attention for the rest of my life was philosophy. The first school of philosophy that captured my imagination was existentialism, and then phenomenology. I wrote my honors thesis on Kierkegaard's idea of indirect communication, and at the time I thought I understood what I was talking about. When I reread it now, though, I am not so sure.

Spiritually I was coasting. I prayed and went to Mass, but I did not identify with the Newman Center culture. I have found that on each campus, religious or secular, there are people who tend to swarm around the religious centers and they form their own kind of subculture. I have never felt at home in one of these groups. The problem as I see it is that the Christian calling contains a paradox. While there is no motive to change the world without a critical stance and the distance that entails, our voices will be viewed with suspicion unless we love the culture we aim to change. By temperament I am less critical and more accommodating than most committed Christians. My instinct is to minimize conflict and to try for the broadest span of human appeal, with confrontation a last resort. The public message given by Christians, though, is very often confrontational in tone. I find this disquieting. Of course, it is true that Christians are called to a set of values that deviate from the historical forces shaping our society at numerous points, so we cannot help but be critics of our culture in many ways. But the danger is that to be taken seriously we cannot be too far removed from the culture we wish to influence. If Christians are perceived as a whining fringe group, we will not have any real effect on that culture. Ideally, we should aim to have one foot in and one foot out. In practice, I am more in than out. This is probably one of my major defects.

My sophomore year at Stanford I had the good fortune to spend two quarters studying at Stanford-in-France in Tours. Previously I had never even been out of California, although travel was one of my fantasies. The experience was so wonderful that I all but forced my own sons to go to Europe twenty years later. As a matter of fact, I have dragged them there twice (soon to be a third time), and although they always enjoy themselves when they are traveling, they are basically homebodies like their father. But to me travel makes a great difference to the way I live my life. As I have already remarked, I believe that coherence among beliefs is only the bare minimum desirable in a well-formed belief system, and the same can be said for the coherence of values. Religion helps to give a set of beliefs and values features that link them to powerful motivations and feelings and thereby aid our quest for wholeness. This is what is meant by integrity in one of its senses. Logical coherence alone can never give us integrity in this sense. Still, if we consider how many different styles of beliefs and values we find within Christianity, there is no doubt that Christian faith alone is insufficient to give us that style of living that is distinctly our own. It is difficult to know what is distinctive about oneself and what one wants to live for without a vivid sense of unfamiliar ways of living. Travel is one way to get such a sense. Reading the literature of other cultures is another way. A third way is living in a culturally diverse city.

I live in Los Angeles, a city that is now in the process of conducting a social experiment never before attempted by any other city in the world. The city's staggering diversity was consciously encouraged by the growth mentality of the last one hundred years, and the demographic flow is incredible. The proportion of foreign-born immigrants has risen to over 40 percent of the population, and in the last thirty years non-Hispanic whites have dropped from 73 percent to 37 percent. Eighty-one languages are spoken in the homes of the children in the L.A. Unified School District; in the Beverly Hills school district the second most common language spoken is Farsi. Now the challenge is to find a way to unify the city in the absence of a common culture and in a period of economic downturn. Since the riots of 1992, there has been continuous and intensely self-conscious scrutiny among all segments of L.A. society on the sources of cultural conflict and potential remedies. While there is no shortage of proposals, I doubt that anybody really knows what will work. In any case, I believe that new styles of applying Christian virtues need to be discovered in order to make our society functional, let alone an environment most conducive to human flourishing.

Graduate School and Motherhood
After graduating from Stanford, I entered the Ph.D. program in phi-

losophy at the University of California at Berkeley. I met Ken in church there and married him my first year of graduate school. That year was probably the most violent in Berkeley's history and was for me a shattering awakening to the lack of wisdom of those in authority. During the first quarter demonstrations were held in support of Eldridge Cleaver, who had been invited and then disinvited to speak on campus; the second quarter saw demonstrations in support of the Third World Liberation Front; and finally, in the third quarter there were the violent and ultimately fatal confrontations over the student takeover of university property to create People's Park. In each case the most emotionally wrenching part of the experience was the recognition that the authorities I had always respected were on the other side. The sense of betrayal was staggering.

The background for these confrontations, of course, was the Vietnam War. If our country could make such a serious moral error, I reasoned, the causes of that error must exist in deep structures of our society that are easy to overlook. Like so many other students of my generation, I began to question all of the traditional institutions I had grown up with, including the church. When the National Guard took over, I was incensed. Fortunately, I did not become alienated from my parents, as happened to so many of my friends, but I did enter adulthood with a strong sense of mistrust of established structures and institutions. In some ways it was even worse for Ken, who went to Berkeley to get an advanced degree in engineering after graduating from the Air Force Academy. It is hard to imagine two places more different in 1968 than the Air Force Academy and Berkeley!

After Ken received his master's degree, he was assigned to an air base in Southern California. I went with him and transferred to the doctoral program at UCLA, commuting three hours a day from Riverside. Life was considerably calmer than it had been at Berkeley, but I remained mistrustful of and alienated from the church. My life changed dramatically two years later when I gave birth to twin boys, an experience that was without a doubt the most amazing of my life. This event was followed four months later by the beginning of the worst year of my life, when Ken was sent on a remote assignment in Korea for thirteen months. It took every bit of my strength to take care of our babies in the way I thought was best, and there was no question of a life outside of them. One day a week my father looked after them so that I could go to UCLA in the afternoon to attend a seminar. That was my only contact with the university or even with the outside world during that year. When Ken returned I was able to do a bit more, but my graduate studies were stretched out over ten years.

While I was pregnant, in the spring of 1972, Alvin Plantinga came to UCLA and gave a seminar while writing *The Nature of Necessity*. Toward the end of the term I was so huge I could barely get in and out of those space-economizing combination desk-chairs that universities use to pack students into classrooms. I did not quite make it to the end, as the boys were born during the last week of class. The course itself was exciting because Plantinga showed me that we do not have to choose between the fashionable technical topics in philosophy and the more enduring metaphysical questions, including those with a theistic focus. It is possible to do both.

I think that Christian philosophers today are faced with a problem in influencing the course of philosophy analogous to the problem I have already mentioned of Christians attempting to influence the culture. To be really effective, one should have one foot in the culture one hopes to influence, and to the philosopher this means that one should always be abreast of current trends in the profession. If possible, we should try to enter the discussions directly and not be content to produce a parallel strain of philosophy that has little interaction with the best of the secular philosophical literature. As a Catholic philosopher primarily trained outside the Catholic philosophical tradition, I have taken that as my principal professional aim.

Most women in philosophy say that graduate school is not kind to women. Among other complaints is that the dialectical method so strongly favored by most departments is adversarial and hence is distinctly masculine. While I did not find the method as unnatural as most women do, I also did not take it as seriously as the men did. One aspect of the method that I have always appreciated is that it assumes that philosophy is not a solitary activity. If one's ideas are worth anything, they ought to be able to withstand dialectical assault. But at the same time, the whole point of the dialectical exchange is to get at the truth, and it is successful only if all parties to the discussion are equally committed to a disinterested search for truth. I have sometimes found, though, that a lot of time is wasted in philosophical discussions by forcing the proponent of a thesis to do most of the work. Let us be honest about this. Socrates loaded his method in such a way that he had the advantage. The questioner *always* has the advantage. It is simply easier to find fault with a position than to propose a faultless position oneself. One problem in the standard dialectical approach to philosophy, then, is that it can be intellectually unfair.

There is another reason many women object to the dialectical method currently practiced, and that is that it can sometimes seem insensitive or even brutish. I am reminded of a passage in Virginia Woolf's novel *To the Lighthouse,* in which Mrs. Ramsay reacts to her husband, a professional philosopher, who has rebuked her for hoping, and allowing their little boy to hope, that they will be able to go to the lighthouse the next day when the evidence suggests that the weather would make such a trip unlikely: "To pursue truth with such astonishing lack of consideration for other people's feelings, to rend the thin veils of civilization so wantonly, so brutally, was to her so horrible an outrage of human decency that, without replying, dazed and blinded, she bent her head as if to let the pelt of jagged hail, the drench of dirty water, bespatter her unrebuked."[4]

Virginia Woolf's words could easily express the reaction of many women to sessions of the American Philosophical Association.

While I would never suggest that women care about the truth less than men do, I do suggest that many women refuse to believe that basic concern for human feelings gets in the way of the search for truth. Although I have no real evidence for this, it seems to me that courtesy and consideration for others are virtues that actually aid us in attaining knowledge. After all, a person who is discourteous and inconsiderate is apt to have the sort of egocentric concern for the good opinion of others that detracts from the openmindedness needed for knowledge. In any case, I agree with Aquinas in his claim that "only he who wants nothing for himself, who is not subjectively 'interested,' can know the truth."

My Return to the Church

Having children forces parents to come to terms with their own beliefs. While our sons were in preschool I had to make up my mind about what I believed. After all, they were going to grow up whether or not I was ready to tell them what kind of faith, if any, I wanted them to have. Even though my dissertation was on natural kinds, and most of my graduate research in philosophy of language, I decided I had to think about the connection between faith and reason and my own reasons for leaving the church. Philosophy makes us yearn for the truth, but it does not always show us how to find it. When it came to parenting, I found that sometimes the most ancient methods are the most trustworthy. If this was true for methods of child rearing, I reasoned, it might be true for other areas of our lives as well, including systems for forming beliefs.

Ken and I began to take the boys to Mass, and I was astonished at the beauty of the liturgy. It is true that there had been liturgical changes during my absence, but the primary change was in me. The natural order of religious belief is not usually to form propositional beliefs first and only later to engage in the faith life of a community. If we disengage ourselves from the practice of faith in order to "find out" if it is justified, there is very little chance that we will ever find out. This should have been obvious to me all along, since it had always been the character of the holy men and women I had known in my childhood that had most impressed me with the veracity of Christianity. When I asked myself what made me believe that a person's philosophy was trustworthy, I decided that ultimately the character of the believer is the most compelling.

I began to search for a theory of the human person that would be as demanding as the hardest-headed philosopher could reasonably expect, while not failing to neglect the importance of the emotions and other noncognitive aspects of the person. All of this eventually worked its way into an epistemological theory that is the focus of my current research. In *Virtues of the Mind* I propose a theory of knowledge based on intellectual virtue. I argue that intellectual virtues, like moral virtues, involve the proper handling of feelings as well as reliable cognitive processes, and that good believing, like good acting, is a matter of behaving the way a person with the Aristotelian virtue of *phronesis,* or practical wisdom, behaves.[5] At the time we came back to the church, however, I had no such theory formulated. It wasn't hard to identify those persons worthy of imitation, but I had no idea how to explain what such persons were doing in their belief formation.

I find the variety of reasons for believing interesting. While I think that the end of believing is to reach the truth and that one has an intellectual obligation to believe in accordance with the evidence, there are many kinds of evidence. Not all of it can be expressed propositionally, and not all of that need be capable of conscious explanation. If I am right that *phronesis* can be extended to practical wisdom in the matter of belief-formation, then a person's reasons for believing in God would be analogous to the reasons why a wise person makes a moral judgment. There may be no set of propositions that explain or justify such a judgment. If there were, moral judgment would be a purely procedural matter and *phronesis* would be unnecessary. Similarly, if *phronesis* operates in the realm of believing, the ultimate justification for beliefs is simply that they are the beliefs a person with *phronesis* would have in the circumstances. The evidence for the truth of the belief is not lacking, but it may not be precisely calculable by any conscious procedure operating on a set of propositions.

I admire the writer G. K. Chesterton for his combination of incisiveness and dramatic flair. Consider what he says about the rationality of religious belief:

> If I am asked, as a purely intellectual question, why I believe in Christianity, I can only answer, "For the same reason that an intelligent agnostic disbelieves in Christianity." I believe in it quite rationally upon the evidence. But the evidence in my case, as in that of the intelligent agnostic, is not really in this or that alleged demonstration, it is in an enormous accumulation of small but unanimous facts. In fact the secularist is not to be blamed because his objections to Christianity are miscellaneous and even scrappy; it is precisely such scrappy evidence that does convince the mind. I mean that a man may well be less convinced of a philosophy from four books than from one book, one battle, one landscape and one old friend. The very fact that the things are of different kinds increases

the importance of the fact that they all point to one conclusion.[6] As I see it, a person who knows how to put together the evidence of a book, a battle, a landscape and a friend has learned something that it is too easy to forget in our intellectually fragmented world. Yes, even philosophers are moved by landscapes and friends. (I'm not so sure about battles.) It takes insight, though, to see these things as evidence.

Philosophers are so used to being praised for intellectual acumen that it always does us good to be reminded that in the last analysis our minds are very small. In the words of Agur in the book of Proverbs:

Surely I am too stupid to be a man.

I have not the understanding of a man.

I have not learned wisdom,

nor have I knowledge of the Holy One.

Who has ascended to heaven and come down?

Who has gathered the wind in his fists?

Who has wrapped up the waters in a garment?

Who has established all the ends of the earth?

What is his name, and what is his son's name?

Surely you know! (Prov 30:2-4 RSV)

Teaching

When I finished my Ph.D. I began teaching at Loyola Marymount University and have been on the faculty there for fourteen years. I was very fortunate to find such a good position so close to home and in a university whose mission I wholeheartedly supported. Teaching at LMU has been a very rewarding experience. Speaking as both a mother and a philosopher, I can say that teaching undergraduates has more in common with the former than with the latter. The satisfaction of giving young minds ideas they never thought about is quite different from the satisfaction of personal discovery. It is probably true that we ourselves do not really understand what we are doing until we can explain it from the beginning to someone who not only does not know any of the background literature but also does not know why anybody would care about such matters. It is also good for us if we learn to appreciate just how far from the ordinary we philosophers are and why philosophy looks so odd to the ordinary person. Teaching does that. It also allows those among our students who are out of the ordinary like ourselves to find that out.

Being a college professor, like being a parent, forces a person to decide what is really important for young adults to know. This has been especially true for me as I have just served on a committee to revise our university's core curriculum at the same time as my own sons are in the university. The natural tendency of many academics is to be intellectually cautious—not to decide what to believe, but to remain as long as possible in the stage of considering the arguments for and against a position. But the next generation is not going to wait for us to make up our minds before growing up. At some point we simply have to make a commitment to the beliefs we want to govern their lives, as well as our goals for their education.

Universities are very interesting institutions. They give us a wide range of intellectual freedom, not only to think whatever we want but to teach whatever we want. At the same time they unwittingly impose their own form of oppression on us. I do not think that so-called political correctness is the result of conscious design; it simply results from the natural laziness and sloppiness of human beings who have grown tired of the intellectual life.

Is there a politically correct version of Christianity? I fear that there is, at least in the academic side of the Catholic Church today. Christianity is presented as the religion of the dispossessed—the poor, the powerless, the downtrodden, the friendless—in short, the unlucky. This is bad news for those of us who are all too vividly aware of our good fortune. I have been treated gently by life for the most part, but nonetheless, I believe that everybody suffers, just not all in the same way. Everyone needs God, but that need comes to consciousness through different paths. The experience of being deprived or treated unjustly is one of them, but the experience of being exceptionally blessed is another. Success-anxiety is a real phenomenon that calls attention to the flimsiness of temporal desires. While those desires remain unsatisfied, it is still possible to maintain the illusion that their satisfaction is sufficient for happiness. When they have been satisfied and a deep lack of satisfaction remains, we are forced to admit that material and professional success, and even good health and a loving family, are not enough. As St. Augustine said, "Our hearts are restless until they rest in thee, O Lord."

Vocatio Philosophiae

Philosophy arises out of wonder, and once we begin it, it does not leave us alone. It puzzles us, confuses us, inspires us, daunts us, satisfies us, causes us doubt. In short, it puts great strain on the emotions while simultaneously taxing reason to the limit and putting demands on the imagination unlike any other human activity. It is one of the principal ways human beings transcend themselves, the others being art, religion and love, and like the other modes of self-transcendence, it is sometimes painful. It should not be surprising, then, that beginners to philosophy often have a love-hate relationship with it. What students often find frustrating, more experienced philosophers find exciting; what students find enervating, the more experienced find invigorating. While there is no doubt such a thing as a talent for philosophy, it requires a commitment not unlike the commitment to a life of music or the arts. Like music, it is deeply pleasurable, but it can also be a vocation.

Philosophy is my vocation. I do not use the word *vocation* lightly since I believe that it is quite literally a summons. In my childhood the concept of vocation was used frequently. We were told in school to be constantly alert to signs from God that we were called to a certain state in life, although the alternatives were limited to the religious life, the married life and the single state. I do not recall anyone speaking of a vocation in such a way that philosophy could be anyone's vocation, although recently two friends and philosophers, Bob Adams and Carroll Kearley, have written of vocation in the sense I mean and have incorporated the concept of vocation into the context of moral duty. One has, I believe, a duty to follow one's vocation, and since I am less inclined than most to find duties in human life, my judgment that I have a duty to be a philosopher is a very strong claim indeed.

When I speak of a vocation I mean a lifelong project that centers a person's life on a particular type of activity and that one feels one has not so much chosen as discovered. Motherhood also centered my life for a very long time, but it will not have this same function for the rest of my life. As I write these words on my sons' twenty-first birthday, I have a strong sense of reaching a milestone myself. I have completed what was central to my life for the last two decades, and while I would still give my life for my sons, I cannot give them the rest of my self, the part that is not defined by being their mother.

During the first ten years of their life I was making my slow way through graduate school, and then began teaching a heavy load at LMU with a two-hour commute from Altadena each day. I was not engaged at all in professional activities outside the university. While I never doubted that I was meant for a life of professional philosophy, I did not regret the fact that my career was on hold. Instead, I searched out all the aspects of motherhood and domestic life that were most creative and emphasized those to the neglect of the more mundane aspects of homemaking. I became an enthusiastic cook and gardener, decorated our house within the limits of our budget, taught religion classes (CCD), participated in parish committees and actively designed my sons' education. When the boys began Suzuki music lessons in first grade, I began a process of daily involvement with their progress on the cello and the oboe that was to last twelve years and ended only when they both decided to forgo careers as musicians. As a member of the American Association of University Women, I was part of an extensive research project on images of girls and women in elementary-school textbooks. The result was a report and slide presentation that was presented at the Conference of the United Nations Decade for Women in Copenhagen in 1980.

During the last ten years the proportion of my time devoted to professional activities has gradually increased while the proportion devoted to my children and other domestic interests has decreased. I have been fortunate to have the opportunity to make the transition smoothly—an academic career is more flexible than most in this respect, and many other women are not so lucky. For me it has been possible to do just about everything I want in life, just not all at the same time.

Self-Transcendence

In my experience everybody loves Plato, but hardly anybody is a Platonist. Plato was right about one vitally important matter, though, and that is his understanding of the urge to self-transcendence, found in numerous places in the dialogues. My favorite is the analysis of love in the *Symposium*. There Socrates defines love as the desire for the perpetual possession of Beauty, or the Good. Plato's brilliant way of connecting love with both the aesthetic and the intellectual urge is one of the most important of the Greek ideas assimilated by Christianity. While philosophers and mathematicians are often faulted for being exceedingly cerebral, both have much in common with artists and mystics. If we all have the same ultimate end, this should not be suprising.

In the broader intellectual culture of the later twentieth century, the Christian vision has been largely lost. What's more, even the vision of our classical Greek heritage has disappeared as well. The result is that the urge to self-transcendence is often inverted. What is perceived as liberating is often constraining; what is perceived as joyful is often saddening; what is perceived as fulfilling often results in emptiness. What people presume to call free inquiry is often simply directionless. It is not always easy to tell in what direction is joy and in what despair, but much of our culture has not yet learned that appearances can be deceiving. G. K. Chesterton, at the end of his powerful book *Orthodoxy*, calls to task the inverted aims of the intellectual agnostic in his devastating prose:

> Joy ought to be expansive; but for the agnostic it must be contracted, it must cling to one corner of the world. Grief ought to be a concentration; but for the agnostic its desolation is spread through an unthinkable eternity. This is what I call being born upside down. The skeptic may truly be said to be topsy-turvy; for his feet are dancing upwards in idle ecstasies, while his brain is in the abyss. To the modern man the heavens are actually below the earth. The explanation is simple; he is standing on his head; which is a very weak pedestal to stand on. But when he has found his feet again he knows it. Christianity satisfies suddenly and perfectly man's ancestral instinct for being the right way up; satisfies it supremely in this: that by its creed joy beomes something gigantic and sadness something special and small.[7]

The Grace
That Shaped My Life

NICHOLAS WOLTERSTORFF

Nicholas Wolterstorff has a joint appointment in the divinity school and the philosophy and religion departments of Yale University. Prior to joining the Yale faculty, Wolterstorff taught for thirty years at Calvin College and also held an appointment at the Free University of Amsterdam. He has been selected to present the forthcoming Wilde Lectures at Oxford and Gifford Lectures in Scotland in defense of religious belief. His many important works include Works and Worlds of Art, Art in Action, Lament for a Son, Until Justice and Peace Embrace, Reason Within the Bounds of Religion *and* On Universals.

*T*he grace that shaped my life came not in the form of episodes culminating in a private experience of conversion but, first of all, in the form of being inducted into a public tradition of the Christian church.

The reformation of the Christian church that occurred in the Swiss cities during the second quarter of the sixteenth century took two main forms. One eventuated in the movement known as Anabaptism. The other became embodied in the churches known throughout Continental Europe as Reformed, and in Scotland as Presbyterian. I was reared in the tradition of the Dutch Reformed Church transplanted to the United States. My parents had themselves in their youth emigrated from the Netherlands. The place was a tiny farming village on the prairies of southwest Minnesota—Bigelow.

Simplicity, Sobriety and Measure

In his book on English dissenting movements, the poet and critic Donald Davie remarks that

> it was . . . John Calvin who first clothed Protestant worship with the sensuous grace, and necessarily the aesthetic ambiguity, of song. And who that has attended worship in a French Calvinist church can deny that—over and above whatever religious experience he may or may not have had—he has had an aesthetic experience, and of a peculiarly intense kind? From the architecture, from church-furnishings, from the congregational music, from the Geneva gown of the pastor himself, everything breathes simplicity, sobriety, and measure.[1]

That's it exactly: simplicity, sobriety and measure. We "dressed up" on the Lord's Day, dressed up *for* the Lord's Day, and entered church well in advance of the beginning of the service to collect ourselves in silence, silence so intense it could be touched. The interior was devoid of decoration, plaster painted white, ceiling pitched to follow the roof, peak high but not too high. The only "richness" was in the wooden furnishings. These were varnished, not painted; as a child I dwelt on the patterns in their unconcealed woodiness—perhaps because, coming from several generations of woodworkers, I was from infancy taught reverence for wood. We faced forward, looking at the Communion table front center, and behind that, the raised pulpit. Before I understood a word of what was said I was inducted by its architecture into the tradition.

Then the consistory entered, men dressed in black or blue suits, faces bronzed and furrowed from working in the fields, shining from scrubbing; this was the Lord's Day. Behind them came the minister. Before he ascended the pulpit one member of the consistory shook his hand; when he descended from the pulpit at the end of the service all the members of the consistory shook his hand, unless they disagreed. We sang hymns from here and there—nineteenth-century England, sixteenth-century Germany. But what remains in my ear are the psalms we sang. Every service included psalms, always sung, often to the Genevan tunes. Sometimes the services were in Dutch; then the older people sang the psalms from memory, always to the Genevan tunes. My image of the hymn tunes was that they jumped up and down. My image of the Genevan psalm tunes was that they marched up and down in stately, unhurried majesty—sometimes too unhurried for me as a child! The minister preached at length, often with passion, sometimes with tears, the content of the sermons—usually doctrine followed by application. He led us in what was known as "the long prayer," during which the consistory stood, eyes closed, swaying back and forth. Four times a year we celebrated the Lord's Supper. In a long preliminary exhortation we were urged to contemplate the depth of our sins and the "unspeakable" grace of God in forgiving our sins through the death and resurrection of Jesus Christ. Then, in silence alive, the bread and wine were distributed. The minister communicated last.

There was no fear of repetition. The view that only the fresh and innovative is meaningful had not invaded this transplant of the Dutch Reformed tradition in Bigelow, Minnesota. Through repetition, elements of the liturgy and of Scripture sank their roots so deep into consciousness that nothing thereafter, short of senility, could remove them. "Our help is in the name of the Lord, who has made heaven and earth," said the minister to open the service, unfailingly.

The cycle for one of the two sermons each Sunday was fixed by the Heidelberg Catechism. This catechism, coming from Heidelberg in Reformation times, had been divided up into fifty-two Lord's Days; the minister preached through the catechism in the course of the year, taking a Lord's Day per Sunday. It was doctrine, indeed, but doctrine peculiarly suffused with emotion—perhaps because, as I now know, it had been formulated for a city filled with exiles. The first question and answer set the tone; decades later they continue to echo in the chambers of my heart:

Q: What is your only comfort in life and death?

A: That I am not my own but belong to my faithful savior Jesus Christ.

A Sacramental Theology

If the aesthetic of this liturgy was simplicity, sobriety and measure, what was its religious genius? The only word I have now to capture how it felt then is *sacramental;* it felt profoundly sacramental. One went to church to meet God; and in the meeting, God acted, especially spoke. The language of "presence" will not do. God was more than present; God spoke, and in the sacrament, "nourished and refreshed" us, here and now sealing his promise to unite us with Christ. Ulrich Zwingli had considerable influence on the liturgy of the Reformed churches; for example, it was he rather than Calvin who set the pattern of quadrennial rather than weekly Eucharist. In part that was because he insisted that the climax of the Eucharist was Communion, and he could not get his parishioners to communicate weekly, accustomed as they were to communicating just once a year; in part it was because he interpreted the Lord's Supper as entirely our action, not God's. But in word and tone the liturgy I experienced was a liturgy of God's action; it was "Calvinistic." During the liturgy as a whole, but especially in the sermon, and most of all during the Lord's Supper, I was confronted by the speech and actions of an awesome, majestic God. Of course, liturgy was our action as well, not just God's. We gave voice, always in song, never in speech, to praise and thanksgiving and penitence. The religious genius of the liturgy was interaction between us and God.

And throughout there was a passionate concern that we appropriate what God had done and was doing. We were exhorted to prepare ourselves so as to discern and receive the actions of God; it didn't happen automatically. It was as if the "secret" prayers of the Orthodox liturgy had been changed into exhortations and spoken aloud; the concern with right doing was the same. And we were exhorted, as we went forth, to live thankfully and gratefully. Max Weber argued, in his famous analysis of the origins of capitalism, that the energetic activism of the Calvinists was designed to secure the success that was taken as a sign of membership among the elect. I can understand how it would look that way to someone on the outside; and possibly there were some on the inside, English Puritans, for example, who did think and speak thus. But it has always seemed to me a ludicrous caricature of the tradition as I experienced it. The activism was rather the activism congruent to gratitude. Sin, salvation, gratitude: that was the scheme of the "Heidelberger." Conspicuous material success was more readily taken as a sign of shady dealing than of divine favor.

My induction into the tradition, through words and silences, ritual and architecture, implanted in me an interpretation of reality—a fundamental hermeneutic. Nobody offered "evidences" for the truth of the Christian gospel; nobody offered "proofs" for the inspiration of the Scriptures; nobody suggested that Christianity was the best explanation of one thing and another. Evidentialists were nowhere in sight! The gospel was report, not explanation. And nobody reflected on what we as "modern men" can and should believe in all this. The scheme of sin, salvation and gratitude was set before us, the details were explained; and we were exhorted to live this truth. The modern world was not ignored, but was interpreted in the light of this truth rather than this truth being interpreted in the light of that world.

The picture is incomplete without mention of the liturgy of the family. Every family meal—and every meal was a family meal—was begun and concluded with prayer, mainly prayers of thanksgiving principally, though not only, for sustenance. We did not take means of sustenance for granted; my family was poor. Food, housing, clothes—all were interpreted as gifts from God—again the sacramentalism, and again, a sacramentalism of divine action rather than divine presence. Before the prayer following the meal there was a reading, usually from Scripture chosen on a *lectio continua* scheme, but sometimes from devotional literature, and often from a Bible-story book. Thus between church and home I was taught to read the Bible as doctrine, as Torah and as narrative; that there might be tension among these never occurred to me.

The Center

The piety in which I was reared was a piety centered on the Bible, Old Testament and New Testament together. Centered not on experience, and not on the liturgy, but on the Bible; for those themselves were seen as shaped by the Bible. Christian experience was the experience of appropriating the Bible, the experience of allowing the Bible to shape one's imagination and emotion and perception and interpretation and action. And the liturgy was grounded and focused on the Bible: in the sermon the minister spoke the Word of God to us on the basis of the Bible; in the sacraments, celebrated on the authority of the Bible, the very God revealed in the Bible united us to Christ. So this was the Holy

Book. Here one learned what God had done and said, in creation and for our salvation. In meditating on it and in hearing it expounded one heard God speak to one today. The practice of the tradition taught without telling me that the Bible had to be interpreted; one could not just read it and let the meaning sink in. I was aware that I was being inducted into one among other patterns of interpretation, the pattern encapsulated in the Heidelberg Catechism; sometimes polemics were mounted against the other interpretations.

The center from which all lines of interpretation radiated outward was Jesus—Jesus Christ. Of course I knew he was human; but the humanity of Jesus Christ did not function much in my imagination or anyone's interpretation. Jesus Christ was the incarnated second person of the Trinity. I must say in all candor (and with some embarrassment) that not until about five years ago, when I read some books on Jesus by Marcus Borg, E. P. Sanders, Ben Meyer, Tom Wright and Gerd Theissen, books that set Jesus within the context of first-century Palestinian Judaism, did Jesus' polemic with the Pharisees finally make sense to me and did Jesus become a genuinely human figure.

Describing precritical modes of biblical interpretation in *The Eclipse of Biblical Narrative*, Hans Frei remarks that "biblical interpretation [was] an imperative need, but its direction was that of incorporating extrabiblical thought, experience, and reality into the one real world detailed and made accessible by the biblical story—not the reverse." Then Frei quotes a passage from Erich Auerbach, in which Auerbach is contrasting Homer with Old Testament narrative:

> Far from seeking, like Homer, merely to make us forget our own reality for a few hours, it seeks to overcome our reality: we are to fit our own life into its world, feel ourselves to be elements in its structure of universal history. . . . Everything else that happens in the world can only be conceived as an element in this sequence; into it everything that is known about the world . . . must be fitted as an ingredient of the divine plan.

Frei then continues with the comment, "In the process of interpretation the story itself, constantly adapted to new situations and ways of thinking, underwent ceaseless revision; but in steadily revised form it still remained the adequate depiction of the common and inclusive world until the coming of modernity."[2] If Frei is right, the mentality in which I was reared was premodern; one of the ironies of history is that it now looks postmodern as well.

The Full Pattern

I remember my father sitting at the dining-room table during the long winter evenings in our house in the village on the Minnesota prairies, making pen and ink drawings. All his life long, I now believe, he wanted to be an artist; but he grew up in the Depression, child of displaced Dutch city dwellers consigned to farming in the New World, and it was never a possibility. There was in him accordingly a pervasive tone of disappointment. He was on intimate terms with wood; but wood was not yet art for him. I have since learned of Christians who see art as a device of "the enemy," something to be avoided at all costs. I have learned of other Christians who are torn in pieces by art, unable to leave it alone, yet told by those around them that art is "from the other side." My father-in-law was one of those troubled lovers of art. But not my father.

I have also learned of Christians for whom the life of the mind is "enemy." That too was not my experience. I take you now on our move from Bigelow to Edgerton, forty-five miles distant, in my early teens. My mother died when I was three. Of her I have only two memories: being held in her lap on a rocking chair when my arms were full of slivers, and seeing her lying still and pale in a coffin in our living room while I ate strawberries. After a few years of loneliness my father remarried and we moved to Edgerton, the village from which my step-mother, Jennie Hanenburg, came. The Hanenburgs were and are a remarkable family: feisty, passionate, bright, loyal. Though our family lived in the village, most of the others were farmers. So after morning church they all came to our house—aunts and uncles, cousins, every-body, boisterous dozens of them. Sweets were eaten in abundance, coffee drunk; and the most dazzling intellectual experience possible for a young teenager took place. Enormous discussions and arguments erupted, no predicting about what: about the sermon, about theology, about politics, about farming practices, about music, about why there weren't as many fish in the lakes, about what building the dam in South

Dakota would do to the Indians, about the local schools, about the mayor, about the village police officer, about the Dutch Festival, about Hubert Humphrey. Everyone took part who was capable of taking part—men, women, teenagers, grandparents. I can hear it now: one aunt saying at the top of her voice, "Chuck, how can you say a thing like that?" And Chuck laughing and saying, "Well, Clara, here's how I see it." Then when it was time to go, everyone embracing.

I must mention especially my Aunt Trena, one of the most wonderful women I have known; she also died young. One Saturday afternoon I walked into her house and heard the Metropolitan Opera playing on her radio; to me as a young teenager it was caterwauling. So I asked her why she was listening to that. Her answer remains for me a marvel and a parable: "Nick, that's my window onto the world." She had never gone to school beyond the fifth grade; she was then trying to finish high school by correspondence.

Reverence for wood and for art in my father; reverence for the land and the animals in my uncles, sometimes even for machinery; longing reverence for music in my aunt; reverence for the life of the intellect in everybody. In the tenth book of his *Confessions* Augustine imagines the things of the world speaking, saying to him: Do not attend to us, turn away, attend to God. I was taught instead to hear the things of the world saying: Reverence us; for God made us as a gift for you. Accept us in gratitude.

It has taken me a long time to see the full pattern of the tradition. I think it was something like this: the tradition operated with a unique dialectic of affirmation, negation and redemptive activity. On the reality within which we find ourselves and which we ourselves are and have made, I was taught to pronounce a differentiated yes and no: a firm yes to God's creation as such, but a differentiated yes and no to the way in which the potentials of creation have been realized in culture, society and self. And I was taught, in response to this discriminating judgment, to proceed to act redemptively, out of the conviction that we are called by God to promote what is good and oppose what is bad, and to do so as well as we can; as an old Puritan saying has it, "God loveth adverbs." The affirmation of what is good in creation, society, culture and self was undergirded by a deep sacramental consciousness: the goodness surrounding us is God's favor to us, God's blessing, God's grace. Culture is the result of the Spirit of God brooding over humanity's endeavors.

The tradition operated also with a holistic understanding of sin and its effects, of faith and of redemption. By no means was everything in society, culture and personal existence seen as evil; much, as I have just remarked, was apprehended as good. The holistic view of sin and its effects instead took the form of resisting all attempts to draw lines between some area of human existence where sin has an effect and some area where it does not. The intuitive impulse of the person reared in the Reformed tradition is to see sin and its effects as leaping over all such boundaries. To the medievals who suggested that sin affects our will but not our reason, the Reformed person says that it affects our reason as well. To the Romantics who assume that it affects our technology but not our art, the Reformed person says it affects art too.

Corresponding to this holistic view of sin and its effect is then a holistic view as to the scope of genuine faith. Faith is not an addendum to our existence, a theological virtue, one among others. The faith to which we are called is the fundamental energizer of our lives. Authentic faith transforms us; it leads us to sell all and follow the Lord. The idea is not, once again, that everything in the life of the believer is different. The idea is rather that no dimension of life is closed off to the transforming power of the Spirit—since no dimension of life is closed off to the ravages of sin. But faith, in turn, is only one component in God's program of redemption. The scope of divine redemption is not just the saving of lost souls but the renewal of life—and more even than that: the renewal of all creation. Redemption is for flourishing.

Third, the tradition operated with the conviction that the Scriptures are a guide not just to salvation but to our walk in the world—to the fundamental character of our walk. They are a comprehensive guide. They provide us with "a world and life view." This theme of the comprehensiveness of the biblical message for our walk in this world matches, of course, the holistic view of sin and of faith.

The grace of God that shapes one's life came to me in the form of induction into this tradition. That induction into tradition should be an instrument of grace is a claim deeply alien to modernity. Tradition is usually seen as burden, not grace. But so it was in my case. If you ask me who I am, I reply: I am one who was bequeathed the Reformed tradition of Christianity.

Calvin College

And bequeathed the benefits of a remarkable institution in this tradition, Calvin College. Institutions are also not customarily seen as instruments of the grace that shapes one's life with God. But so it was in my case.

I had entered what seemed to me a world of dazzling brightness. In part it was a journey into self-understanding. For here, in this college of the tradition, I began to understand the tradition and thus myself. I learned how to live with integrity within this tradition, within any tradition—how to discern and embrace its fundamental contours while treating its details as adiaphora, how to discern and appropriate what is capable of nourishing life in one's own day and how to let the rest lie, how to empathize with the anxiety and suffering embodied in one's tradition and how to celebrate its accomplishments.

More important than coming to understand the tradition, I saw the tradition at work in some remarkably intelligent, imaginative and devoted teachers. I came with the conviction that I was called to make my thoughts captive to Jesus Christ. But now I was plunged deep into the culture of the West—its literature, its philosophy, its theology, its science; everything; nothing was off-limits. The challenge constantly placed before us was to struggle to understand this massive inheritance "in Christian perspective." And more than that: ourselves to embody Christ in culture—ourselves to compose poetry and write philosophy and paint paintings that would breathe the Spirit of Christ. There are two cities, said one of our teachers, Harry Jellema, with gripping charisma, using the language of Augustine, there are two cities—then he would switch to the Latin—the *civitas Dei* and the *civitas mundi*. Your calling is to build the *civitas Dei*.

Here too nobody was offering evidences for the truth of Christianity, arguments for the inspiration of Scripture, proofs for the resurrection of Jesus, best explanation accounts of Christian faith. The challenge set before us was to interpret the world, culture and society in the light of Scripture—to describe how things look when seen in Christian perspective, to say how they appear when the light of the gospel is shed on them.

It was heady stuff; and we students were as energized and instructed by each other as by our teachers. In my sophomore year I met Alvin Plantinga; we became at once dear friends and have remained that ever since. More important, from that time on we have engaged together in the project of Christian philosophy, parceling out the work, learning from each other—but let me be candid, I learning more from Al than Al from me. There was one college class in which Al and I were the only students, a course in Kant's "pure critique" taught by Harry Jellema. A few years back, Al gave the Gifford Lectures; a few years hence, I am slated to give them. Harry Jellema would have chuckled with delight at learning that all the students in one of his classes had become Gifford Lecturers. Too bad he's no longer alive—though perhaps he knows without my telling him. He was the pioneer, breaking up the sod for the second and third generations, for people like O. K. Bouwsma and William Frankena and Henry Stob and Al and myself, and lots of others; I continue to think that he was maybe the most profound of us all. Certainly the most charismatic.

No doubt some students were bored stiff with all this heady stuff. And some were there for reasons quite different from ours: they too had grown up in the tradition, but were angry with it, infuriated by all its rough edges. Their interest was not Nietzsche interpreted in the light of the tradition but Nietzsche for use as ammunition against the tradition. The arguments we had were wonderful!

I must say a word about Abraham Kuyper, who was in many ways the spiritual eminence behind the college. Kuyper was a turn-of-the-century Dutchman whose creativity came to expression in many areas—church, politics, academia, journalism. For our purposes, what was important was Kuyper's model of theory-construction. Since Aristotle, everybody in the West had regarded proper theorizing as a generically human activity. To enter the chambers of theory one must lay aside all one's particularities and enter purely as a human being. Our religions, our nationalities, our genders, our political convictions—

we are to take them off and line them up in the entry. Of course we are never successful at this; always there are some peculiarities that we have failed to strip off. Part of what our peers in the room must do, whenever they notice that, is call it to our attention. It follows that proper theorizing does not eventuate in Muslim sociology or feminist philosophy or Marxist literary criticism or Christian literary criticism, but simply in human sociology, human philosophy and so forth.

Kuyper didn't believe it—didn't believe it was possible. He didn't think one could shed one's nationality or one's social class; but he especially insisted that one could not shed one's religion. A person's religion, on Kuyper's view, was not an inference or a hypothesis but a fundamental determinant of that person's hermeneutic of reality. Of course the hermeneutics of reality shaped by two different religions do not, by any means, yield differences of interpretation on everything; but unless the religions in question are very close, they yield enough differences to have consequences within the field of theorizing. Thus Kuyper thought that the goal of constructing a generically human philosophy was vain; philosophy, and academia generally, is unavoidably pluralistic. The only circumstance under which that would not be true would be that in which Christians, say, would practice amnesia about their religion while doing philosophy, and then remember it when arriving home or at church. Such amnesia Kuyper could not tolerate.

I believed this when first I learned of it in college days; I believe it still. It is a fascinatingly "postmodern" perspective; when I first read Thomas Kuhn's *The Structure of Scientific Revolutions* my main reaction was "Well, of course." I should add that sometimes Kuyper articulated his view in a much more "expressivist" form than I have given it above. That is to say, sometimes he talked as if the development of philosophy occurred, or should occur, just by expressing in philosophical form one's religious convictions. That seems to me mistaken. To become a philosopher is to enter the ongoing practice of philosophy. That practice is a malleable practice; though one is shaped, one also shapes. But no philosopher ever just gives expression to his inner self. And the Christian who engages in philosophy will seek to learn from the practice and its tradition as well as to contribute to the shaping of that practice.

Later I spent thirty years of my life as a teacher at Calvin College. Or better put, as a member of that community of Christian learning. That community has been for me an instrument of grace, supporting me in my Christian reflections—challenging, correcting, supplementing, encouraging, chastising, disciplining. To know who I am, you must know that I was bequeathed the opportunity of being a member of that community. It was an instrument of grace. I miss it deeply. But a call is a call.

Cries of the Oppressed

A notice appeared in my mailbox at the college in the spring of 1978, inviting me to attend a conference in Chicago on Palestinian rights at the end of May, sponsored by Christians. To this day I do not know who sent it. I had celebrated with everyone else I knew the astounding victory of Israel in 1967; over the years, though, I had become more and more uneasy with Israel's treatment of the Palestinians. But I did nothing about this unease, did not even, as I recall, express it to anyone other than my wife. Now this invitation. The semester was over, I didn't feel like starting summer work yet, Chicago was only about a three and a half hour's drive away; so I went.

I had not knowingly met a Palestinian before; and my image of Palestinians was that they were all Muslims. Here in one place there were about 150 Palestinians; and obviously a good many of them, I have no idea how many, were Christians. They poured out their guts in rhetoric of incredible passion and eloquence. They spoke of how their land was being wrenched away from them, and how no one cared. They said that the land in which Jesus walked would soon have no more Christians in it, squeezed out by a Zionism supported by the West and Muslim fundamentalism in reaction. They asked why we in the West refuse to hear their cry. The U.N. representative of the PLO was given permission to come, but was forbidden by the State Department to speak to all of us at once; he might speak only to groups of five people or fewer. A person who had worked for the U.S. State Department in Israel and, while there, had been commissioned to prepare a report on the torture of Palestinians in Israeli jails, rehearsed the central parts of her report; she had been fired by the State Department a few days before.

I felt cornered, confronted—confronted by the word of the Lord telling me that I must defend the cause of this suffering people. My tradition yielded me the category: it was a call. Not to answer the call would be desecrating disobedience.

I have not changed my profession. But I have gone to the Middle East several times. I have bought and read yards of books. I subscribe to out-of-the-way journals. I became chair of the board of the Palestine Human Rights Campaign. I have written; I have spoken. It hasn't always been pleasant; the Palestinians are both immensely lovable and difficult to defend. But it is a sacred call. And I do all in my power, when answering the call, to remember the pain, the anxiety and the rights of the Jewish people.

During the academic year 1980-81 Allan Boesak was at Calvin as our multicultural lecturer. He became, and remains, one of my dearest friends in all the world. I dedicated my book *Until Justice and Peace Embrace* to him; I cannot do better, to say what I found in him, than to quote what I said in my dedication:

for my dear friend Allan Boesak,

black Reformed pastor and theologian from South Africa,

in whose speech

I have heard

both

the cries of the oppressed

and the Word of the Lord

I had been to South Africa in 1975 to attend a conference on behalf of Calvin College at the University of Potchefstroom. What I saw and heard there made me very angry; but it was almost exclusively whites that I talked with. Beginning with Allan, I have met the blacks.

Very little in my background had equipped me to deal with these experiences. Of course I believed that it was the calling of us who are Christian philosophers to develop a Christian theory of justice. But here I was confronted with injustice. Or rather—that's still too abstract—I was confronted with the faces and voices of people suffering injustice.

These experiences have evoked in me a great deal of reflection and reorientation. Justice has become for me one of the fundamental categories through which I view the world. I think of justice not so much as a virtue but as a condition of society: a society is just insofar as people enjoy what is due them—enjoy what they have a legitimate claim to. Previously the fundamental moral category for me was responsibility. Now I have come to see that the moral domain is an interplay between rights and responsibilities. To the Other in my presence I have responsibilities; but also the Other in my presence comes bearing rights. The violation of moral responsibility yields guilt; the violation of moral rights yields injury. The proper response to guilt is repentance; the proper response to moral injury is lament and outrage.

Slowly I began to see that the Bible is a book about justice; but what a strange and haunting form of justice! Not our familiar modern Western justice, of no one invading one's right to determine one's life as one will. Rather the justice of the widow, the orphan and the alien. A society is just when all the little ones, all the defenseless ones, all the unprotected ones have been brought back into community, to enjoy a fair share in the community's goods, and a standing and voice in the affairs of the community. Biblical justice is the shepherd leaving the corral to look for the hundredth one and then throwing a feast when the one is found.

I hadn't seen their faces before, I hadn't heard their voices; that's what changed me. I have come to think that there is little passion for justice if the faces of suffering are hidden from view and the voices muffled. But horrible to know and say: in the presence of some of those faces and some of those voices, I have discovered in myself not empathy but loathing, fear and resentment. Who shall deliver us from this bondage?

Lament for a Son

This was all before. I now live after, after the death of our son, Eric. My life has been divided into before and after.

To love is to run the risk of suffering. Or rather, in our world, to love is to suffer; there's no escaping it. Augustine knew it well; so Augustine recommended playing it safe, loving only what could neither die nor change on one—God and the soul. My whole tradition had taught me to love the world, to love the world as a gift, to love God through and in the world—wife, children, art, plants, learning. It had set me up for suffering. But it didn't tell me this: it didn't tell me that the invitation to love is the invitation to suffering. It let me find that out for myself, when it happened. Possibly it's best that way.

I haven't anything to say beyond what I've already said in *Lament for a Son*. There's a lot of silence in the book; no word too much, I hope. In the face of death we must not chatter. And when I spoke, I found myself moving often on the edges of language, trying to find images for what only images could say. The book is extremely particular; I do not speak about death, only about Eric's death. That's all I could do. But I have discovered, from what readers have told me, that in its particularity lies universality.

I see now, looking back, that in writing it I was struggling to own my grief. The modern Western practice is to disown one's grief: to get over it, to put it behind one, to get on with life, to put it out of mind, to insure that it not become part of one's identity. My struggle was to own it, to make it part of my identity: if you want to know who I am, you must know that I am one whose son died. But then, to own it redemptively. It takes a long time to learn how to own one's suffering redemptively; one never finishes learning.

Though there are strands in the Reformed tradition for which sovereignty is God's principal attribute, I don't think I ever thought of God much in terms of sovereignty. God was majesty for me, indescribable majesty. And graciousness, goodness; God is the one who blesses, blessing calling for gratitude. To be human is to be that point in the cosmos where God's goodness is meant to find its answer in gratitude: John Calvin told me that.

Now everything was different. Who is this God, looming over me? Majesty? I see no majesty. Grace? Can this be grace? I see nothing at all; dark clouds hide the face of God. Slowly the clouds lift. What I saw then was tears, a weeping God, suffering over my suffering. I had not realized that if God loves this world, God suffers; I had thoughtlessly supposed that God loved without suffering. I knew that divine love was the key. But I had not realized that the love that is the key is suffering love.

I do not know what to make of this; it is for me a mystery. But I find

I can live with that. The gospel had never been presented to me as best explanation, most complete account; the tradition had always encouraged me to live with unanswered questions. Life eternal doesn't depend on getting all the questions answered; God is often as much behind the questions as behind the answers. But never had the unanswered question been so painful. Can I live this question with integrity, and without stumbling?

It moved me deeply to discover one day that John Calvin alone among the classical theologians had written of the suffering of God. Whenever he wrote of it, it was, so far as I could discover, in the same context: that of a discussion of injustice. To wreak injustice on one of one's fellow human beings, said Calvin, is to wound and injure God; he said that the cry of those who suffer injustice is the cry of God.[3]

To Be Human

There's been a grace that's shaped my life. It came to me in the form of being inducted into a tradition of the Christian church, and in the form of participating in an institution, and in other ways as well which I haven't mentioned: in the form of persons such as my wife, my children, my friends.

But was it grace I experienced when I heard God saying to me, in the voice of the Palestinians and the South African blacks, you must speak up for these people? When God confronted the reluctant Jeremiah with his prophetic call, was that grace? And was it grace I experienced when my son was killed?

God is more mysterious than I had thought—the world too. There's more to God than grace; or if it's grace to one, it's not grace to the other—grace to Israel but not grace to Jeremiah. And there's more to being human than being that point in the cosmos where God's goodness is meant to find its answer in gratitude. To be human is also this: to be that point in the cosmos where the yield of God's love is suffering.

Notes

Clark: Introduction

[1]April 7, 1980.

[2]Although under 20 percent of professional philosophers are women, a substantial number of women were invited to contribute to this project.

[3]Published in *Faith and Philosophy* 1, no. 3 (1984): 253-71.

[4]For a discussion of Plantinga's views on the problem of evil and the rationality of religious belief, see Kelly James Clark, *Return to Reason* (Grand Rapids, Mich.: Eerdmans, 1990), pp. 57-91, 118-58.

[5]The *Retractations* 2.6 as found in *Augustine: Confessions and Enchiridion*, ed. and trans. Albert C. Outler (Philadelphia: Westminster Press, 1955), p. 24.

[6]Leo Tolstoy, *Confession*, trans. David Patterson (New York: Norton, 1983), p. 18.

[7]Frederick Buechner, *Godric* (San Fransisco: Harper & Row, 1980), p. 99.

[8]Buechner, *Godric*, p. 40.

[9]Job 19:25-26. The interpretation of this passage is widely disputed. Does the Redeemer mentioned here refer to God or to something like a defense attorney who will vindicate him against the accusations of God? Or is it a statement of faith, that in spite of his lack of understanding of divine justice, he trusts that God is his Redeemer and, in the end, he shall see God? Either interpretation makes a profound contribution to honest confessional literature.

[10]Augustine, *The Confessions*, bk. 2, chap. 3.

Basil Mitchell: War and Friendship

[1]*Bhagavadgita*, trans. W. O. D. Hill (Oxford, 1928), fourth reading, vv. 18-21.

[2]Ibid., second reading, v. 38.

[3]Ibid., second reading, v. 31.

[4]Ibid., third reading, v. 35.

Alvin Plantinga: A Christian Life Partly Lived

[1]In *Alvin Plantinga*, ed. James Tomberlin and Peter van Inwagen (Dordrecht, Netherlands: D. Reidel, 1985), pp. 3-97.

[2]My thanks to Neal and Kathy Plantinga, Eleonore Stump, Trenton Merricks and Leonard Vander Zee for wise counsel and good advice on this dicey project.

[3]*Mistakenly* so-called in my opinion. These five points summarize the declarations of the Synod of Dort (1618-19); they essentially distinguish one kind of seventeenth-century Calvinist from another kind (and do not at all obviously represent what John Calvin himself had in mind). A number of the Reformed churches have adopted the Canons of Dort as one of their confessional standards; my own church, the Christian Reformed Church, takes the Belgic Confession and the Heidelberg Catechism as well as the Canons as its standard. The former two can properly be said to embody what is essential to Calvinism, but the latter really addresses a seventeenth-century internecine quarrel among Calvinists. It is by no means obvious that the right side won at the Synod of Dort; and even if the right side *did* win, is it not at best dubious to take as a standard for confessional unity such highly specific and detailed pronouncements on matters of great difficulty about which the Bible itself is at best terse and enigmatic?

[4]See, for example, J. Fodor's "Methodological Solipsism Considered as a Research Strategy in Cognitive Psychology," *The Behavioral and Brain Sciences* 3 (1980): 68; and Stephen Stich's *From Folk Psychology to Cognitive Science* (Cambridge, Mass.: MIT Press, 1983), chap. 8 and elsewhere. See also P. Churchland, "Eliminative Materialism and Propositional Attitudes," *Journal of Philosophy* 78 (1981); Fred Dretske, *Knowledge and the Flow of Information* (Cambridge, Mass.: MIT Press, 1981); J. Fodor, *Psychosemantics* (Cambridge, Mass.: MIT Press, 1987); B. Loar, *Mind and Meaning* (Cambridge, U.K.: Cambridge University Press, 1981); and Z. Pylyshyn, *Computation and Cognition* (Cambridge, Mass.: MIT Press, 1984). Robert Cummins goes so far as to call this view—that representations have causal efficacy only with respect to their syntax, not with respect to their semantics or content—the "received view" (*Meaning and Mental Representation* [Cambridge, Mass.: MIT Press, 1989], p. 130). In *Explaining Behavior* (Cambridge, Mass.: MIT Press, 1988) Fred Dretske takes as his main project that of explaining how it could be that beliefs (and other representations) play a causal role by virtue of their contents.

[5]Of course we Calvinists didn't restrict our antipathies to fundamentalists. At Calvin in those days there was a wholly deplorable battle between the "Dooyeweerdians," the largely Canadian followers of the Dutch philosopher Herman Dooyeweerd (led by H. Evan Runner), and the rest of us. We were thus prepared to be evenhanded in our acrimony.

[6]In fact there was current among the older generation the idea that smoking was not only permissible, but quasi-obligatory, an attitude summed up in the Dutch verse

Die niet roken kan,

Dat is geen man.

(Loosely translated: he who can't smoke is not a real man.) My father was offered a job at Wheaton in the 1940s or 1950s; he replied that while he could easily enough give up the occasional beer, he couldn't even consider giving up cigars; the whole idea was unthinkable.

[7]See my "Evolution, Neutrality, and Antecedent Probability: A Reply to Van Till and McMullin," *Christian Scholars Review* 21 (September 1991): 90.

[8]I speak of the "burden" of rearing our four children; in fact these children—Carl, married to Cindy Kok and now a professor of film at Hollins College; Jane, married to John Pauw and an associate pastor of a Presbyterian church in Seattle; Harry, married to Pamela van Harn and a professor of computer studies at the University of Pittsburgh; and Ann, married to Raymond Kapeyn and director of education, youth ministry and outreach at a Christian Reformed church in Grand Rapids—are for us a source of enormous joy and satisfaction.

[9]I hope I have since learned better, in part from the example of younger people, including in particular some graduate students at Notre Dame.

[10]A diffidence he of course shed some seventeen years ago; since then he has become an inspiring and peerlessly valuable leader among Christian philosophers.

[11]See my *God and Other Minds* (Ithaca, N.Y.: Cornell University Press, 1967, rev. ed. 1991), chap. 7, "Verificationism and Other Atheologica."

[12]At present the Yale philosophy department is in receivership; the administration has appointed a member of the statistics department as its head, and a committee of faculty members not including members of the philosophy department is overseeing the attempt to rebuild it.

[13]In *Faith and Rationality*, ed. A. Plantinga and N. Wolterstorff (Notre Dame, Ind.: University of Notre Dame Press, 1983).

[14]As it used to be called; now, I gather, it is called "bipolar affective disorder."

[15]Though with respect to the *probabilistic* atheological argument from evil, as opposed to the claim that the existence of evil is logically incompatible with the existence of an almighty, all-knowing and perfectly good God; the probabilistic argument is vastly more difficult to deal with, if only because probability is such a confusing and ill-understood morass. (See chaps. 8 and 9 of my *Warrant and Proper Function*.)

[16]See my "Justification in the Twentieth Century," in *Philosophy and Phenomenological Research* 50, supplement (Fall 1990). In *God and Other Minds*, then, I was implicitly rejecting classical foundationalism as well as accepting it; for obviously a person flouts no epistemic duty in believing that there are other minds, whether or not there is good argumentative support for that belief.

[17]Another name for "warrant" is Chisholm's "positive epistemic status."

[18]As well as the Payton Lectures at Fuller Theological Seminary in 1987, the Norton Lectures at the Southern Baptist Theological Seminary in 1988 and the Wilde Lectures given at Oxford in 1988.

[19]*Warrant: The Current Debate* and *Warrant and Proper Function* (New York: Oxford University Press, 1993).

[20]See my "Advice to Christian Philosophers," published by the University of Notre Dame and in *Faith and Philosophy* 1 (July 1984), my Stob Lectures, *The Twin Pillars of Christian Scholarship*, delivered at Calvin in November 1989 (and available in pamphlet form from Calvin College), and also "When Faith and Reason Clash: Evolution and the Bible" and "Evolution, Neutrality and Antecedent Probability: A Reply to Van Till and McMullin," both in *Christian Scholars Review* 21 (September 1991), for a development of these ideas. (I hope to write a book on Christian philosophy, if I ever get finished with the books I'm currently writing.) Here I mention just one example of the way in which current science may run clearly contrary to Christianity: according to Herbert Simon (*Science* 250 [December 1990]: 1665ff.) the *rational* thing for a person to do is to act so as to increase one's personal fitness, that is, so as to maximize the probability that one's genes will be widely disseminated. (Thus a paradigm of rational behavior would be that of Dr. Cecil Jacobson, a specialist in fertility problems who was convicted in 1992 of fraud for using his own sperm to inseminate some seventy-five women who came to him for treatment. True; this behavior landed him in jail and disgrace; but it certainly increased his fitness.) But people like Mother Teresa or the Little Sisters of the Poor, says Simon, raise a problem: Why do they act as they do, going so clearly counter to the rational way to behave? Simon's answer: "bounded rationality" (that is, not to put too fine a point on it, stupidity) together with docility. I should think no Christian could even for a moment take seriously either the proposed account of rationality or the preferred explanation of the behavior of people like Mother Teresa. See pp. 83 and 98 of "Evolution, Neutrality and Antecedent Probability."

[21]Of course, I don't mean to hold up myself as a model here: quite the contrary. A few

years back I several times found myself thinking about a certain person, and feeling obliged to call him and speak with him about Christianity; this was a person for whom I had a lot of respect but who, I thought, had nothing but disdain for Christianity. I felt obliged to call this person, but always did my best to put the thought out of my mind, being impeded by fear and embarrassment: what would I say? "Hello, have you found Jesus?" And wouldn't this person think I was completely out of my mind, not to mention really weird? Then later I heard that during this very time the person in question was in the process of becoming a Christian. I had been invited to take part in something of real importance and refused the invitation out of cowardice and stupidity.

John Rist: Where Else?

[1]Anna has corrected my memory and improved my style and the clarity of my presentation. I am also grateful to Joseph Boyle for showing me how I had managed to misrepresent my own appropriation of Augustine in an earlier draft.

Stephen T. Davis: Passing the Baton

[1]If anyone is caused pain by what I write in this essay, I hope that person will forgive me. More important, I ask God to forgive me if I have written anything here that is false or misleading. I confess I was unaware until trying to write this essay how spiritually dangerous efforts of this sort can be. The constant temptation is to write things that are self-serving or hypocritical.

[2]I had always been puzzled why the writers of the Heidelberg Catechism of 1563 entitled part three of that document (which is about the Christian life) "Thankfulness." Since 1975 this has been much less mysterious to me.

[3]One of the most enjoyable things I've ever done in adult Christian education was in April and May 1991. I led a group of curious but serious Presbyterians at our family's home church in a six-week study of Thomas à Kempis's The Imitation of Christ.

[4]I would like to thank my wife, Charis Davis, my pastor, Rev. Ron Kernaghan, and five members of the faculty Christian group at the Claremont Colleges (Dave Bosley of Harvey Mudd College, Don Griesinger and Joe Maciariello of the Claremont Graduate School, Joe Schreiber of Claremont McKenna College and Don Zenger of Pomona College) for their wise counsel and helpful comments on an earlier draft of this essay.

Nicholas Rescher: In Matters of Religion

[1]"Language has been given to man to disguise his thoughts."
[2]Blaise Pascal Pensées 233.

Frederick Suppe: Becoming Michael

[1]Anthony deMello, Sadhana: Way to God; Christian Exercises in Eastern Form (New York: Doubleday, Image, 1978).
[2]See Francis Vanderwall, Water in the Wilderness: Paths of Prayer, Springs for Life (New York: Paulist, 1985), chap. 2, sec. 1.
[3]See Francis Vanderwall, Spiritual Direction: An Invitation to Abundant Life (New York: Paulist, 1981).
[4]DeMello, Sadhana, pp. 42-43.
[5]Ibid.
[6]Ambrose G. Wathen O.S.B., Silence: The Meaning of Silence in the Rule of St. Benedict (Washington: Cistercian Publications, 1973), pp. 58-59.
[7]DeMello, Sadhana, p. 25.

[8]C. S. Lewis, *Surprised by Joy* (San Diego: Harcourt Brace Jovanovich, 1956), pp. 218-19.

[9]Thomas Philippe, *The Contemplative Life*, trans. C. Buonainto, ed. E. D. O'Connor (New York: Crossroads, 1990), pp. 23-24.

[10]Ibid., p. 27.

[11]David Keirsey and Marilyn Bates, *Please Understand Me: Character and Temperament Types* (Del Mar, Calif.: Prometheus Nemesis, 1984), p. 49. "NT" refers to one of the four temperaments (NT, NF, SP, SJ) as measured by Myers-Briggs type scales. Each temperament has four personality types, for a total of sixteen types, formed out of the opposition pairs Introverted vs. Extroverted, iNtuitive vs. Sensible, Thinking vs. Feeling, Perceiving vs. Judging. My personality type is INTJ ("introverted-intuitive-thinking-judging") and my temperament type NT ("intuitive-thinking"). These scales and associated typologies are based on Jungian analysis.

[12]Ibid., pp. 114-15.

[13]Nicholas Wolterstorff, *Lament for a Son* (Grand Rapids, Mich.: Eerdmans, 1987), p. 89.

[14]So far as I can determine, the abuse has gone on for four generations.

[15]J. D. Salinger, *Franny and Zooey* (New York: Bantam Books, 1961), p. 115.

[16]Though my older brother does report that on one or more occasions she came to my aid when my father was abusing me psychologically.

[17]See my *The Semantic Conception of Theories and Scientific Realism* (Urbana: University of Illinois Press, 1989), pp. 10-15.

[18]For details about these days, see *Semantic Conception* and the Dedicatory Epistle to my *Facts, Theories, and Scientific Observation*, forthcoming 1995.

[19]Keirsey and Bates, *Please Understand Me*, p. 56.

[20]Lewis, *Surprised by Joy*, pp. 17-18.

[21]The phrase is due to N. R. Hanson; see his *Observation and Explanation: A Guide to Philosophy of Science* (New York: Harper & Row, 1971), p. 45.

[22]A. Schaef, *Escape from Intimacy: Untangling Addictions to Sex, Love and Romance, Relationships* (New York: Harper & Row, 1989), pp. 102-5.

[23]St. Ignatius of Antioch, Bishop and Martyr, in *Liturgy of the Hours* (New York: Catholic Book Publishing, 1975), 3:324.

[24]In Catholic teaching, "the contracting parties, not the officiating priest, are the ministers of the sacrament. Moreover it has always been recognized by the Church that in certain cases, provided by Canon Law, marriage may be contracted and the sacrament received without the presence of a priest" (G. D. Smith, *The Teaching of the Catholic Church* [New York: Macmillan, 1949], p. 1067). Those circumstances include those where a priest is not available to perform the ceremony and none is expected. Having argued that our relationship could be a valid marriage *if* celebrated, I next argued that the church's refusal to perform the celebration constituted the unavailability of a priest and thus it could be sacramentally valid, though not licit, for us to marry ourselves.

[25]Published as A. Kosnick, W. Carroll, A. Cunningham, R. Modras and J. Schulte, *Human Sexuality: New Directions in American Catholic Thought* (Paramus, N.J.: Paulist, 1977).

[26]That is, he was saying that there were present impediments to the marriage of the sort that that constituted grounds for an annulment in the case of heterosexual, Church-sanctioned marriages.

[27]New American Bible (Washington, D.C.: Confraternity of Christian Doctrine, 1970), hereafter NAB-1970.

[28]Unless indicated to the contrary, all scriptural quotations in this essay are from The New American Bible with Revised New Testament (Nashville: Catholic Bible Press, 1987).

[29]Ralph McInerny, *The Basket Case: A Father Dowling Mystery* (New York: St. Martin's, 1987), p. 40.

[30]Lewis, *Surprised by Joy*, p. 171.

[31]See Eugene Kennedy, *Tomorrow's Catholics, Yesterday's Church: The Two Cultures of American Catholicism* (New York: Harper & Row, 1988).

[32]Lewis, *Surprised by Joy*, pp. 207-8.

[33]See Jean Genet, *The Thief's Journal*, trans. Bernard Frechtman (Evanston, Ill.: Greenleaf, 1965), pp. 220-25, 231, 263; see also Jean-Paul Sartre, *Saint Genet: Actor and Martyr*, trans. Bernard Frechtman (New York: Mentor Books, 1963).

[34]Keirsey and Bates, *Please Understand Me*, p. 56.

[35]For a survey of them, see David Shi, *The Simple Life: Plain Living and High Thinking in American Culture* (New York: Oxford University Press, 1985).

[36]Derek Humphry, *Let Me Die Before I Wake: Hemlock's Book of Self-Deliverance for the Dying* (Los Angeles: Hemlock Society, 1984; distributed by Grove Press).

[37]Wolterstorff, *Lament*, p. 19.

[38]St. Augustine, *Confessions*; as in *Liturgy of the Hours*, 4:1357.

[39]This would have been true several years earlier, but a change of priest had occurred and it proved to be a very rich and vibrant spiritual environment—one that was a great aid in rebuilding my faith.

[40]E. P. Sanders, *Jesus and Judaism* (Philadelphia: Fortress, 1985).

[41]For the latter see Part IV of my *The Semantic Conception of Theories and Scientific Realism* (Urbana, Ill.: The University of Illinois Press, 1989) and especially my *Facts, Theories, and Scientific Observation*, two vols., forthcoming 1995.

[42]But not a gift *from* God.

[43]Evagarius Ponticus, *The Praktikos and Chapters on Prayer*, trans. and ed. J. E. Bamberger (Spencer, Mass.: Cistercian Publications, 1970), p. 101.

[44]Keirsey and Bates, *Please Understand Me*, pp. 49, 50, 186-87.

[45]Philippe, *Contemplative Life*, pp. 57-58.

[46]The very notion is problematic. See R. M. Adams, "The Problem of Total Devotion," in *Rationality, Religious Belief and Moral Commitment: New Essays in Philosophy of Religion*, ed. R. Audi and W. Wainwright (Ithaca, N.Y.: Cornell University Press, 1986), pp. 169-94.

[47]*Liturgy of the Hours*, 3:296.

[48]John Cassian, as quoted by Henry Suso, *The Exemplar, with Two German Sermons* (New York: Paulist, 1989), p. 138.

[49]Philippe, *Contemplative Life*, p. 84.

[50]Ibid., p. 31.

[51]William of Thierry, *The Mirror of Faith*; as reprinted in *Liturgy of the Hours*, 4:1778.

[52]I am grateful to the following persons who have commented on drafts of this or a larger manuscript from which it has been adapted: Michael Buckley S.J., David Burrell C.S.C., Kelly Clark, John Dunne C.S.C., Joe Godfrey, Ms. Kelly Hamilton, Rev. Michael Himes, John Jenkins C.S.C., Mark Jordan, Shabir Kamal, Tony Kayala C.S.C., Jeremy Langford, Kathy Lossau, Rev. Ernan McMullin, Steve Norton, Cornelius O'Boyle, William Ramsey, Barbara Suppe, Benjamin Suppe, Bob Suppe, John Suppe and Paul Weithman. As so frequently has been the case, the comments and wisdom of my brother-in-Christ Bas van Fraassen have brought me up short and been a source of growth, inspiration and insight.

The writing variously was done while on a General Research Board research leave from the University of Maryland at College Park, a sabbatical leave from both the Baltimore and the College Park campuses of the University of Maryland, and while holding the Senior Scholar Fellowship at the Notre Dame Center for Philosophy of Religion. I am grateful for all this support.

I wish to acknowledge the spiritual direction given me by the late Rev. Joseph D. Easter, the late Father Edward Buttgen, Father Ernan McMullin, Father Thampi (Tony)

Kayala and Father Michael Buckley S.J. at crucial junctures in my life, as well as the ministry of many other priests and nuns under more ordinary circumstances.

Finally I want to thank God for not giving up on me.

Richard Swinburne: The Vocation of a Natural Theologian

[1]Some of the more philosophical passages that follow are taken from a small pamphlet, *Evidence for God*, published by Mowbrays and the Christian Evidence Society, 1986, in which I summarized one or two of the main ideas of *The Existence of God*. I am grateful to the society for permission to reuse this material, which I have also reused elsewhere in various forms.

[2]See my summary of and commentary on this work, "The Argument from Fine-Tuning," in *Physical Cosmology and Philosophy*, ed. J. Leslie (New York: Macmillan, 1989); republished as Appendix B in *The Existence of God*, rev. ed. (Oxford, U.K.: Clarendon, 1991).

[3]See the revised edition of *The Existence of God*, pp. 152-60 and chaps. 10 and 11, for the detailed arguments.

Mortimer J. Adler: A Philosopher's Religious Faith

[1]Other relevant anticipations will be found in *Philosopher at Large* (New York, Macmillan Publishing Company, 1977; Collier Books, 1992), chap. 14, and especially pp. 314-17.

[2]See ibid.

[3]See ibid.

[4]See ibid., p. 317.

[5]See my *Truth in Religion: The Plurality of Religions and the Unity of Truth* (New York: Macmillan, 1990), p. 109.

[6]Ibid., pp. 109-10.

[7]The point I have just made indicates the significant difference between Aristotle's pagan, philosophical theology, written in total ignorance of the Old and New Testaments, and the pagan, philosophical theology of those who try to prove the existence of a God that, in the light of sacred Scriptures, is seen as the Creator of this radically contingent cosmos.

Aristotle's God is the *primary* cause of motion in a universe that he conceived as eternal or everlasting, whereas the God of the Old and New Testaments is the *only* cause of being of a cosmos that would totally cease to be without that causation at every instant of its existence.

This does not mean that modern pagan philosophical theology proves the existence of the God believed in by persons of Jewish, Christian or Islamic faith. Such faith attributes to God many properties that exceed the power of rational proof; but starting from the radical contingency of the cosmos, philosophical theology affirms the indispensable existence of its ex nihilo creative cause.

[8]In Greek the title is π ερy οὐράνου; in Latin, it is *De Caelo*.

[9]One may ask why Holy Scripture is filled with metaphorical—not analogical—language that gives many of its narrative passages the aspect of myth rather than of factual historical truth. Does not such metaphorical language impel readers of Scripture to use their imagination rather than their intellect?

The answer given by Thomas Aquinas to these questions is very much to the point. He wrote:

It is befitting [for] Holy Writ to put forward divine and spiritual truths under the likenesses of material things. For God provides for everything according to the capacity of its nature. Now it is natural to man to attain to intellectual truths through sensible things, because all our knowledge originates from sense. Hence in

283

Holy Writ spiritual truths are fittingly taught under the metaphors of [sensible] material things.

In this respect, Aquinas goes on to say, Holy Writ is like poetry, but it differs from poetry in that sacred Scripture "makes use of metaphors as both necessary and useful" for the learning of divine and spiritual truths (Thomas Aquinas, *Summa Theologica*, pt. 1, q. 1, art. 9, Response and Reply to Obj. 1).

Linda Trinkhaus Zagzebski: Vocatio Philosophiae

[1]Nietzsche is an exception.

[2]John Henry Newman, *Apologia Pro Vita Sua*.

[3]See "Boys and Girls Apart," *World Press Review* 39 (September 1992). The success of Hillary Rodham Clinton has drawn media attention to this issue recently.

[4]Virginia Woolf, *To the Lighthouse* (New York: Harvest/Harcourt Brace Jovanovich, 1989), p. 32.

[5]For those readers unfamiliar with Aristotelian ethics, *phronesis* is a virtue usually translated "practical wisdom." It involves the ability to see the morally relevant features of a particular case and to make good judgments in the concrete situation. It is a virtue that is not precisely describable as the following of any set of rules, nor is the decision procedure used by a person with *phronesis* fully conscious.

[6]G. K. Chesterton, *Orthodoxy* (New York: Doubleday/Image Books, 1959), p. 180.

[7]Ibid., pp. 159-60.

Nicholas Wolterstorff: The Grace That Shaped My Life

[1]Donald Davie, *A Gathered Church* (New York: Oxford University Press, 1978), p. 25.

[2]Hans Frei, *The Eclipse of Biblical Narrative* (New Haven, Conn.: Yale University Press, 1974), pp. 3-4.

[3]When I mentioned these passages to one of the theologians of the tradition, he reacted sharply and said that of course Calvin did not intend such language to be taken seriously!